TAKE MY WORD

TAKE MY WORD

*Autobiographical Innovations of Ethnic
American Working Women*

ANNE E. GOLDMAN

UNIVERSITY OF CALIFORNIA PRESS
BERKELEY   LOS ANGELES   LONDON

University of California Press
Berkeley and Los Angeles, California

University of California Press, Ltd.
London, England

© 1996 by
The Regents of the University of California

Library of Congress Cataloging-in-Publication Data

Goldman, Anne E., 1960–
    Take my word : autobiographical innovations of ethnic Ameri-
can working women / Anne E. Goldman.
        p.   cm.
    Includes bibliographical references (p.   ) and index.
    ISBN 0-520-20096-9 (acid-free paper) — ISBN 0-520-20097-7
(acid-free paper : pbk.)
    1. Women's studies—United States—Biographical meth-
ods.   2. Working class women—United States—Biography.
3. Minority women—United States—Biography.   4. Ethnol-
ogy—Biographical methods.   5. Autobiography—Women
authors.
I. Title.
HQ1186.U6G65   1996
331.4'08'693—dc20   95-6078
                                                      CIP

Printed in the United States of America
9 8 7 6 5 4 3 2 1

For David
(doctor, cyclist, and endurance storyteller)
whose courage and sweetness we remember

Contents

Preface

Historically, the authority of working-class writers has often been erased by the generic byline "Anonymous." Contemporary American literature goes unsigned only rarely (with the significant exception of immigrant narrative), but as cultural studies, feminist, and ethnic studies scholars have pointed out, not every signature is equally recognizable. This book considers a number of such unfamiliar scripts: personal narratives by ethnic American women who for all practical purposes remain anonymous because their work, developed out of such genres as oral history, political documentary, and cooking, not only transgresses the boundaries of the literary canon but falls altogether outside of what is generally considered "literature."

Reading beyond the frame of traditional autobiography is useful for scholars who study the work of American ethnic women; it makes the literary field richer by opening up a wide range of new source texts. It also demands we rethink rigidly teleologic models of literary history which equate ethnic literature with contemporary literature by celebrating the recent work of writers of color to the exclusion of the literary traditions their books grow out of. In arguing for a wider autobiographical field we describe a wider spectrum of the ways and means by which people in the twentieth century speak themselves into textual existence. This wide-angle critical lens also historicizes the techniques of contemporary writing. Recognizing the subtlety with which New Mexican culinary narratives of the 1930s and 1940s simultaneously exploit and critique the commercialization of nuevomexicano culture, for instance, prevents us from automatically assuming that the more recent the narrative, the more rhetorically complex it must be. Fabiola Cabeza de Baca's 1949 cookbook *The Good Life*, which describes food preparation in order to historicize familial relations and community ties, anticipates Mexican writer Laura Esquivel's best-selling novel *Como Agua para Chocolate/Like Water for Chocolate* by some four decades. Appreciating the ways in which Cabeza de Baca's culinary text doubles (triples) as an essay in cultural criticism and as an autobiographical document also allows us to contextualize the generic "border crossings" of contemporary Chicana writers like Cherríe Moraga, whose two personal narratives, *Loving in the War Years* (1983) and *The Last Generation* (1994), fuse essay, poetry, and fiction in order to develop contextualized self-portraits, and Gloria Anzaldúa, whose own multigenric autobiography *Borderlands/La Frontera* was published in 1987. Similarly, understanding how Rose Pesotta's recollections of organizing work in *Bread upon the Waters* (1944) sidestep publishers who favor the assimilationist parable by substituting the language of class for that of ethnic identity offers a way to read the complicated relations between progressive political practice and Jewish tradition in contemporary texts like Kenneth Kann's 1993 oral history collection, *Comrades and Chicken Ranchers: The Story of a California Jewish Community*.

This book, then, glosses the "literary" qualities of "extra-literary" texts—books marketed under the rubric of sociology, labor history, or cultural studies—in order to explore how the desire to speak autobiographically is negotiated in narratives that simultaneously write the self and represent the culture(s) within which that self takes shape. I have selected these personal narratives in order to introduce readers to a series of uncelebrated writers—ethnic American women who speak for themselves but whose racial identity and working-class status have often prompted readers to speak for them instead—and to foreground the rich and varied rhetorical strategies they develop to script and to speak their lives.

To this end, the first two chapters consider how Hispanas writing at midcentury and African American women publishing in the 1970s use cooking as a metaphor for a kind of cultural authority that opens a space for individuation as well. In *The Genuine New Mexico Tasty Recipes: Old and Quaint Formulas for the Preparation of Seventy-Five Delicious Spanish Dishes* (1939) and *The Good Life: New Mexico Traditions and Food* (1949), Cleofas Jaramillo and Fabiola Cabeza de Baca insist on a proprietary interest in the reproduction of tradition while at the same time exploiting the cookbook as an opening for memory. Cultural critique is an aim of Jessica Harris's 1989 *Iron Pots and Wooden Spoons: Africa's Gifts to New World Cooking* as well. As the title of her book implies, Harris suggests we see intercultural contact not as one-directional but as a series of cross-fertilizations. Other cookbooks by black American women interrogate the relationship between ethnography and autobiography, between languages that define a cultural "we," that is, and those that articulate an "I." In *Vibration Cooking: Or, The Travel Notes of a Geechee Girl* (1970) and *Spoonbread and Strawberry Wine: Recipes and Reminiscences of a Family* (1978), VertaMae Smart-Grosvenor and Norma Jean and Carole Darden develop their respective identities as contemporary African American women within very different familial, communal, and historical contexts.

Chapters 3 and 4 focus on the rhetorical patterns speakers of a number of collaborative narratives use in order to further their own interests despite editorial pressures that position them as cultural icons rather than distinct individuals. In *La Partera: Story of a Midwife* (1980), Jesusita Aragón remembers growing up at the turn of the century near Las Vegas, New Mexico. In the process she reflects on the devastating impact the early death of her mother had on her own youth, as well as describing her practices as a working midwife. Onnie Lee Logan's life history in *Motherwit: An Alabama Midwife's Story* (1989) offers readers another portrait of rural childhood and develops an identity fostered both by her editor's interest in her work and by her own criticisms of the physicians who have obstructed this practice.

The final chapters discuss how the impulse toward distinction is scripted in a range of Jewish texts, those prompted by the turn-of-the-century interest in slumming (what autobiography critic William Boelhower identifies in the work of Jacob Riis as a fascination with immigrant Americans as the "new ethnic substitute for the now vanquished Indian"),[1] as well as those most avowedly collective of narratives, the memoirs of Jewish labor organizers active in the International Ladies Garment Workers Union (ILGWU) in the 1920s, 1930s, and 1940s. Curiously, the recollections that insist most vehemently on their subjects' successful assimilation into (Anglo) American life (books like Mary Antin's *The Promised Land* [1912] and Elizabeth Levin Stern's *My Mother and I* [1917]) undermine their own melting-pot plots by meditating on the inescapable hold memories of Russian life exercise over their present identities. The autobiographies of ILGWU activists like Rose Schneiderman (*All for One*, 1967) and Rose Pesotta (*Bread upon the Waters*, 1944) develop a different relation between class and ethnic affiliations, using their alliance with progressive politics as a substitute *for* rather than a dismissal *of* Jewish tradition, culture, and identity.

This book lists a single author on its cover page, but in many ways it has been a collaborative project. First, I would like to thank my family: Susan and Dave Faust, Michael, Barbara, Charles, Julie, and David Goldman, Julia Wada, and Jody and Zoe Pollak, who collectively and singly have supported my work by putting up with my worries and preoccupations—but also by taking me outside of work altogether. My parents have both influenced this book in more ways than I can count or even know, but I acknowledge two particulars here: the ways my mother, Barbara, prompted its first two chapters by teaching me how cooking can be a language for more than food, and the extent to which the willingness of my father, Michael, to question what look like intellectual axioms has provided me with a critical model of my own. My brother Charles has patiently assisted me in my efforts to become computer-literate (not an altogether completed task), in one unforgettable instance spending more than two hours on the telephone helping me recover the manuscript after I accidentally deleted all of my computer files. My brother David celebrated my work by making sure I attended my doctoral graduation. My sister, Susie, a good listener always, provided lively contestatory responses to my arguments.

Many other people and institutions have supported this book. In its initial stages, the project was funded by a Chancellor's Fellowship at Berkeley and a Woodrow Wilson Grant in Women's Studies. More recently, an Ahmanson/Getty Postdoctoral Fellowship at UCLA in 1993 gave me the time necessary to finish the book. I am particularly grateful to Clark Library Director Peter Reill, and to Valerie Matsumoto and George Sánchez, who coordinated the Fellows, for their enthusiastic support of my work. At the University of California Press, I would like particularly to thank Doris Kretschmer, for her warm encouragement, Laura Driussi, for her continued patience and hard work, and Jane-Ellen Long, for her scrupulous attention to the manuscript.

At the University of California at Berkeley, Carlos Camargo, Barbara Christian, Giulia Fabi, Sandra Gunning, Kate McCullough, Lori Merish, Judith Rosen, and Susan Schweik all provided me with careful critical readings of portions of the manuscript. Elizabeth Abel encouraged me to submit what became in 1990 my first academic publication; her gifted teaching and her support of my work have been important to me. Mitch Breitwieser and Barbara Christian have similarly encouraged this project since its inception. Dialogues with Hertha Wong about collaborative narrative, together with her own work on Native American autobiography, have improved my chapters on edited texts. The personal and professional friendship of Alyson Bardsley, Leslie Delauter, Nora Johnson, and Judith Rosen has helped me keep faith during difficult periods. Lori Merish's support of my arguments is all the more appreciated for the fact that we never agree. Cindy Franklin, likewise, has been a generous friend and colleague as well as a model for innovative teaching. I owe a particular debt to Sandra Gunning, whose sense of humor and keen critical eye I can always count on, notwithstanding our distance from one another.

Finally, it is my pleasure to acknowledge the people without whose help this book would have been impossible. Teacher and colleague Genaro Padilla has put up with my intellectual *cabezonada* for years and has accorded this project, and indeed all of my work, the careful and demanding critical scrutiny all scholarship requires. By always asking the right questions, he has immeasurably enriched this study. My daughter Zoe graces my days with her lively chatter and blesses my life with her affectionate companionship. And my husband Jody has with love and patience supported and encouraged my every endeavor. Thank you, Jody, for being there for me every time.

Introduction

Autobiography, Ethnography, and History: A Model for Reading

Redefining Autobiography

When does cultural description further self-expression and when does it defeat autobiographical purpose? This book traces the complicated relationship between identity, culture, and language; between the desire to speak autobiographically and the pressures ethnography exerts upon this desire. Cookbooks, labor histories, and edited narratives of women working as midwives and healers may not seem to qualify as autobiographies. Rather than foregrounding the "I," they appear to celebrate a collective, focusing on ethnic culinary traditions, on the medical services midwives and healers provide in poor communities, or on the struggles of labor activists to improve working conditions for their members. Yet, as I try to show here, the women who speak in these books use the languages of folklore, of social critique, and of historical tribute to speak on their own behalf as well. Their personal narratives manage to be socially engaged without submerging individual voice in collective history.

Choosing books with such titles as *The Good Life: New Mexico Traditions and Food, All for One,* and *La Partera: Story of a Midwife* for a study of autobiography obviously implies arguing to expand the definition of the genre.[1] Reading autobiographical gestures in narratives that are not confessional or even "literary" also implies locating such impulses historically. If the desire to make the self in language is a constant, the kinds of languages available to people change across time, culture, and region.[2] Writing a distinctive "I," for ethnic Americans particularly, often means writing against the grain: of an East Coast publishing establishment that defines "Mexican" through the writings of white traveler-surveyors from New England who were more interested in mapping what they successively called "the "frontier" and "the Golden State" than in reading the personal narratives of "native Californians";[3] of nativist accounts of American identity that present "Jew-town" as a strange and exotic setting, while simultaneously offering the assimilationist bildungsroman as the only literary template by which immigrant autobiographers could gain access to publishing;[4] of a century of editorial insistence that the distinctive personal histories of black Americans are valuable only insofar as they illustrate a unitary sociological "them"; of critical and theoretical accounts of American women's autobiographies that either celebrate "community" across diverse ethnic texts, or else leave out ethnic women altogether.[5]

In the chapters that follow, I trace the forms this generalizing tendency takes in a number of different discursive and historical circumstances, as a means of contextualizing the strategies women autobiographers use to insist on their own self-distinction. In a recent essay on the politics of contemporary Chicana literature, Sonia Saldívar-Hull argues that Mexicana readers must "look in nontraditional places for our theories: in the prefaces to anthologies, in the interstices of autobiographies, in our cultural artifacts, our *cuentos,* and . . . in the essays published in marginalized journals."[6] My reading strategy, like Saldívar-Hull's, looks to nontraditional kinds of autobiography in order to demonstrate the range of rhetorical maneuvers writers use to insert their presence into contexts that discourage sustained autobiographical voicing. At the same time, this method enumerates what feminist critic Sidonie Smith has recently called "the pressure points" women in turn place on "traditional autobiography as it presses [them] into a specific kind of autobiographical subject."[7] And I consider as well how current critical readings of such nontraditional autobiography often reproduce the generalizing pressures the writers have experienced, how such readings embody what Sidonie Smith and Julia Watson characterize as the propensity to "see the colonized as an amorphous, generalized collectivity."[8]

Thus this study questions recent theories that celebrate the self-in-relation at the same time as they slight forms of subjectivity that emphasize the distinctive qualities of the self. For instance, some critics of ethnic autobiography too easily conflate a cultural plural (a "we" derived out of and taken for granted by the disciplines of ethnography, sociology, and anthropology) with this discrete "I," just as some feminist scholars argue that a gendered "we" defines the subject in autobiographical writing by women. My own reading practice follows Sau-ling Wong's recommendation, in *Reading Asian American Literature,* to work toward "a scrupulous grappling with textual complexities" as a means of avoiding ahistorical generalizations about the feminine subject.[9] The focus of this book on the particularizing gestures of a number of women autobiographers is, of course, first a response to what I perceive to be the writers' own impulses to authorize the self in discursive contexts that discourage self-distinction. But it is also a response to the direction of current theorizing about personal narrative, which makes the need to specify a particularly urgent theoretical project in and of itself.

Rethinking the Politics of "Accommodation"

Here I would like to illustrate my own argument for specificity by way of the folkloric work of two Hispana writers who published at midcentury in New Mexico. The memoirs of Fabiola Cabeza de Baca and Cleofas Jaramillo exemplify the relation between autobiographic impulse and ethnographic necessity. Charting the development of the self, Cabeza de Baca's *We Fed Them Cactus* (1954) and Jaramillo's *Romance of a Little Village Girl* (1955) describe in the process the communal traditions and cultural practices upon which identity is grounded.[10] Before publishing their more sustained autobiographical narratives, however, both Cabeza de Baca and Jaramillo wrote a series of cookbooks—books which describe not only food but folklore, books which reproduce recipes along with memories of holiday preparations, religious events, and family celebrations. It is these books, I would argue, that enable the more self-possessed prose of the later memoirs.

Like the subtlety of ethnic women's self-presencing strategies more generally, which take place within the context of (variously) inhospitable publishing circumstances, the self-disclosing gestures these narratives contain are articulated against the grain of a language that discourages them, a language made famous by expatriates like D. H. Lawrence and folklorist-writers like Mary Austin, who eulogized the turquoise skies of New Mexico and lamented, with unctuous aesthetic relish, its "ever-declining" civilization. As Genaro Padilla argues, such romanticizing language, ostensibly celebratory of the land and its native inhabitants, actually deprived them of speech, "setting them into the sediment of the earth instead of relating to them as social subjects, mystifying and mythifying their cultural practices, reducing their social history, ignoring their individuality."[11] The grandiloquent prose of writers like Lawrence and Austin is clearly meant to pay homage to the grand Southwestern vistas the visitors found so inspiring, yet the romanticism of their writings suggests that their gaze was at times more enthusiastic than discriminating. In their preference for panoramic overview rather than close reading, their eye for the large outline rather than for fine detail, they tend to the sweeping statements that characterize ethnographic narrative more generally. In their capacity for overstatement, that is, the eulogies of these newcomers to New Mexico at midcentury typify other writing by nonnatives about natives, their own literary language borrowing from the disciplines of sociology and anthropology in its tendency to objectify people and to exoticize their cultural practices. And while the particular forms this ethnographic model takes vary with historical circumstance, its implications for autobiography are regrettably constant: to reduce the nuanced cadences of particular voices to one generic note.

In the face of the literary establishment's definition of Southwestern narrative, the cookbooks Jaramillo and Cabeza de Baca published provided them with a suitably nonthreatening framework within which to work toward self-expression.[12] Presenting itself in relation to ethnic community rather than claiming center stage, the authorial "I" in these texts is a modest presence. But if the authors' voices are unobtrusive, as they slip quietly in and out of recollections that mark familial and racial affiliation, both Cabeza de Baca and Jaramillo claim identities for themselves in their culinary narratives, which act as a kind of prelude to the more sustained autobiographical voices of the later memoirs.

Critic Ramón Saldívar argues that "contemporary Chicano narratives and other forms of novelistic discourse are . . . self-consciously crafted acts of social resistance,"[13] but close reading of apparently accommodationist texts reveals oppositional voicing there as well. As the Personal Narratives Group argue, "many women's personal narratives unfold within the framework of an apparent acceptance of social norms and expectations but nevertheless describe strategies and activities that challenge those same norms."[14] Cabeza de Baca's *The Good Life*, for example, exploits this subtle strategy. Announcing in her preface that "the fondest memories of my life are associated with the people among whom I have worked," she inserts herself into a text that does not really require her presence, establishing life history at the center of a book ostensibly dedicated to celebrating a communal idea of culture. Situations that discourage autobiographical voicing will of necessity demand such rhetorical maneuvering. Open resistance may be the endpoint in a literary teleology that assumes that the most advanced political maneuver is always the most explicit one. Yet, as Raymund Paredes suggests in his own account of Chicano literature, "The members of an ethnic or racial minority, deprived of material goods and sophisticated technology, rely on their wits to survive in an oppressive society."[15] In contexts that make plain speaking impossible, writers still manage to speak their mind.

I am not suggesting an either/or interpretive framework (either "progressive," "multi-voiced," "dialogic," and "resistive" or "conservative," "univocal," "monologic," and "accommodating"). To my mind, most authors do not *either* simply "re-elaborate" *or* simply "rewrite" "the received behavioral script of the rhetorically well-defined American self," as William Boelhower suggests in a recent essay on ethnic autobiography in the United States.[16] Rather, their texts both exert pressure upon and must contend with the languages available to them. Determined to express their own presence in such contexts often means, as I have suggested, that such authors have to speak "on a bias," across the grain of narratives explicitly dedicated to ethnography, to history, or to cooking.

In the cookbooks of Cabeza de Baca, as in the works of many of the other women I consider in this project, resistance is often masked. Autobiographers like Cleofas Jaramillo, Onnie Lee Logan,[17] and Rose Schneiderman make use of metaphors that sustain a characteristically feminine humility, yet a closer look at the rhetorical patterns that govern their narratives reveals a critical awareness that is often at odds with the status quo. Rose Pesotta likens her organizing work for the International Ladies' Garment Workers Union to "housekeeping," but when this disclaimer precedes her request to an overconfident young volunteer to sweep the floor of the common room, we can see her remark for what it is: a directive designed to quash his masculine arrogance. Likewise, Rose Schneiderman's coy reference to her diminutive stature only makes her account of herself as the first woman representative on a federal labor committee look a more grandiose accomplishment. If these women advance their arguments cautiously—obliquely, circuitously, through repetition and accretion rather than direct appeal—their criticism is ultimately no less pointed for being articulated in coded form.

Nor are their own interests as autobiographers less marked for being developed in texts ostensibly dedicated to historical documentation. Or to cultural inquiry: I have suggested that people make their opportunities where they find them, and for women of color, especially, such openings have often taken shape in an ethnographic publishing context that ignores the specificities of individual voices in order to draw general, and abstract, claims about the way "culture" operates.[18] Whether these claims are advanced as explicitly anthropological, as sociological studies premised on a distinction between "domestic" and "foreign" communities, or as "purely" literary, the outcome is the same. Comprehensive patterns, not the particularities of inflection, are the object, and those under examination are characterized—if not caricatured—as cultural icons, exemplars of traditions left over from primitive times, racialized identities where race is not one variable in a wider field but an absolute value, sufficient in and of itself. Many of the collaborative texts I discuss in Part 3 of this book take shape in this context, one in which the editorial agenda, despite affirmations to the contrary, attempts to rewrite the autobiographical particulars of the speaker as representative of a tradition—a tradition generally styled as an anachronism from some vaguely pretechnological time. When she associates the interest of Jesusita Aragón's life history with her status as "the last of the traditional, Hispanic midwives in the area,"[19] editor Fran Leeper Buss provides a case in point. For Buss, Aragón functions as a cultural icon, a museum piece who evokes memories of an earlier, "lost" era. The same desire to return to a presumably simpler, bucolic scene characterizes the relation between editor and speaker in *Motherwit: An Alabama Midwife's Story*, another interracial collaboration. Despite Onnie Lee Logan's numerous references to the thriving practices of other midwives, editor Katherine Clark persists in styling this "granny midwife" as "the last . . . in Mobile and one of the last in Alabama" (xiii). Once again autobiography works in the service of ethnography as Logan's discrete history becomes, in the editor's introduction, the history of all human evolution and change; "performing a service as old as the human race," she is described as moored by the currents of time, "caught in the flux of a changing culture . . . an unusual victim of historical 'progress' " (xiii).

The pressures of ethnographic discourse upon autobiographers are not exerted solely on those in joint publishing ventures, nor are they produced only by editorial agenda. In "Autobiography as Guided Chinatown Tour? Maxine Hong Kingston's *The Woman Warrior* and the Chinese American Autobiographical Controversy," Sau-ling Wong argues that writing for an interethnic audience encourages ethnographic representation that often ends by commodifying cultural practice:

Removed from Chinese culture in China by their ancestors' emigration, American-born autobiographers may still capitalize on white curiosity by conducting the literary equivalent of a guided Chinatown tour: by providing explanations on the manners and mores of the Chinese American community from the vantage point of a "native."[20]

This kind of autobiography, which forces the subject to serve as cultural ambassador for an audience eager for a peek at "exotic" rites and "foreign" practices, defines the field so that even those personal narratives that refuse to act as literary tour guides may nevertheless get read as such. Wong goes on to suggest that "from an intraethnic point of view, the writing of autobiography may be valued as a means of preserving memories of a vanishing way of life, and hence of celebrating cultural continuity and identity; in an interethnic perspective, however, the element of *display,* whether intentional or not, is unavoidable."[21] Yet the very "involuntary intertextuality" that she so acutely identifies as characteristic of the reception of Chinese American narratives—and that, I would argue, is typical of other ethnic autobiographical traditions as well—may inform intraethnic readerships too.[22] Or, rather, anyone whose writing gets marketed under this ethnographic rubric will inevitably have to contend with its tradition of objectification and its tendency to hurry the postmortems on those cultures diagnosed as dying or in distress.[23] And, given the imperial frame of reference within which this language has its origin—and continues to flourish—virtually any effort to define the self in relation to ethnic community runs the risk of being glossed by others as more a cultural sign than an autobiographical presence.

All for One and One for All:
Complicating the Relationship
Between Affiliation and Self-Distinction

Nevertheless, identity (likeness?) cannot be defined without reference to difference, cannot be theorized independently of class, of geography, of gender—or of ethnicity. Poststructuralists have insisted on the contingent nature of the "I," but they have generally chosen as illustrations the classic literary examples: Woolf, Flaubert, Balzac, Shakespeare.[24] For the women considered in this study, however, writers neither celebrated nor even marginal to canonical literature, so much as "extra-literary," the cultural "we" and the autobiographical "I" always stand in relation. And despite historical situations which trivialize their contributions as women and language contexts which discourage self-representation, they rely on a conjunction of singular and collective voicing in order to develop subjectivity.

The following very different autobiographical introductions—the first from Zora Neale Hurston, the second from Jade Snow Wong—demonstrate the complicated relation between affiliation and distinction:

I maintain that I have been a Negro three times—a Negro baby, a Negro girl and a Negro woman. Still, if you have received no clear cut impression of what the Negro in America is like, then you are in the same place with me. There is no *The Negro* here. Our lives are so diversified, internal attitudes so varied, appearances and capabilities so different, that there is no possible classification so catholic that it will cover us all, except My people! My people![25]

By turns, the family coaxed and ridiculed the recalcitrant member, but Jade Snow grew more grimly stubborn as their pressure became greater. Thus in the one Wong family picture complete with its in-laws, the camera recorded Jade Snow, defiant and tense, with the only head of straight feminine hair in the group of curly-topped, relaxed, smiling faces.[26]

Zora Neale Hurston's "I" may initially look bolder on the page than the more oblique self-presentation Jade Snow Wong offers readers, but the first-person pronouncements of *Dust Tracks* and the "she" who is described for us in *Fifth Chinese Daughter* equally defy easy attempts at classification. Despite the ambivalence with which they invoke their affiliations with racial community, family, and female networks, both writers insist on their own self-distinctiveness precisely in relation to these ties that bind.

This desire to frame the self as unique—even iconoclastic—has been considered by traditional autobiography criticism to be one of the essential characteristics of personal narrative.[27] Yet this very effort to maintain difference—in relation to race, to family, to sex—has brought down upon both Hurston and Wong the most severe admonishments, albeit in different critical contexts. Hurston has often been indicted as unwilling to engage the facts of racial politics in her self-revelatory writings, and her insistence on a portraiture that defies community affiliation has been labeled as self-deceiving and untruthful to the spirit of a genre dedicated to uncovering the "truth" about identity.[28] Moreover, Frank Chin has chastised Wong for choosing to write autobiographically, defining the genre as unalterably Christian, white, and Western, and thus false to the experience of the Chinese in the United States.[29]

Assigning an historical truth-value to personal narrative accords it privileged status as a "record" and denies that it is subject to the general rules of language, to be applied equally to literature and documentary. Yet in calling attention to the historical context within which both books are produced, these comments do serve an important critical function. The responses of blacks to the Second World War, conceived as either a patriotic or an imperialist project, certainly inform Hurston's book, despite her inability, because of publishing strictures, to invoke it explicitly. And though Chin's sanctions against Wong are derisively framed, his insistence on the relation between history and literature underscores how crucial it is to rewrite a historical record which to a large extent still remains whitewashed. Memory often provides a viable alternative to such a history, as autobiography theorist Françoise Lionnet suggests in her discussion of Hurston.[30] The association between autobiography and history, then, should not be reduced to a question of foreground versus background; texts are informed, not determined, by history.

Linked to this issue of text and context is another question of boundaries: of "inside" and "outside" and the relation between them. If the criticisms of Hurston and of Wong tend to overstate the degree to which the subjects of *Dust Tracks* and *Fifth Chinese Daughter* celebrate iconoclasm and resist racial identification,[31] their insistence on the relation between the "I" and the "we" does raise one of the crucial questions of contemporary autobiography criticism, particularly of what are called (as if white authors are somehow raceless) "ethnic" texts.[32] Just how is the self of personal narrative, as it works toward self-formation, engaged in affiliation as well? To what degree is the "us," described by Hurston as at once irrelevant to the "me" and yet implicated in its development, the subject of autobiography? To what extent is Wong's "membership" the focus of a narrative which ostensibly refuses its sanctuary?

With respect to the narratives this study foregrounds, I would argue that in privileging the "we" over the "I," recent responses which celebrate the collective in the theory and criticism of ethnic literature, autobiography, and gender studies run the risk of oversimplifying the relation between distinction and affiliation as surely as did the ethnographic publishing conditions under which these books were first produced.[33] My own concern is to move toward redressing this balance by retrieving those impulses toward self-presencing which I believe remain an essential characteristic of life writings. But I wish to hold to the notion of "balance" here, not to reinstate the idea of the isolationist "I" which lies at the heart of traditional definitions of the autobiographical canon. Rather than fix the subject of a given text as either illustrative of a privileged self, distinguished from others in bold relief, or as an example of the "we" that is metonymic of a collective, identity might more effectively be appraised with reference to a continuum. This flexible model has the advantage of supporting multiple self-positionings that can provide critiques of bipolar theories. Notwithstanding their different discursive and historical contexts, for instance, the texts I consider here all challenge conventional notions of the genre. Politically engaged, they tend to frame consciousness less as contemplative than as involved with social conditions, community affiliations, and historical circumstances. But drawing connections between "me" and "us" and maintaining distinctions between "us" and "them"—the latter as much of a concern as the former for the writers and speakers discussed in the following chapters—does not preclude the kind of self-formation traditionally considered autobiographical. The practice of self-contextualization, that is, does not prevent people from speaking their own idiosyncratic selves into textual existence. On the contrary, as I have already suggested in my comments on Fabiola Cabeza de Baca's *The Good Life,* acknowledgment of affiliation often provides the basis from which the "I" authorizes herself to speak.

Revising the Subject
of Traditional Autobiography

I am interested here in amplifying such strategies toward self-presencing. My work could not have developed, however, without the two decades of committed attention to revising and enriching that earlier model. Susan Friedman cites Regina Blackburn as defining " 'The "self" of black autobiography' " as " 'a conscious political identity, drawing sustenance from the past experience of the group.' "[34] This contextualization is a crucial revision of earlier versions of subjectivity which refused to recognize how the "I" is implicated and informed by circumstance. Similarly, Arnold Krupat's description of Native American autobiography as a tradition in which "the self most typically is not constituted by the achievement of a distinctive, special voice that separates it from others, but, rather, by the achievement of a particular placement in relation to the many voices without which it could not exist,"[35] if an overgeneralized critical portrait, corrects a monochrome version of personal narrative that defines only the self of the writings of the Puritans and their descendants—Jonathan Edwards, Benjamin Franklin, Henry Adams—as achieving autobiographical distinction.[36]

My own study builds upon this reevaluation of personal narrative. Critics like Blackburn and Krupat, as well as other scholars—William Andrews, Françoise Lionnet, Genaro Padilla, Joanne Braxton, Hertha Wong—have already responded to constricted definitions of the genre by delineating traditions of their own using more politically and historically engaged criteria of inclusion.[37] It seems to me time to examine more closely the range of self-representation exhibited by texts both within *and* across such critical categories. This project is historicist in that it honors the racial and cultural distinctions that underwrite, in part, the impulse toward self-formation in the writings of Jewish American, Chicana, and African American women, but it is more concerned with outlining the range of strategies particular narratives employ than it is in developing a general argument about a tradition of women's autobiography. My interest is in analyzing the strategies women with little access to textual positions

of authority use to develop their voices, and, in keeping with this privileging of the will to autobiographical presence, I have tried to approach selected narratives as "agents as well as effects of cultural change," to adopt
the phrase Carolyn Porter uses in her critique of the New Historicism.[38]
In practice this has meant a focus more on the particular than on the
general; a concern less with finding a textual common denominator than
with considering the range of rhetorical patterns distinct narratives provide
and with redefining what constitutes writing about the self—always with
an eye toward the discursive and historical contexts in which such scripting
is conceived, produced, and read.

Cultural Engagement
and Autobiographical Practice

*Cogewea then told of an amusing incident. . . . The irrepressible
camera man was there and he thought to obtain a rare picture
of a band of stampeding buffaloes, bearing directly down upon
him. He secured his negative alright, but with lowered horns
the animals charged and he had scant time to spring into the
branches of a nearby tree, where he hung, thus narrowly escaping with his life. A noted "Cowboy Artist" was in close proxim-
ity and he drew a sketch of the discomfited man swinging to
[sic] the tree with the rushing buffaloes passing under him. It
was, perhaps, a more interesting picture than the camera could
have secured.*

Mourning Dove, *Cogewea, the
Half-Blood: A Depiction of the
Great Montana Cattle Range*

Often, locating the personal pronoun in cultural terms means writing it in
an ethnographic language that appears self-defeating. Yet like the "amusing incident" relished by Cogewea in which an aspiring ethnographer finds
himself caricatured by the "half-blood" cowboys whose way of life he ex-
pects to memorialize,[39] the anecdotes and memories related by the women
of this study often encode criticisms of the ethnographic scripts they appear to underwrite. Consider Cleofas Jaramillo, caustic on the subject of
"Americans" who reproduce "Spanish" recipes without including all the
ingredients necessary to make them edible; while furthering the commodi-

fication of nuevomexicano culture, she demands that it be orchestrated by Mexicanos themselves. Or Onnie Lee Logan, whose invocations of the editorial apparatus surrounding the telling of her story elide and call attention to the heavy-handed supervisory strategies by which two kinds of self-appointed "midwives"—medical and literary—seek to control her work. Or Rose Schneiderman, whose warmest recollections serve to reconfigure the insistently Jewish family life that is being whitewashed by the commercial frame within which her narrative of union labor is published.

At their most successful, the speakers and writers considered here maneuver between autobiographical and political-cultural texts, between "I" and various forms of "we." This study, then, documents those impulses toward self-presencing that counterpoint as well as contravene the pressures ethnographic discourse exerts upon autobiographers. In part, what enables such autobiographers simultaneously to represent culture and to write the self is their insistence on the work involved in both activities. Focusing on the reproduction of culture as a conscious labor rather than as "something . . . often unsuccessfully repressed or avoided,"[40] they often stress the extent to which the traditions of their particular communities have been appropriated by others—and therefore need to be reinterpreted by themselves. In an essay on African American women's autobiography, Elizabeth Fox-Genovese has suggested that "to write the account of one's self is to inscribe it in a culture that for each of us is only partially our own,"[41] but if they recognize the sociopolitical stakes involved in producing life history, these autobiographers are not content to cede discursive authority to cultural outsiders. And in the process of insisting that they retain the rights to represent cultural practice, such writers confer upon themselves the status to argue their claims. Cultural critique, that is, gives them their opportunity, as women, to speak at all. In voicing their opinions about a collective with which they are affiliated, whether they broadcast these opinions or argue them sotto voce, they accord themselves the agency and presence necessary for autobiographical distinction.[42]

Michael Omi claims that "where political opposition was banned or useless . . . transformation of the racial order, or resistance to it, was perforce military."[43] Yet the quiet but none the less decisive cultural engagement Evelyn Nakano Glenn describes suggests that this formulation is too narrow. According to Glenn, Japanese and Japanese American women acted not only as "conservators" but also as "mediators" of cultural change in the

United States: "Employed women, especially those working as domestics, helped introduce selected aspects of American culture, such as home decoration and living arrangements."[44] Making changes in home decoration may seem a modest exercise of authority, but in an environment that is less than encouraging of self-articulation and that provides almost no leisure in which to create on a grander scale, that it happens at all is telling.

The recognition that Japanese American women can articulate a cultural polemic through their domestic practices demands a rethinking of the distinction between public domain and private sphere more generally and points toward the necessity of historicizing the private as thoroughly as the public. Yet postmodern theorists have denied the political efficacy of such resistive articulations. Fredric Jameson, for instance, mourns the apparent failure of all cultural critique: "Not only punctual and local countercultural forms of cultural resistance and guerrilla warfare but also even overtly political interventions . . . are all somehow secretly disarmed and reabsorbed by a system of which they themselves might well be considered a part, since they can achieve no distance from it."[45] The problem with such a systemic formulation, however, is that it denies the very real authority of individual agency—or it assumes a model of consciousness that credits its subjects with a singular incapacity to accommodate their speech to their listeners or to "speak out of both sides of their mouths" at once.[46] But, as the coded critique of Rose Pesotta, the ethnographic circumlocutions of Zora Neale Hurston, and the rhetorical wiliness of VertaMae Smart-Grosvenor's formulations of identity[47]—or even, to cite an older illustration of such strategizing, the Trojan Horse—make clear, resistance is often most potent when it is masked, most effective when it is formulated using the language of accommodation.

In order to evaluate the political work redefining culture does for personal narrative, we need a more nuanced conception of identity. Just as autobiography critics need not reduce the relation between distinction and affiliation to an either/or equation, identification of structural principles does not have to make individual lives irrelevant. Racial identity is, after all, as Michael Omi characterizes it, composed of a "complex of individual practices. . . . The panoply of individual attributes—from one's patterns of speech or tastes in food or music to the economic, spatial, familial, or citizenship 'role' one occupies—provides the essential themes for political organization."[48] Likewise, culture need not be formulated as an apocalyptic struggle between conqueror and conquered, but can instead be seen as a network of relations—hierarchically striated and often at odds, yes, but providing intellectual and spiritual sustenance nonetheless. As theorist John Brenkman articulates this: "Individuals . . . are members of several interlaced collectivities, so that their social identities are formed by and their discursive participation occurs within several potentially conflicting cultural practices/traditions at once."[49]

The narratives of the Jewish labor organizers discussed in chapters 5 and 6 display a particularly curious working out of ethnic identity. In this instance, the language of class speaks on behalf of culture as well. Published during the First World War, when to act "American" meant to choose between a very limited number of cultural scripts, many Jewish writers—Elizabeth Hasanovitz, for instance, whose autobiography was initially serialized by *The Atlantic Monthly* in 1917 and 1918, and Rose Cohen, whose personal narrative was published in 1918 as part of George H. Doran Company's American Immigration Library—were able to construct American selves only by disaffiliating themselves from a Jewish culture identified as a political anachronism. In these books and others like them, the "Americanization" of the self, which requires a renunciation of Jewishness, is overtly framed as a story of class rise. Rose Pesotta's history of her involvement with the International Ladies' Garment Workers Union, *Bread upon the Waters* (1944) and Rose Schneiderman's recollections of struggle in *All for One* (1967) are equally class-conscious, but here working-class affiliations are celebrated rather than denied. In turn-of-the-century Russia, after all, to agitate for labor reform was virtually to announce yourself as Jewish-identified, since a disproportionately high number of Russian socialists were Jewish. This association, coupled with the fact that Jewish culture in the United States has historically been a working-class culture, suggests that those writers who choose steadfastly to represent themselves as part of the working poor express a kind of filial piety in the process. If there appears to be little explicit focus on Jewishness in these books, holding on to a working-class identity nonetheless enables these writers to maintain a secular kind of Jewish cultural practice.

What I wish to suggest by emphasizing the multiple and shifting nature of cultural forms and collective affiliations is that the identity that is predicated upon them is equally particularized. Its articulation takes different forms in different contexts, so that at various points in a narrative the same autobiographical subject may provide us with multiple formulations of, for instance, racial identity. The ethnic "I" of VertaMae Smart-Grosvenor's culinary autobiography *Vibration Cooking*, for example, provides readers with what would be theorized as both essentialist and constructionist conceptions of blackness. Such apparently contradictory conceptions are a problem only when we consider race or other determinants of identity as "pure" categories. Dispense with this kind of abstraction, and what looks like inconsistency soon begins to read as flexibility, the kind of flexibility that allows for a richer conception of the "I" and a more nuanced version of the self's relation to ethnicity.

Smart-Grosvenor's refusal to generalize about racial identity—or, more specifically, her insistence on providing readers with multiple generalizations—is illustrative here. Denying both ethnography's claims on the subject as "representative" and an autobiographical model which would deprive the self of racial identity, she insists: "I don't have culinary limitations because I'm 'black.' On the other hand, I choose to write about 'Afro-American' cookery because I'm 'black' and know the wonderful, fascinating culinary history there is. And because the Afro-American cook has been so under-appreciated." Announcements like this one pull the complacent reader up short by making any easy formulation of race impossible. Or consider the following remark in which the autobiographer's insistence on her self-distinction is framed using a language that locates this idiosyncratic "I" squarely within black speech traditions: "Black people been eating that traditional New Year's Day dinner for years. That's why I'm not having no more open house on New Year's Day. I'm going to try something new" (4).

Ethnic identity may be a constant, but its forms are constantly changing, since this particular relationship between "I" and "we" depends upon a number of other factors, including geography and gender, work and sexuality, generation and class status and historical circumstance. In his celebrated study of Asian American history, Ronald Takaki explains how Korean children growing up on the sugar plantations of Hawaii begin to speak pidgin more fluently than Korean, creating "a new identity associated with Hawaii,"[50] while in José Villareal's novel *Pocho*, Richard's Mexican-born father simultaneously wonders at the racism of a high school teacher and affirms his own sense of mexicanidad: "What the hell makes people like that, anyway? Always worried about his being Mexican and he never even thought about it, except sometimes, when he was alone, he got kinda funnyproud about it."[51]

What all of these examples are designed to suggest is that we conceptualize race—and every other determinant of identity—not as a pure and irreducible category, but instead as formed by and informing the whole range of social, historical, political, and cultural circumstances within which the subject locates herself. Evelyn Brooks Higginbotham questions the tendency of feminist criticism to privilege gender as the single most important determinant of identity. Gender, she suggests, was for nineteenth-century American women "both constructed and fragmented by race. Gender, so colored by race, remained from birth until death inextricably linked to one's personal identity and social status. For black and white women, gendered identity was reconstructed and represented in very different, indeed antagonistic, racialized contexts."[52] Her own counterprivileging of race as the more significant term of the equation runs the risk of creating different but equally significant overgeneralizations, however. As she herself indicates, any assessment of the ways in which race and gender inform identity must be framed historically. But privileging one term inevitably abstracts it in such a way as to render it ahistorical, reframing the contingent and material as a universal category that transcends the individual lives it sets out to explain.

This is not to suggest that I am interested in reinstating gender as the critical category of choice. Clearly, making "gender relations primary is to assume that they create a set of universal experiences more important than those of other inequalities," as Elizabeth Higginbotham, Maxine Baca Zinn, Lynn Weber Cannon, and Bonnie Thornton Dill maintain.[53] Privileging gender in this way is "inadequate," autobiography critic Julia Watson argues, given that women's positions "with respect to ethnicity and class and their modes of self-identification are not only divergent but organized within a structure of power relations."[54] While a certain number of globalizing statements are almost unavoidable in any discussion, I am more concerned to develop ad hoc, local observations about given narratives, privileging neither race nor gender as the dominant determinant of identity but instead acknowledging the range of inflections the combination of these factors—and others—can impart to different texts at different times. An ever more refined method of abstraction may be the mode of inquiry

favored by much contemporary theory, but this study works instead toward
a theory of the concrete, focusing closely on a series of individual voices
and their permutations, refusing to make broad claims about autobiographical narrative by women but honoring the particular, distinct pres-
ences which the writers and speakers of individual narratives have worked
so hard to achieve.

Generalizing statements are clearly useful in establishing the autonomy
of particular autobiographical traditions, however. "Reading by ethnicity,"
as Sau-ling Wong argues, "is a necessary act of . . . identity-building for
those whose literatures have been rendered invisible by subsumption."[55]
The distinction Elizabeth Fox-Genovese draws between personal narrative
by black and by white women ("Much of the autobiographical writing of
black women eschews the confessional mode—the examinations of personal motives, the searchings of the soul—that white women autobiographers so frequently adopt")[56] is helpful in establishing the work of African
American women as an autonomous narrative tradition that needs to be
studied in its own right and on its own terms. Yet in circumscribing a
given autobiographical genre, such statements run the risk of ignoring
other narrative forms with which women experiment. To consider black
women's writing, again, the meditations of Charlotte Forten in the journals
she kept through the mid-1850s comment on the Port Royal experiment
and the political circumstances of the freedmen living there but also develop a voice as rigorously "soul-searching" as are the reflections of Alice
James in the diary she wrote some thirty years later. Marita Golden's 1983
autobiography oscillates between ethnographic description and an analysis
of the "personal motives" that drew its author to Nigeria and back home
following the birth of her son and a failed marriage. And Maya Angelou's
1986 appraisal of the relations between Africans and African Americans
discloses as many personal "confessions" as political critiques.[57]

Delineating autobiographical traditions by particular groups of women
requires, of necessity, limiting them as well. When scholars begin to make
generalizations about the practices of women writers as a whole, however,
the drawbacks attendant upon their conclusions are potentially more serious, their summarizing claims more likely to slight a greater range of self-
representational strategies. The tendency of some feminist autobiography
theory to celebrate the feminine self-in-relation rightly critiques the andro-
centric quality of much autobiography theory, but at the same time it

leaves us with a model of the subject so abstracted as to transcend social conditions. Mary G. Mason's description, for instance, obscures as much as it reveals:

The self-discovery of female identity seems to acknowledge the real presence and recognition of another consciousness, and the disclosure of female self is linked to the identification of some 'other.' This recognition of another consciousness—and I emphasize recognition rather than difference—this grounding of identity through relation to the chosen other, seems . . . to enable women to write openly about themselves.[58]

For a great many women, as I have suggested earlier, the relation between "recognition" and "difference" is far more complicated, writing "openly" an impossibility—even with the authority affiliation provides. Take, for instance, the records of Jewish labor organizers considered in this study. If we assume, as does Margo Culley, that women writers in general "submerge the personal in some 'larger' purposes in order to become the vehicle for conveying a message about history,"[59] we are likely to hear these narratives only as voice-overs for the ongoing struggles of organized labor. Acknowledging the discursive constraints under which such activists as Rose Schneiderman and Elizabeth Hasanovitz labored leads to a different reading of their memoirs, a reading which in reaccentuating context underscores quality of voice as well.

Careful scrutiny thus suggests that we transform the terms of Culley's equation, identifying Schneiderman's and Pesotta's focus on their engagement in the collective labor contest as a means of justifying their interest as autobiographical subjects. Ostensibly celebrating the power of unified struggle, such writers thereby establish a sense of their singular authority. Elizabeth Hasanovitz's *One of Them: Chapters from a Passionate Autobiography* invokes the united response of hundreds of workers—in order to demonstrate how their solidarity supports her individual claim as shop steward.[60] Rose Schneiderman documents the founding of the National Women's Trade Union League but makes this bit of union history contingent upon personal history: "And so, with the blessings of labor and laymen the National Women's Trade Union League was born, an organization which was to be the most important influence in my life."[61] And Rose Cohen's autobiography *Out of the Shadow* compares the anonymity of one form of collective consciousness—the dispirited sense of herself as one of the hospital "dependents"—to the recognition that working-class community gives to her as an individual.[62]

Recognizing the range of autobiographical models and the rhetorical strategies used to develop them in these three narratives alone—personal histories produced under similar publishing constraints by women of the same ethnic background—should not mean that we deny their interest as texts by women. If, as feminist critic Jill Mathews asserts, " 'There can be no unified history of women,' " the field of women's autobiography is only the more compelling for the number of different histories with which it does provide us.[63] Acknowledging each woman's narrative as a distinct working out of the "struggle of memory against forgetting"[64] suggests the need to theorize history differently as well, as Sarah Rice does in her autobiography *He Included Me:* "Right now what we are doing is making history. You might not ever be in a book, but you are making history. History is things that happened in the past, and things that you do every day, as long as you live, that's history."[65]

Fabiola Cabeza de Baca puts this another way in *We Fed Them Cactus,* when she glosses for us what constitute significant events in the llano country of Northeastern New Mexico:

Money in our lives was not important; rain was important. We never counted our money; we counted the weeks and months between rains. . . . We would remember an unusually wet year for a lifetime; we enjoyed recalling it during dry spells. Rain for us made history. It brought to our minds days of plenty, of happiness and security, and in recalling past events, if they fell on rainy years, we never failed to stress that fact. The droughts were as impressed on our souls as the rains. When we spoke of the Armistice of World War I, we always said, "The drought of 1918 when the Armistice was signed." (11–12)

In this quiet but nevertheless radical statement, Cabeza de Baca restructures the relation between history and personal narrative. Rather than being a universal organizing principle, an abstraction against which individual lives are measured, history is redefined as a contingent phenomenon, constructed, and constructed differently, by the very individual subjects it has in more scholarly philosophical accounts found wanting in authority. Accepting of the mundane as well as the monumental, investing daily life with the attention and dignity typically accorded only to the sweeping changes of governments or the rise and fall of civilizations, "history" in this formulation is twin to life history, not the master narrative engineered to supplant it. Explanations like Rice's and Cabeza de Baca's and responses like the one Ron Takaki records (" 'What is it you want to know?' an old Filipino immigrant asked a researcher. 'Talk about history. What's that . . . ah, the story of my life . . . and how people lived with each other in my time' ") grant a value to private life more commonly reserved for the public sphere.[66] Perhaps this awareness will make it easier not only for Gertrude Stein but also for Rose Schneiderman—and Onnie Lee Logan and Cleofas Jaramillo and Jesusita Aragón—to receive the autobiographical recognition they deserve.

Part One

Defining Genre:
Culinary Autobiography

Chapter One

"I yam what I yam"

Cooking, Culture, and Colonialism
in New Mexico

Culinary Art, Literary Art:
The Cookbook as Autobiography

*Books were rare. My mother had one, which she kept in the
cedar box. It had a faded polychrome drawing on the cover
with the title* La Cocinera Poblana, *a cookbook which had be-
longed to Grandmother Isabel. We did not need it for cooking
the simple, never-changing meals of the family. It was the first
book from which Doña Henriqueta ever read to me. The idea of
making printed words sound like the things you already knew
about first came through to me from her reading of the recipes.
I thought it remarkable that you could find oregano in a book
as well as in the herb pot back of our house.*

Ernesto Galarza, *Barrio Boy*

*I still think that one of the pleasantest of all emotions is to know
that I, I with my brain and my hands, have nourished my beloved few, that I have concocted a stew or a story, a rarity or
a plain dish, to sustain them truly against the hungers of the
world.*

M. F. K. Fisher,
The Gastronomical Me

At first glance, Ernesto Galarza's description of his reading primer and
M. F. K. Fisher's recollections of her work as a mother and a wife make

3

an unlikely literary pairing, discordances yoked together by my own critical violence.[1] Yet as personal narratives they speak to one and the same end: food. In twin attempts to keep their readers off balance, words are equated not only with metaphysical intangibles (this would be predictable, in literary texts), but also with the transient and material pleasure of eating: for Galarza, who underscores his working-class status, these foods are "simple"—"frijoles, chile piquín and panocha" (33); for a clearly more affluent Fisher they include "rarities" as well as "plain dishes."

This chapter, which focuses on cookbooks by Mexicanas, argues that writing about food preparation provides the authors of such titles as *The Genuine New Mexico Tasty Recipes* (1939) and *Historic Cookery* (1949) with the literary occasion for writing about ethnic community and personal identity as well.[2] Before developing this thesis, however, I would like to make a critical detour through Fisher's culinary autobiography. Canonical reading for food professionals and the pièce de résistance of culinary narratives, *The Gastronomical Me* may initially strike readers as less than revolutionary. Yet the paragraph cited above levels the hierarchy of labor; Fisher represents the writing of literature and the cooking of a dinner as equally satisfying and equally significant forms of work. What is perhaps more important than the equation made between the products of the writer's "brain" and "hands," however, is the pride both forms of work engender in the speaker. Behind the domestic and literary labors foregrounded in this personal narrative, another form of work is operating: that process of self-reflection whose end product is articulation of the self. Reappraise this apparently unassuming paragraph on cooking and creativity with an eye on the "I," and you will find that, far from being restrained, it is insistently present.

The very title of Fisher's autobiographical foray insists that to write about food is to write about the self as well. In these wartime reminiscences "the hungers of the world" provide a compelling metaphor for love and desire; the author writes of her own wants and those of the numerous people she encounters on her travels over two continents. Fisher describes with equal relish her consumption of caviar and cod, boeuf bourguignon and frijoles, and these culinary equations provide her with a means of asserting the existence of the less palpable hungers we all share. Erasing differences of class and culture along with distinctions between writing and cooking, Fisher implies that in producing a discrete "I" she is in fact representing, at least to a certain extent, "us" and "them" as well.

What appeared during the Second World War as a humanistic effort to resist the divisive polemics of fascism and Nazism becomes in the post-modern frame of reference itself a (cultural) imperialism: if the well-meaning Anglo-American appreciates the products of different peoples' culinary labor, she nevertheless consumes them and, in so doing, makes them a part of herself. If I have not persuaded you that the edible metaphor may in fact accord with the seriousness of the occasion, let me rephrase this formulation more conventionally. By writing about the food and, by implication, the cultures of people distinct from herself in an acquisitive way—as desirable to sample because they are "exotic"—Fisher represents such "foreign" traditions as commodities to be (literally) assimilated for her own use.

The compiler of cookbooks as artist? Perhaps. But as political critic? We do not often rank cookbooks as literature, let alone as the occasion, whether covert or explicit, for political commentary. We may be readier to grant the connections between cooking and creative expression in a more diffuse sense, interpreting the gendered labor of the kitchen as feminine artistry. "She could paint with one hand / Studying grapes and peaches / A bowl of pears she would later / Cut, peel and stew for dinner," Joan Aleshire begins her "Exhibition of Women Artists (1790–1900)," affirming both the homely labor involved in feeding "the colicky child" and the heroic work of transforming this domestic practice into the subject of art.[3]

Students of American folk art have for some time been insisting that we acknowledge the previous centuries' "song fests . . . sewing, and sharing [of] favorite recipes" not merely as testaments to the exigencies of women's lives but as creative expressions in their own right. The editors of *Artists in Aprons* argue that because such domestic art of the eighteenth and nineteenth centuries did not explicitly contravene dominant social values but, rather, appeared to conform to the prescribed domestic role of women, its producers could often work relatively freely, undeterred by many of the obstacles set in the paths of professional women artists.[4] Writers on women's culinary texts agree. Alan Grubb's assessment of late-nineteenth-century Southern cookbooks as having generally been "published locally and in limited editions" suggests that modesty of scale may be, at least in part, what allows women to use this genre as a literary entrée.[5] His acknowledgment that the authors' prefaces reveal "the life stories of these women and those for whom they wrote" calls attention to the way in which collective affirmation can open into personal narrative, while his description of Jessie C. Benedict's *The Blue Ribbon Cook Book* (1904) as autobiographical as well as culinary—"We learn, somewhat surprisingly (in that her book is otherwise simply a recipe book), how her own experience as a homemaker laid the basis of her subsequent 'career' "—anticipates the hybrid texts home economist Fabiola Cabeza de Baca was to write in New Mexico some four decades later.[6] Tey Diana Rebolledo's distinction between storytelling and story writing is also useful here: "It was acceptable for women to be the storytellers, although not the story writers," she argues of midcentury Hispanas like Cabeza de Baca and Cleofas Jaramillo; thus "the passing on of recipes" was a folkloristic activity specifically coded feminine.[7]

As Rebolledo and other literary critics are beginning to argue, the exchange of recipes may communicate more than the culinary. In "Recipes for Reading: Summer Pasta, Lobster à la Riseholme, and Key Lime Pie," Susan Leonardi analyzes recipes as "highly embedded discourse akin to literary discourse,"[8] and she identifies this language practice as a gender-inflected one:

In the earlier *Joy*, the establishment of a lively narrator with a circle of enthusiastic and helpful friends reproduces the social context of recipe sharing—a loose community of women that crosses the social barriers of class, race, and generation. Many women can attest to the usefulness and importance of this discourse: mothers and daughters—even those who don't get along well otherwise—old friends who now have little in common, mistresses and their "help," lawyers and their secretaries—all can participate in this almost prototypical feminine activity. (342–43)

Before commenting on this compelling reappraisal of an apparently mundane practice, I would like to juxtapose against it two additional comments about recipe-sharing, framed not by food critics but by food writers:

While calling upon and taking one of my Spanish recipe cookbooks to one of my neighbors, our conversation for the moment centered around Spanish recipes. "Have you seen the article in *Holland Magazine* written by Mrs. D?" she inquired. I had not seen it, so she gave me the magazine to take home to read it. It was a three-page article, nicely written and illustrated, but very deficient as to knowledge of our Spanish cooking. In giving the recipe for making *tortillas* it read, "Mix bread flour with water, add salt." How nice and light these must be without yeast or shortening! And still these smart Americans make money with their writing, and we who know the correct way sit back and listen.[9]

Diana Kennedy, the authoritative cultural missionary for the foods of Mexico, has been decorated with the Order of the Aztec Eagle, the highest honor of its kind bestowed on foreigners by the Mexican government. In addition to this now classic and definitive cookbook, she is the author of *The Tortilla Book*, *Mexican Regional Cooking*, and *Nothing Fancy* and she travels widely promoting authentic Mexican cuisine.[10]

So aptly does Kennedy, the "ultimate authority, the high priestess, of Mexican cooking,"[11] personify the "smart American" of Jaramillo's cultural critique that if three decades did not separate the promotional paean from the political complaint, it would be tempting to resolve the twin images of Ms. Kennedy and Mrs. D into a single overzealous evangelical. That the author of *The Art of Mexican Cooking: Traditional Mexican Cooking for Aficionados* and the now anonymous writer for *Holland Magazine* are in fact not one but two distinct missionaries for the intercultural faith does not, of course, date Jaramillo's criticism. Rather, the persistence of American forays into foreign ground—cultural rather than geographical here—merely makes such a critique more pointed.

Leonardi's thesis that a cookbook is a literary production deserving of critical comment is compelling. But in light of passages like the two quoted here, her affirmation of recipe-sharing as a practice uniting women across "social barriers" begs to be reconsidered. Precisely because art—in this case, the art of cooking—is produced, as Leonardi herself indicates, within a specific social context, it encodes a political problematic. I would like to refocus inquiry on the "barriers of class, race, and generation" which Leonardi invokes only to transcend, in order to suggest that we read the "embedded discourse" of the cookbook not as an archetypally feminine language but rather as a form of writing which, if gender-coded, is also a culturally contingent production. What kind of ideological impulses are operating in a cookbook like *The Art of Mexican Cooking: Traditional Mexican Cooking for Aficionados*, whose title calls attention to the representation of a specific culture and the authority of "aficionados" to reproduce it in a text circulated for the benefit of English speakers? When does recipe-sharing, that is, become recipe-borrowing, with only a coerced "consent" from the domestic "help?"[12]

While *The Gastronomic Me* may strike some critics of autobiography and ethnography as a peculiar kind of self-reflexive text, the equations its author establishes between the presentation of recipes and the articulation of a self are clearly not idiosyncratic to M. F. K. Fisher. If writing of global food traditions in this case fashions the speaker-writer as culture plunderer, describing regional food traditions can enable self-reflexive writing to invoke "a sense of place and belonging," as Tey Diana Rebolledo indicates of the folkloristic narratives of Cleofas Jaramillo.[13] Developed out of a distinct geographical locale, a recipe may invoke a context rich in historical resonance, political association, and cultural permanence. Or, as Ntozake Shange explains of the recipes interwoven into her 1982 novel *Sassafras, Cypress and Indigo:* " 'I didn't want readers to skip over the recipes. . . . I wanted those recipes to create a place to be.' "[14] The reproduction of recipes provides "a direct link to history," as Marialisa Calta writes in a review of Laura Esquivel's best-selling novel *Like Water for Chocolate* (1992): "Everyone's past is locked up in their recipes. . . . The past of an individual and the past of a nation as well."[15]

Particularly for ethnic women writers, whose race or class may seem to preclude access to "high art" and its literary forms, the very domestic and commonplace quality of cooking makes it an attractive metonym for culture. For such autobiographers, presenting a family recipe and figuring its circulation within a community of readers provides a metaphor that is nonthreatening in its apparent avoidance of overt political discourse and yet culturally resonant in its evocation of the relation between the labor of the individual and her conscious efforts to reproduce familial and cultural traditions and values. The reproduction of such dishes as okra gumbo and huevos rancheros works to maintain cultural specificity in the face of assimilative pressures that attempt to amalgamate cultures in the "melting pot." At the same time, the series of imperatives the exchange of any recipe requires—the "cut" and "soak," "simmer" and "season" which enable readers to reproduce the writer's culinary art—gesture toward a sense of authority. These directives—orders, really—bespeak a kind of command, however limited in scope. The preliminary kind of authority exercised here suggests that reproducing a recipe, like retelling a story, may act both as cultural practice and autobiographical assertion; it may, as Esquivel asserts, recollect "the past of an individual and the past of a nation as well." The act of passing down recipes from mother to daughter, then, not only provides an apt metaphor for the reproduction of culture across generations but also creates a figurative home space from within which the "I" can begin the process of self-articulation.[16]

The recollections of Jesusita Aragón, a midwife working in Las Vegas, New Mexico, demonstrate this conjunction of cooking practice and self-assertion. Ostracized by her family after she gave birth to two children as a single mother, Aragón recounts her difficult circumstances in such a way as to demonstrate her eventual triumph over them. Her narrative, as edited by Fran Leeper Buss in *La Partera: Story of a Midwife,* works to resituate the exile, the family ec-centric, called "Amigo" by the father who would have preferred a son, in a position central and indispensable to a more expansively defined community which encompasses both the women she helps in labor and her familial relations.[17] Significantly, reconciliation with her grandmother takes place over the careful and loving preparation of a meal:

After my grandfather died, I ask her, "Who are you going to stay with, Grandma?" She says, "My sons, not you." But she didn't last too long with them. No, she went back to me. And I buy a little goat, and I have green chili, and I make tortillas, a good supper. When she came she said, "Oh, it smells good here." And I told her, "Yes, come in. You can eat with me, too." And she said, "I won't go back to my sons again. I will stay with you. If you want me to." And I told her, "Yes, you're welcome." (45)

The savor of "good" food indicates the moral lesson this recollection provides: Aragón's own goodness in forgiving her grandmother for her persistent censure.[18] Documenting her strength and resourcefulness in the face of familial neglect, the description of the carefully prepared supper enables the speaker to locate herself in the authoritative position of mother to her grandmother, providing this maternal predecessor with spiritual and cultural nourishment.

The connection between culture and identity toward which Ralph Ellison's "I yam what I yam" gestures in *Invisible Man* appears repeatedly in the culinary autobiographies of American women. In her cookbook *Iron Pots and Wooden Spoons: Africa's Gifts to New World Cooking,* Jessica Harris recollects her mother's cooking and implicitly attests to the relationships among cooking, culture, and colonialism. "My mother, who trained as a dietician but was discouraged from work in the food presentation field in which she excelled because of her race, took her talents home," Harris writes. "Each night was a feast. No frozen dinners or cake mixes ever crossed our threshold. Made-from-scratch cakes, flaky pie crusts, and intricate finger sandwiches went along with the traditional African-inspired foods that my father loved."[19]

Maya Angelou more explicitly invokes food as the signifier of political well-being. Indicting what she sees as the Ghanaian penchant for things European, a West African woman in *All God's Children Wear Traveling Shoes* decries the absence of rice—a traditional African staple—at the university cafeteria as a way of critiquing the inability of Ghanaian culture-makers to use indigenous culture as the foundation for a healthy body politic: " 'No rye?' Again, 'No rye? What fa country you peepo got? . . . You peepo, you got your Black Star Square. You got your university, but you got no rye! You peepo!' She began to laugh sarcastically. 'You make me laugh. Pitiful peepo.' "[20]

The invocation of a specific food speaks on behalf of cultural nationalism here. The elaboration of cooking techniques may equally provide a means of articulating an ethnic subject, however.[21] In her 1945 autobiography, *Fifth Chinese Daughter,* Jade Snow Wong devotes a considerable portion of one chapter to an extended description of a Chinese dinner she cooks for an interracial group of schoolmates. A narrative of assimilation gives way, for one reading moment, to an affirmation of cultural difference, as the author reproduces her recipes for "egg foo young" and "to-mato-beef" in extended detail. In her follow-up to her description of cooking techniques, Wong clearly indicates that she designs this kind of cultural reproduction to be circulated for the benefit of a non-Chinese audience when she follows up her description of cooking techniques with this proverbial gesture: "[She] found that the girls were perpetually curious about her Chinese background and Chinese ideologies, and for the first time she began to formulate in her mind the constructive and delightful aspects of the Chinese culture to present to non-Chinese" (161). While this coda explicitly reaffirms on the gastronomic level the ideology of the melting pot her "perpetually curious" readers might well expect to see reinstated, the very attention to a specific cultural practice as figured through a feminine discourse apparently bereft of political implications opens a space—if only at the subtextual level—within which the author can affirm a tradition decisively Chinese American. In effect, this passage declares Jade Snow Wong's intention to shape her friends—and her readers'—perceptions of Chinese American culture.[22]

More important, by constructing an empowering image of cultural tradition out of her own cooking labor, the autobiographer writes herself into a prominent place in the narrative. Her apparently casual invitation to dinner, accepted with alacrity by friends Wen-Lien, Teruko, and Harriet, allows her to assert herself as deserving of attention as it simultaneously implies their cultural deficit: "Within half an hour, her comrades had raised Jade Snow high in their estimation. To be worthy of this new trust, Jade Snow racked her brains to decide what dishes she could cook without a Chinese larder" (158). This apparently tentative appropriation of the limelight is repeated several pages later when the writer describes a dinner she cooks for a group of world-renowned musicians staying with her employer, the dean of Mills College. Again the explicit text works to erase cultural difference while the underlying message affirms both Chinese culture and the author's autobiographical presence:

That was a wonderful evening. . . . For the first time Jade Snow felt an important participant in the role of hostess. Because of everyone's interest in the kitchen preparations, she soon lost her shyness in the presence of celebrities and acted naturally. There was no talk about music, only about Chinese food. And Jade Snow ceased thinking of famous people as "those" in a world apart. She had a glimpse of the truth, that the great people of any race are unpretentious, genuinely honest, and nonpatronizing in their interest in other human beings. (172–73)

Ostensibly celebrating "universal" moral values, her praise of the performers nevertheless allows Jade Snow Wong to construct a subject who, if located in the modest role of "hostess," is yet "important" as the recipient of the homage of "famous people." Significantly, it is the representation of racial difference that enables this kind of self-assertion. Like the talk of the musicians, the chapter itself speaks not so much about the accomplishments of the celebrities, nor even about the virtues people share regardless of race, but instead "about Chinese food."[23]

The Conflict over Culture:
Some Discursive Contexts

I would like to explore this symbiosis of autobiographical act and cultural affirmation in a reading of cookbooks by two New Mexican writers, Cleofas Jaramillo and Fabiola Cabeza de Baca.[24] The folkloristic narratives Jaramillo published over the course of two decades, beginning in 1939 with a collection of stories she called *Cuentos del Hogar* and culminating in 1955 with her sustained autobiographical project, *Romance of a Little Village Girl*, insist upon an identity informed by region, community, and history. So, too, Cabeza de Baca's narrative of her youth on a ranch near Las Vegas, New Mexico, *We Fed Them Cactus*, explains selfhood as developing out of a specific geographical locale which the book places, if obliquely, in a political context. Like these texts, though less explicitly, the culinary histories both women published also define an engaged subjectivity, anticipating the later personal narratives by providing for the beginnings of an autobiographical assertion that is matrixed geographically, culturally, and socially. They demonstrate, too, how *political* circumstance—in this case the struggle for control of Mexican culture that succeeds the struggle for proprietorship of Mexican land—helps to shape both the way people conceive of themselves and the manner in which they speak this sense of self-assertion. Self-reflection in both narratives is accordingly complicated by political and literary history—by the demands of the publishing world and of the languages available to Hispanas writing during the first half of the twentieth century.[25]

Working as a home demonstration agent for New Mexico from the 1910s through the 1930s, Fabiola Cabeza de Baca published, in addition to *We Fed Them Cactus* and a number of cookbooks celebrating nuevomexicano traditions, a series of pamphlets through the New Mexico State Agricultural Extension Service that were designed to instruct rural Hispanas in the new housekeeping and cooking methods currently being promoted by the U.S. government following the passage of the Smith-Lever Act in 1914.[26] Her activities as an "agent" placed her in the position of cultural mediator between the Hispanos—whom the state clearly considered her a representative *of* as well as *for*—and the Anglo-American business interests that were being promoted by the government's discourse of technological "advancement." To the extent that they recirculate this language of "the march of progress," Cabeza de Baca's two pamphlets "Bo-letín de Conservar" (1931) and "Los Alimentos y Su Preparación" (1934) reflect the compromising—as well as compromised—role their author oc-cupied in working on behalf of a government agency as eager to assume ignorance, incivility, and inability on the part of its Hispano residents as it was willing to trumpet the advantages of Eastern farm and housekeeping methods over the nuevomexicano and Native American practices more ap-propriate to the arid environment Anglo "pioneers" were attempting to improve through industrialization.

In "Canning Comes to New Mexico: Women and the Agricultural Ex-tension Service 1914–1919," historian Joan Jensen characterizes the re-sponse of Hispanas to the work of Cabeza de Baca and other home dem-onstration agents as less than enthusiastic. "Hispanic women, unlike Anglo women, did not feel at home in school houses or public buildings. They also preferred meeting without Anglo women. 'It is not possible to com-bine demonstrations for English and Spanish-speaking people even when they can all be reached by one language,' wrote one agent, 'because the Spanish-speaking people will not come to a meeting called for both. They are very retiring and can best be reached in small groups' " (213). It is not difficult to read in this recalcitrance a resistance to the pressures of assimi-lation that were being exerted upon the women by means of a critique of their domestic work practices. Jensen herself acknowledges that the state's efforts to emphasize the virtues of "modernization" encoded a very conser-vative cultural agenda. Focusing here on the government's interruption of Navajo tradition by forcing families to send at least one child away to boarding school, she comments:

At the McKinley County School for Navajos, for example, matrons apparently taught the young girls to can in 1918, though there was little chance that they would use these skills on the reservation. It was, however, part of the national program to replace traditional skills of the Indian woman with skills that would make them more dependent upon the Euro-American culture and occupy the place women were assigned in that culture. (205)

But what of Cabeza de Baca's own efforts to further the march of prog-ress through the state of New Mexico? In marked contrast to later publica-tions celebrating the nuevomexicano past as an Edenic era of abundance, prosperity, and self-sufficiency (consider, for instance, the author's two cookbooks, *The Good Life: New Mexico Traditions and Food* and *Historic Cookery,* both published in 1949), "Los Alimentos y Su Preparación" reproduces the future-oriented discourse of progress employed by the state, often as justification for land fraud, illegal business practices, and the attempt at cultural obliteration. Paralleling changes in food preparation with changes in "civilization," Cabeza de Baca introduces this domestic instruction manual with an assertion half apologetic, half imperative: "Cada día hay una nueva invención y nuevos descubrimientos de la ciencia y todos estamos listos para adoptarlos" (Every day there is a new invention and new scientific discoveries and we are all ready to adopt them).[27] Framing assimilation as the inexorable and inevitable outcome of history, Cabeza de Baca reproduces the state's teleology of industrial growth: "En esta época de progreso y descubrimientos científicos hay que seguir la marcha, no sólo en el modo de vivir, sino que también en el modo de comer" (In this era of progress and scientific discoveries it is necessary to follow the trend, not only in one's style of life, but also in one's style of eating) (3). The politics of cooking here make a virtue of necessity, as progress sweeps from the urban to the rural sector:

para progresar en el modo de vivir debíamos que estar listos para aprender como alimentarnos para conservarnos saludables. ¿De qué sirve tener los mejores automóbiles, las mejoras carreteras, las mejores escuelas, y todo lo mejor del mundo si no falta la salud? El pueblo que no se alimenta propiamente no puede producir y mantener una civilización próspera y fuerte. (4)

In order to progress in our way of life we must be ready to learn how to eat in order to maintain our health. What use does having the best cars, the best highways, the best schools, and the best of everything in the world serve if we don't have our health? The town that doesn't nourish itself properly can't produce and maintain a prosperous and strong civilization.

Eating "properly" is to good bodily health what building the best cars, highways, and schools is to a strong body politic. Despite Cabeza de Baca's emphasis on the relation between good nourishment and good health—and here one marvels at the fortitude with which the preceding four centuries of Hispanos have prospered, bereft, apparently, of this capability—learning how to eat "properly" has a great deal more to do with accommodating to cultural change than it does with building strong bodies twelve ways.

The bright tone of this pronouncement notwithstanding, the appeal to assimilate carries with it a cost. Writing to women, the home demonstration worker defines cultural accommodation in the language of home management. Good table manners signify superior comportment, she asserts, and

Una persona que tiene buenos modales en el modo de comer considerá superior a una que no los tiene. Es una de las pruebas de tener educación o buena crianza. Si la madre enseña a sus hijos seguir buenos modales de mesa cada día, no tendrá que avergonzar cuando tengan huéspedes. (44)

A person who has good table manners will be considered superior to one who doesn't have them. This is one of the proofs of having an education or being well brought up. If the mother teaches her children to use good table manners every day, she will not have to be ashamed when she has guests.

Superiority or shame: the subjugated must become convinced of their own desire for subjugation.[28] Here women, the reproducers of culture because of their work of child-rearing, are urged to internalize the political dictates—framed as moral lessons—of the state discourse on home improvement. Cooking does not so much embody culture in this text, it turns out, as obliterate it. If "Los Alimentos y Su Preparación" explicitly appeals to its female readers' experience of maternal obligation, the pamphlet, complete with photos depicting the proper way to use knife, fork, and spoon and instructions detailing the "Reglas para Poner y Como Servir la Mesa" (Rules for Setting and Serving at the Table) (41), ultimately addresses its audience not as parental educators but as children themselves, culturally speaking, requiring instruction in the new rules of the Anglo table.

Cooking and Colonialism: Speaking Against Cultural Appropriation

The public worker must be sympathetic with people she works with regardless of their background or extraction; she must respect their customs, their habits and beliefs; and foremost she must know that though individuals may differ, people are people in any language, race, or creed.

Fabiola Cabeza de Baca,
"New Mexican Diets"

A pamphlet on table manners may seem a rather slight subject with which to examine how cultural appropriation figures in works by American women writers. Yet, like Jaramillo's complaint about tortilla-making, which associates the authenticity of a recipe with the integrity of a culture, Cabeza de Baca's juxtaposition of "el modo de vivir" with "el modo de comer" is a gesture made repeatedly by Hispano writers concerned with the maintenance of cultural practices in the wake of the 1848 United States conquest of northern Mexico.[29] For women, this attention to the pressures of acculturation often takes the form not of explicit political statements but, rather, of a kind of composite genre: a combination of familial reminiscence and personal narrative, of descriptions of custom, history, food, and folklore. In the three decades between the 1930s and the 1950s, both Fabiola Cabeza de Baca and Cleofas Jaramillo published narratives integrating recipes "with accounts of folk life, as if the female sense of rootedness and place is passed down through the distinctive foods nature offers," as Tey Diana Rebolledo has noted.[30] This attention to "rootedness" and "place," I would suggest, framed as it is in a feminine culinary discourse apparently far removed from the sphere of political contention, nevertheless provides the two writers, whose sex and position within landed families would discourage the voicing of explicit discontent with Americano policy, with a means of critiquing it.

Home economics, in other words, serves as a suitably genteel forum for theorizing about the social and political economy. In "New Mexican Diets" Cabeza de Baca develops this nutritional pedagogy quite explicitly, as the essay's concluding lesson, excerpted above, makes clear.[31] In this piece Cabeza de Baca juxtaposes the dietary changes occasioned by the Spanish "conquest" with the shift in food preparation following the "American occupation," in order to establish a syntactical parallel which is political as well, a comparison which equates the first conquest with the second, denying those historical euphemisms that redefine a hostile military invasion as a welcomed or at least unresisted "annexation." Setting "Spanish" and "American" takeovers in apposition allows Cabeza de Baca to define them as oppositional as well. The "Spaniard" both "improved" the eating habits of Native Americans, she suggests, and adapted to theirs: "Like all pioneers [the Spaniard] had to be resourceful and adaptive; therefore, he learned the food habits of the Indians. Likewise, the Indian adopted many of the food habits of the Spaniard." Not so with the "American" takeover. While "some of the urban people adopted the food habits of the newcomers," de Baca writes, "the isolated rural population changed little."

Through a critique of the inferior nutritional quality of these "poorer urban diets," diets explicitly linked to the "newcomers," she simultaneously indicts the cultural impoverishment of the nonnatives who followed "the coming of the railroad" and affirms native cultural practice. In addition, she refuses to accede to racist jeers like the following: " 'Give [the Spanish people] beans and chili and that is all they need.' " Instead of reading such modest needs as a sign of poverty, she insists, we should see such collective "self-reliance" as a means of countering ethnocentrism and of honoring cultural integrity. In arguing that "the people were not poor since they owned their homes, produced all their foods, and with a little additional income that the men could pick up were self-sufficient" (668), Cabeza de Baca thus exploits the edible trope in order to reaffirm the strategic value of cultural separatism.

Published just seven years later, the author's *Historic Cookery* appears more sentimental than argumentative. Descriptions of food and its preparation resonate with nostalgia for an Edenic past; as with Proust's concisely symbolic madeleines, evocations of flavors and cooking methods work efficiently to recall an entire way of life. "Try the recipes," she urges. "And when you do, think of New Mexico's golden days, of red chile drying in the sun, of clean-swept yards, outdoor ovens, and adobe houses on the landscape. Remember the green valleys where good things grow. And think too of families sitting happily at tables" (2). Yet, like its more obviously tutelary predecessor, this cookbook evokes the flavors of the past in order to critique the cultural present. Echoing the "New Mexican Diets" reading of "our basic foods—chile, beans . . . and whole grain cereals" as "increasingly popular" because "highly nutritious" (1–2), the author reaffirms the value of New Mexican cultural practice. "Chile drying" and "clean-swept yards" are indications of a well-ordered life; descriptions of the domestic economy, where "good things grow," reflect the health of the Hispano community before it was besieged by Anglo land speculators, its culture "re-covered" by white intellectuals.

Clearly Cabeza de Baca's description of familial and community harmony is modeled after nonnative accounts of Hispano culture, its nostalgic evocation complicit in a folkloric discourse that romanticizes both the land and its people as suspended in a kind of glorious sunset of fast-fading primitive rituals. Yet by defining cultural practice as conscious choice, she asserts the cultural agency of the New Mexicans whose lives she depicts.[32]

Emphasizing the labor that is involved in the reproduction of cultural practices, in other words, however sentimentalized and class-conscious such representations may be, does work (at least on the textual level) against the politics of assimilation, insisting on a historically grounded sense of cultural specificity and maintaining an ethnic difference which in turn provides the self with a certain authority to speak. Thus the rose-colored tribute to "New Mexico's golden days," with its description of "historic" (read "unadulterated") Hispano cooking and pointed lack of reference to more contemporary cooking methods enables Cabeza de Baca to develop an unspoken comparison between the richness of traditional nuevomexicano life and the paucity of the presumably nonnative reader's "modern" cultural practices.

That the brief but tartly phrased admonishment of *Romance of a Little Village Girl*, with its proprietary emphasis on "our Spanish cooking," is, like Cabeza de Baca's romance of sun and adobe, aimed at Anglo appropriation of Hispano culture more generally becomes clear if we look more closely at the text by Jaramillo that precedes its publication. A response in part to the aplomb with which the Mrs D's of her day marketed recipes not of their own making, *The Genuine New Mexico Tasty Recipes* is not simply a catalogue of recipes correcting the absence of yeast and shortening. Instead, by employing food and food preparation within the context of personal narrative as metonyms for the whole of traditional Hispano cultural practice, it reaffirms and maintains that practice. After a series of "Spanish" recipes—and note that this formulation is itself a colonial one, suppressing Native American contributions to New Mexican culture[33]—Jaramillo reprints a series of chapters from *Shadows of the Past*[34] describing, as Genaro Padilla notes, "familial and community occasions that contextualize the very preparation and consumption of food" (55).

It is such a cultural context—and, more specifically, who is authorized to describe it—that is at issue in this text. The very title of the book, with its insistence on authenticity, foregrounds nuevomexicano tradition, as represented by the culinary, as subject to appropriation. To assert that the recipes in one's cookbook are the genuine article is, after all, to imply that fabrications—nonauthentic recipes—exist. Emphasizing the antiquity of her collection (the subtitle reads, "Old and Quaint Formulas for the Preparation of Seventy-Five Delicious Spanish Dishes"), Jaramillo ensures that the bloodlines of her culinary products are pure, or nearly so.[35]

"In this collection of Spanish recipes," she announces, "only those used in New Mexico for centuries are given, excepting one or two Old Mexico recipes" (1). While this attention to cultural commodification may clearly be read as a critical move on Jaramillo's part, the very act of eulogizing Hispano tradition as "quaint"—an artifact, that is—suggests that this critique is itself intended to be circulated extra-culturally. As Padilla argues:

On the one hand, *Tasty Recipes* represents the popularization of ethnic cuisine, and, in that respect, represents a desire to cater to members of the dominant culture. On the other, Jaramillo contextualizes consumption in an explicitly cultural manner, and, therefore, suggests how intimately food is related to lived cultural experience. Hence, we discover a form of culinary resistance—Anglo-Americans can follow the recipe and still not eat nuevomexicano cooking. (55)

Yet, in *The Genuine New Mexico Tasty Recipes,* food is invested not only with a cultural register ultimately inaccessible to the nonnative, but with a more overtly political signification as well. By historicizing his sister's evocation of food traditions, Reyes N. Martínez in his introduction to the book directs readers to draw connections between good nutrition and good government:

The early settlers introduced certain kinds of foods to this section of the country, which, although occasionally used now, are not appreciated for their nutritive and health value. No one questions the evidence of the superior physical ruggedness of the past generations of that era in comparison with that of their descendants of the present day, who, although enjoying the advantages of modern science and research along the lines of dietetics, do not generally attain the natural constitutional ruggedness of body that tradition tells us their ancestors possessed. (28)

Compare this insistence on the better health of previous generations with the future-extolling text of Cabeza de Baca's "Los Alimentos":

Hay personas que afirman que nuestros antepasados guardaban mejor salud y vivían más años sin saber nada de la propia nutrición: estas eran las excepciones. Esto puede ser verdad hasta cierto punto. . . . El modo de vivir de nuestros antepasados era más favorable para la salud. Con el progreso y civilización de la nación, el modo de vivir ha cambiado y el resultado es que el modo de comer tiene que cambiar. (4)

There are people who argue that our ancestors kept themselves in better health and lived longer without knowing anything about proper nutrition: these were the exceptions. That can be true up to a certain point. . . . Our ancestors' lifestyle was more healthful. With progress and the civilization of the nation, the way of living has changed and the result is that the way we eat has to change.

Taking up the dominant culture's discourse of progress—that language of "dietetics" adopted in "Los Alimentos" to justify apparently unavoidable cultural accommodations—Martínez's appeal to science turns this language of the inevitable back upon itself. Here, affirming "the advantages of modern science" does not celebrate the encroachment of Anglo business interests upon a rural state of small landholders and self-sufficient homesteads, but, rather, critiques such a political situation as unhealthy. Martínez's historical distinction between "early settlers" and "their descendants of the present day," between "natural constitutional ruggedness" and the artificial "advantages of modern science," thus encodes a racial inflection as well. The loss of cultural integrity and authority is articulated through a parable about the devaluing of "traditional foods." Resonating with Jaramillo's insistence on the authenticity and antiquity of her collection, Martínez's generational focus here suggests that, like the Spanish colonists themselves, foods can have a lineage; the genuine landholders, whose land grants derive from the rulers of sixteenth-century Spain, eat *The Genuine New Mexico Tasty Recipes*. Just as those foods introduced by the *conquistadores* and enjoyed by their descendants resulted in good health, so abandoning them and replacing them with modern ("white") substitutes will produce a people who are less constitutionally sound. Clearly I am distorting the studiedly neutral tone of Martínez's brief historical commentary by subjecting it to such extensive analysis and sardonic paraphrasing. Nevertheless, because the passage simultaneously draws an implicit parallel between cooking and culture and refuses to glorify science despite a publishing environment celebrating its advancements, it does embody a certain resistance to the rhetoric of assimilation.

Even a cursory glance at the contemporary literature produced by non-natives demonstrates that such a critique is neither inordinately defensive nor unfairly acerbic. Like Jaramillo's own preface to *The Genuine New Mexico Tasty Recipes*, Erna Fergusson's introductory remarks to her 1934 *Mexican Cookbook* stress the authenticity of her culinary catalogue. "The recipes in this book," she affirms, "are limited to those which were in common use when the province of New Mexico was a part of the Republic of Mexico."[36] Like the folklorist author of *Shadows of the Past* and *Cuentos del Hogar*, Fergusson is concerned to demarcate, using food as a signifier, a series of cultural traditions: "Nothing more surely reflects the life of a people," Fergusson asserts, "than what they ate and how they prepared it" (4).

Yet, while Jaramillo's project is to recover nuevomexicano customs in a gesture of ethnic pride, however muted, Fergusson's interest is precisely in appropriating such practices on behalf of "national interests." Defining Mexican food in her foreword as "part of the Southwestern diet . . . since the 'American Occupation,' " the author traces the acceptance of "slowly-cooked and richly condimented dishes" by "people who could not even pronounce their names" in order to insist that such recipes "represent Mexican cookery that belongs to the U.S." Cultural appropriation is thus justified by a political event, the military takeover of Mexico by the United States. Fergusson's awareness that her coercive culinary history of the Southwest does in some measure reiterate the forced invasion of the region she speaks of becomes clear later in the book, when she prefaces a series of recipes for tortillas with this derisive but nonetheless anxious comment about cultural authority: "The only way to be sure of making *tortillas* correctly is to have a line of Indian ancestry running back about 500 years" (88). If her recipes for corn and wheat tortillas lack yeast, then, readers have been duly warned.

Yet it is cultural rather than culinary blunders that are most arresting here. In her chapter on "Mexican Cooking Then and Now," a history of cooking methods, Fergusson expends a substantial amount of narrative energy justifying the " 'American Occupation' " by juxtaposing the "modern cook in a modern kitchen" with the "primitive conditions" of traditional domestic life (3, 5). If Cabeza de Baca's "Los Alimentos" reluctantly espouses the new housekeeping and cooking methods as inevitable given the forward movement of "el progreso y civilización de la nación," Fergusson's text actively maligns Hispano cultural practices through a series of racist clichés. Consider, for instance, the caustic sarcasm of this passage:

The menus are based on meals as served at a gentleman's table before the general adoption of American ways. Then eating was a serious matter, interfered with only by famine, war, or Lent. The day began with a preliminary breakfast in bed; coffee or chocolate and sweet rolls. About nine o'clock came the real breakfast which included eggs or meat and more bread and coffee. After that the *Señora* put in her heavy work of unlocking cupboards, storerooms, and chests; of dispensing food for the day; and of directing her servants. Naturally she felt fagged by 11 and ready for the *caldo colado* or clear soup, which came as a pick-me-up at that hour. (6)

Small wonder, given this kind of representation of the nuevomexicano rancheros, that Jaramillo felt called upon to exact literary justice. The romantic picture of wealthy family life described for us in the pages of *The Genuine New Mexico Tasty Recipes,* a scene of "warm harvest sunlight" and "golden wheat and oats, stacked high on round, earthen . . . threshing grounds" (21), is thus in some measure a defensive portrait, its emphatically celebratory rhetoric a compensatory literary strategy. The impression of rural life here is one of busy industry and "self-sustaining" plenty, a harmony of blue corn and yellow wheat, a perpetual "Indian summer" where "servants and children" enjoy the harvest plenty in a bucolic landscape unmarked by time (21). This "historical amnesia" which, as Genaro Padilla notes, is characteristic of Jaramillo's work as a whole, clearly works as a palliative for the all too immediate economic losses and cultural conflict suffered by landed families like hers during the early years of the century. So, too, the author's insistence on maintaining a feudalistic stability of rich and poor works as an implicit indictment of the contemporary, less happy relation between Hispanos and Anglos. In such a context of cultural contention, the sentimentalized picture of "*peones* [working] happily, taking great interest in doing their best for the *patrón,* whom they held in great esteem and respect" (24), provides a critique of race relations precisely contingent upon a suturing of class conflict. Likewise, given the collective loss of self-confidence post-1848, the representation of Jaramillo as authoritative subject is to a certain extent dependent upon the objectification of "Lupe" as "our Indian cook" (23). The proprietary address subsumes both ethnic and class divisions, constructing a whole Hispano Subject greater than the sum of its cross-cultural parts.

This glowing picture of village life is not exclusive to Jaramillo's *The Genuine New Mexico Tasty Recipes* but in fact characterizes both Cabeza de Baca's *Historic Cookery* and her 1949 celebration of Hispano food and custom, *The Good Life: New Mexico Traditions and Food,* as well. I have previously argued that in her earlier pamphlets undertaken as home economist for the state, the author neglects traditional domestic life in order to espouse the changes sanctioned by the government's agricultural "improvement" program. In *The Good Life,* by contrast, Cabeza de Baca does not look forward to some future technological utopia but instead gazes backward, recovering a history untranslatable in the dominant culture's lexicon of industrial progress.[37] Ethnographic description in *The Good Life,* as in Jaramillo's *Tasty Recipes,* then, is nostalgic rather than analytic, with such chapter headings as "Winter's Plenty," "Christmas Festivities," and "The Wedding" celebrating that "happiness and abundant living" (4) the author describes as characteristic of the Hispano past. The emphasis on cultural self-sufficiency invoked by the "full splendor" of an "Autumn Harvest" recalls both the author's own *Historic Cookery* and Jaramillo's *Tasty Recipes,* as well as a series of other Mexicano personal narratives post-1848, in which the cataloguing of farm and field provides an implicit contrast between a harmonious, richly lived past and a more difficult present (5).[38]

While the language of *The Good Life* often shrouds historical struggles in a romantic fog, the reader-response dynamic that the text sets up provides Cabeza de Baca with a means of articulating, albeit quietly, a form of cultural critique. The cookbook is particularly well suited for this kind of critique because it exhorts readers to gloss its text not only as a series of declarative statements (if we read without actually trying the recipes) but as a set of performative acts as well (when the recipes are not only read but reproduced). Ntozake Shange points to this kind of reading dynamic when she suggests that if a reader of her novel *Sassafras, Cypress and Indigo* should cook " 'Rice Casserole #36,' a recipe of the title character . . . or her 'Favorite Spinach,' that reader 'can be right in her kitchen, right in the book.' "[39] Similarly, literary critic Susan Leonardi notes: "Like a narrative, a recipe is reproducible, and, further, its hearers-readers-receivers are *encouraged* to reproduce it, and, in reproducing it, to revise it and make it their own" (344). Leonardi is able to equate "reproducing" with "sharing" only by ignoring the inequities of power across "the social barriers of class, race, and generation" (342), but her emphasis on the performative aspect of cookbook reading is nevertheless a useful one for ethnographic inquiry. If the exhortation to reproduce a recipe may create a community, it may also call attention to the boundaries of such an affili-

ation, asking readers to question the conflations *and* the distinctions between the community constructed within the text itself and the community
of readers created outside it.

Encouraging readers to reproduce, revise, and make a recipe their own
enables Cabeza de Baca to call attention to cultural commodification in
The Good Life; the text appears to encourage its audience to make "New
Mexican Traditions and Food" their own, yet its author ultimately provides
obstacles to such appropriation. "In order to have the dishes taste as one
has eaten them in the New Mexican homes or genuine New Mexican restaurants, one must use New Mexican products," she counsels (45). As in
Jaramillo's text, here "genuine" not only authenticates the writer but also
works as a barrier to the reader. Ostensibly allowing for the possibility of
extra-cultural access, on another level this admonishment to use "New
Mexican products" divides nonnative readers from the Hispano community
the book itself so wholeheartedly celebrates, thus resisting cultural abstraction and insisting on rootedness and a sense of place. Appending a glossary
of Spanish terms to the book allows Cabeza de Baca to remind her readership that reproducing the recipes of *The Good Life* does not necessarily
lead to cultural ownership. "The words in this glossary may have other
meanings," she asserts, "but the one given here explains the meaning as
used in this composition" (81). By calling attention to what is left over, the
remainder that escapes translation, the author problematizes cultural access, depicting a web of associations and meanings ultimately ungraspable
by the nonnative speaker.[40]

Depictions of class conflict further complicate the text's representation
of culture. As in Jaramillo's *Tasty Recipes,* cultural harmony in *The Good
Life* is largely achieved at the expense of a sustained appraisal of class
relations. This is not to say that relations between rancheros and peones
are ignored, however. As in the author's later *We Fed Them Cactus,* in
The Good Life anxiety about class conflict is relieved not by being over-
looked but by being contained. Curiously, it is art that effects this defusing
of class conflict in both of Cabeza de Baca's texts: consistently a laborer-
artist simultaneously articulates the threat to the social order and resolves
it. In *The Good Life,* the relation between art and politics is figured in
Tilano, guitar-playing goatherder for Don Teodoro. His introduction early
in the narrative indicates both the affiliation of manual and mental labor
and the marginal status such a worker occupies. Note how this description

of the making of *ristras* (strings of dried red chiles) situates Tilano: "Men, women, and children joined in the task. Each one, seated on the ground, deftly started tying the pods. Tilano, the goat herder and storyteller, stood at the door waiting for his chance to get in a word" (6). As with Santiago, the grumbling ranch hand of *We Fed Them Cactus* whose critique of class inequities is replaced by the harmonies of his own corrido-singing, Tilano is encouraged to forget his political complaints when the patrón's wife, Doña Paula, urges him to exercise his musical skills instead:

"The *Aleluyas* say that there is no future in being a Roman Catholic and they told me that if I joined them I would not have to herd goats for you for such low wages, Don Teodoro." . . .

"Why don't you play the guitar for us Tilano," said Doña Paula. . . . Tilano did not need coaxing. No sooner had Doña Paula spoken than Tilano was playing familiar strains. Some of the young folks joined in by singing which made Tilano so happy that he forgot the *Aleluyas*." (6–7)

Cabeza de Baca's representation of art as the palliative to political ills is a very traditional one. To the extent that it is defined by the laboring goatherd rather than the leisured gentleman, however, it carries with it quite radical implications. It is the cooks and *curanderas* (healers), after all, who in producing stories and recipes reproduce the cultural practices which constitute the folkloric reminiscences of both *We Fed Them Cactus* and *The Good Life*. Granted, the figure of the working musician in *The Good Life* ultimately underwrites the rule of the wealthy by creating an art that reveals class conflict only to contain it. Nevertheless, what we see in both works are narratives sustained by the very people they explicitly work to keep down.

While the relationship between the Turrieta family and their servants structures *The Good Life,* this insistently affirmative picture of social harmony is itself sustained through a gendered metaphor of class obligations. If the culinary reminiscences in this text depict ethnicity as something that is actively reproduced, it is the working alliance between Señora Martina and Doña Paula through which such cultural labor is represented. Chapters titled "Autumn Harvest," "Christmas Festivities," and "Lent" celebrate nuevomexicano traditions through the year, but the labor involved in preparing for such cultural events remains a constant throughout the text. Indeed, the emphasis of the narrative is precisely on that labor, rather

than on the depictions of Hispano customs that the chapter titles would
lead the reader to expect. And if it is through the representation of work
itself—always a community effort in this text—that Cabeza de Baca locates
Hispano ethnicity, it is the characteristically feminine labor of cooking to
which she calls attention—both as signifying nourishment (material and
moral) and as the active labor involved in providing for such cultural sustenance.

Although the book's nostalgic representation of cultural plenitude is
contingent upon the joint labors of Señora Martina and Doña Paula, the
vantage point from which readers observe this alliance does not accommodate both female subjects equally. We are initially introduced to "Señá
Martina," as she is familiarly called by Doña Paula, not as a distinct individual but, rather, as the type of the ageless, timeless curandera: "The
medicine woman seemed so old to Doña Paula and she wondered how old
she was. No one remembered when she was born. She had been a slave
in the García family for two generations and that was all any one knew.
She had not wanted her freedom, yet she had always been free" (14).
Eulogizing her as "the medicine woman" positions Señora Martina with
respect to Doña Paula, wife of the ranchero, and establishes a smoothly
harmonious picture of relations between classes and cultures.

Succeeding references to "The Herb Woman," however, emphasize not
only Señora Martina's willingness to work on behalf of Doña Paula ("After
greeting Doña Paula she sat down beside her and without being asked,
she took over the task of slicing small squashes into circles in preparation
for drying" [13]), but her resistance to cultural authority as well. It is Señora Martina who voices opposition to acculturation, as this process is signified by changes in the practices of medicine. While Doña Paula, whose
voice is closely linked with that of the narrator, may argue on behalf of
accommodation ("Diphtheria is contagious Señá Martina. It is better to let
the doctor treat that" [15]), the curandera responds: "Be as you say—but
I cured all my children without assistance from the doctor which I could
not have afforded anyway. . . . Today [Juanito, my youngest] is as well as
any one can be, although deaf, he is a healthy man" (15). If Señora Martina's stubbornness is treated a trifle sardonically here, the amount of narrative energy expended upon this figure suggests that her criticism of contemporary medical practices serves a significant function in the text.[41] And
comments like the following more explicitly contrast the well-being of the
previous generations with the difficulties their modern counterparts face:

"When I was young," Señora Martina recalls, "there were no doctors and we lived through many sicknesses" (14). Comparing the competence of the curandera with the incapability of (presumably Anglo) doctors, I would argue, enables Cabeza de Baca to articulate a muted cultural critique. In addition, the meticulous detail with which the author lists herbs and their curative properties not only provides *The Good Life* with a model of cultural authenticity and antiquity but conveys practical information as well.[42]

In "Tradition and Mythology: Signatures of Landscape in Chicana Literature," Tey Diana Rebolledo notes that "in Hispanic folklore the curandera has always had more freedom of movement than other women. Cabeza de Baca saw the herb woman as not only freer but clearly outside the confines of society."[43] Yet her "freedom" seems to me questionable, since it is defined on behalf of the class that benefits most from her labor, and her marginal status does more to provide the author with the measure of a wealthy Hispano society than it does to elevate this working-class figure herself. I would suggest that it is precisely Señora Martina's distance from the voice of the narrator, her position as cultural Other vis-à-vis the Turrieta family, that enables Cabeza de Baca to maintain her own position as cultural mediator in a narrative location that provides her with authority over her non-Hispano readership and simultaneously allows a (muted) critique of Anglo imperialism. This eulogy to the herb woman simultaneously provides Cabeza de Baca with a means of containing cultural difference (the relations between Hispanos and indígenos remain harmonious, in implicit comparison with the current Mexicano-Anglo conflict) and with a way to articulate political difference (post-1848) without compromising the influence of her well-connected narrator. Señora Martina's censure of the medical establishment (" 'I hope to live another year, for when I am gone my remedies go with me and the doctors will get fat from your generosity' " [18]) thus exploits the author's culinary trope for culture to provide her with a critique of it.

Season to Taste:
Autobiographical Idiosyncrasy in
Culinary Narrative

Perhaps El Hoyo, its inhabitants, and its essence can best be explained by telling you a little bit about a dish called capirotada. *Its origin is uncertain. But it is made of old, new, stale, and hard bread. It is sprinkled with water and then it is cooked with raisins, olives, onions, tomatoes, peanuts, cheese, and general leftovers of that which is good and bad. It is seasoned with salt, sugar, pepper, and sometimes chili or tomato sauce. It is fired with tequila or sherry wine. It is served hot, cold, or just "on the weather" as they say in El Hoyo. The Garcías like it one way, the Quevedos another. While in general appearance it does not differ much from one home to another it tastes different everywhere. Nevertheless it is still* capirotada. *And so it is with El Hoyo's* chicanos. *While many seem to the undiscerning eye to be alike it is only because collectively they are referred to as* chicanos. *But like* capirotada, *fixed in a thousand ways and served on a thousand tables, which can only be evaluated by individual taste, the* chicanos *must be so distinguished.*

Mario Suarez, "El Hoyo"

In this analysis of *The Good Life* I have suggested that a cookbook can reproduce the means to more than material nourishment, that it may reproduce as well those cultural practices and values that provide a community with a means of self-definition and survival. I would argue in addition that essays like "New Mexican Diets" and books like *The Good Life* may produce not only a communal subject but an individual authority as well. Granted, in "New Mexican Diets" the advancement of the first person is oblique, requiring an interpolation of the "I" in place of the apparently more generic "extension worker" Cabeza de Baca uses to signify herself throughout this piece. Nonetheless, she takes advantage of the language of ethnography to mark a distinctly autobiographical presence, as can be seen by the series of personal achievements celebrated in the narrative—the author's resumé, if you will, in coded form. Not only are both pamphlets listed here ("A canning bulletin in Spanish was published in 1930 and one on 'Food and Its Preparation' in 1932"), they are acclaimed as second only to liturgical texts for rural women: "Next to her prayer books, the rural Spanish-speaking woman treasures these two booklets" (668). Nor are Cabeza de Baca's practical applications any less influential. Her recommendations on canning, for instance, have been widely accepted: "Within five years, half the farm families owned pressure cookers, and many also had tin-can sealers. More varieties of vegetables were being raised." A decade later, "Nearly every farm family owns or has access to a pressure cooker" (668).

Autobiographical authority in *The Good Life* is at once more explicit and, because it is more exposed, delineated in more measured tones. The subtitle insists that recipes speak a cultural history, yet the preface establishes an individual record of activities on behalf of this collective. Despite the titular focus on "New Mexico Traditions," the preface begins, not by evoking the cultural or physical geography of the state, but instead by providing us with a page-long introduction to the writer herself, naming the father and grandfather who raised her, the ranch where she grew up, and the schools she attended in the United States and abroad, as well as describing her work as a home economist and a schoolteacher; in short, invoking the people, places, and adult activities that form the basis of her autobiography, *We Fed Them Cactus*. Thus two languages drive the narrative. If the text grounds its authority in its capacity to provide readers with an "example" of the good life as lived by Hispanos in midcentury, it simultaneously offers a representation of a particular life as lived by Fabiola Cabeza de Baca, writer, teacher, and home economist. This conflation of ethnographic and autobiographic discourse, of the exemplary and the idiosyncratic, is marked throughout the preface, which moves constantly between descriptions of "our Spanish forebears" and references to the subject who in speaking of them associates herself with nuevomexicano traditions. The first two sentences, for example, negotiate between an ethnographic subject and an autobiographical speaker in order to define a life lived contextually: "The recipes which are a part of *The Good Life* and the family traditions from which the recipes have developed have been a part of my life. They have been a part of the lives of Hispanic New Mexicans since the Spanish colonization of New Mexico" (v). The equation of community traditions with personal development established here is reinforced in the sentences that follow, where a distinctly autobiographical recounting of birthplace and upbringing is itself made representative of "the good life" (v). Toward the close of the preface, readers are again reminded that the structure of this cookbook is contingent upon the personal when Cabeza de Baca insists that the recipes she has selected are themselves derived from the foods "I knew as a child in my grandmother's home" (vi).

Since the play of discourses often operates at the level of the sentence, deciding whether to privilege the language of ethnography or that of autobiography as the ultimate narrative strategy remains at issue. To a certain extent this recounting of the individual life as a representative one is shaped by the demands of audience. Yet while the author literalizes the two roles of the self (as representative of the cultural record, and as illustrative of singularity) by providing readers with two distinct subjects, she avoids sacrificing a commitment to self-assertion through syntax that refuses to subordinate the singular "I," but that instead positions ethnic practice as contingent upon the personal. The following sentence, for instance, posits a singular "I" situated within a community of which the Turrieta family is paradigmatic: "This simple story of the Turrieta family, the family in *The Good Life*, revolves around the observance and traditions of what could have been any Hispanic family in a New Mexican village during that period of my work as a home economist" (v–vi). If Cabeza de Baca's assertion of representativeness ("what could have been any Hispanic family") establishes the text as an ethnographic record, she links, curiously enough, her own life to the larger frame of reference within which the Turrieta family is located. Time is measured not by the sweep of armies across the desert or the dictates of politicians but by the discrete labor of the self: "that period of my work as a home economist."

A similar relationship between the personal and the collective is established in the closing sentences of the preface: "The fondest memories of my life are associated with the people among whom I have worked. The ways of life expressed in the book and the recipes which are a part of those lives have helped make for me *The Good Life*" (vi). Here the subject is interpolated through work; more specifically, through that literary labor which mediates between two cultures. Yet the unexpected intrusion of the speaking subject—"for me"—where we might have expected to read without this formulation demands that we read the text not only as a cultural record but as a self-reflexive narrative as well.

Like Margaret Abreu's 1940 article "In the New Mexico Kitchen," where a recipe for menudo begins as cultural representation and closes by affirming autobiographical presence,[44] culinary narratives like Cabeza de Baca's "New Mexican Diets" and *The Good Life* confound the line traditionally drawn between autobiography proper, where the subject is presumed to constitute herself as unique, and ethnography, whose post-colonial origin has situated the subject as representative of a culture, typically a culture of "dying breeds." In so doing, these works insist on the cultural practices which in part construct the self without privileging those qualities of the subject that are considered representative and without glossing over articulations that are either ambivalent or set in opposition to the "I" as an ethnic "type." By making ethnicity concrete, by representing it as it is experienced by the individual rather than invoking Culture as an abstraction, such autoethnographic texts discourage cultural appropriation, whether it be within the domain of economics or of criticism. For those literary critics interested in ethnicity theory, the "hybrid" texts of writers such as Cleofas Jaramillo and Fabiola Cabeza de Baca—where the subject is situated in context but is at the same time quite obviously a presence the reader cannot ignore—may discourage that form of critical imperialism (whether explicit or phrased as nostalgia for a golden, primitive past) that is encouraged by some "purer" forms of ethnographic criticism, in which the (cultural) subject under investigation is always romanticized as either an artifact or about to become one.

Chapter Two

"Same Boat, Different Stops"

Re-collecting Culture in Black
Culinary Autobiography

Coming Home:
Culinary Artistry and the Politics of Place

*This largest forced migration [the Atlantic slave trade] in the
history of mankind would transport untold numbers of African
slaves from all areas of the continent to the New World, where
their condition of servitude would result, more often than not,
in their being responsible for the cooking in the Big Houses of
the countries to which they were sent. Their service in the
kitchen would, directly and subtly influence the tastes of most
of the New World.*

> Jessica Harris, *Iron Pots and Wooden
> Spoons: Africa's Gifts to New World
> Cooking*

*Sweet potato pies, a good friend of mine asked recently, "Do
they taste anything like pumpkin?" Negative. They taste more
like memory, if you're not uptown.*

> Leroi Jones (Amiri Baraka),
> "Soul Food"

Revising history to invoke cultural authority, redrawing borderlines ("Africa," "the New World," "uptown") to insist on prior claims over contested
spaces, redefining idiosyncratic representation—memory—with its origins
in culture and the social—in a generalized sense, many of the same con-

cerns which mark the culinary narratives of Hispanas of the 1930s and 1940s find currency in post-civil rights writings of black Americans on food: consider Leroi Jones' essay "Soul Food" (1962)[1] or VertaMae Smart-Grosvenor's culinary autobiography *Vibration Cooking* (1970),[2] for instance, as well as more contemporary African American women's cookbooks: Norma Jean and Carole Darden's *Spoonbread and Strawberry Wine* (1978) or Jessica Harris's *Iron Pots and Wooden Spoons* (1989), to name but two. As in Mexicana formulations where food becomes a metonym for culture, the edible in black American women's culinary autobiography is used to reconstruct cultural history, to ground familial reminiscence, and to figure autobiographical authority. Both kinds of "embedded discourse" interest themselves in revising master representations of history, in which people of color are most often figured as transient actors, the "homeless" of hegemonic texts. Likewise, we can read in midcentury Hispana and contemporary African American women's texts a similar attention to the mechanics of cultural commodification. Just as the writings of Cleofas Jaramillo and Fabiola Cabeza de Baca critique Anglo appropriation of Hispano culture, VertaMae Smart-Grosvenor calls attention to the exchange value of "soul food," implicating herself in this transaction when she describes her appearances on a televised Ethnic Week cooking series (xvi–xvii), and when she remarks in the introduction to her book, "Everybody's mama's cousin wanted a free copy of *Vibration Cooking*. After all, wasn't I exploiting and getting rich off their family recipes?" (xiv).

Although critical responses to hegemony mark the culinary autobiographies of both New Mexican and black women, their self-referencing strategies obviously speak to and out of distinctly different concerns and contexts. Chicano literature is engaged with the reappropriation of a culture changed but nevertheless maintained on its home ground. As the new proprietors of Mexican culture, Anglo literature works in the Southwest post-1848 to legitimize a violently acquired political tenure; the disruptive context and consequences of the Mexican-U.S. war are reflected in language which attempts to underwrite land seized by force with a kind of authorizing cultural "title." This history is differently refracted, of course, through a century of Mexicano narrative post-conquest. Californio literature, for instance, from María Amparo Ruiz de Burton's 1885 novel *The Squatter and the Don*, through Lorna Dee Cervantes's "Poema para los Californios Muertos" (1981) occupies itself in large part with redefining and asserting the rights of the "native" population of the state, providing glosses on what constitutes culture and supplying representations of, as well as responsibility for, political agency and change.[3]

The literature of black Americans demonstrates a very different relation to place, not insisting upon the cultural legacy and political responsibilities of a long-settled community, but re-collecting a culture scattered along with its people in the aftermath of the African diaspora. The task of distinguishing between what is "African" and what is "American" so as to define a series of black traditions indigenous to the United States thus takes on a particular urgency not shared by contemporary Chicano narrative and Mexican literature *del otro lado*.[4] It is not surprising, given this historical problematic, that African American autobiographers of the nineteenth and twentieth centuries often explore the relationship between subjectivity and place. Concern with what constitutes "home" is reflected in the critical literature as well: Joanne Braxton writes of the feminine tradition that "for the black woman in American autobiography, the literary act has been, more often than not, an attempt to regain that sense of place in the New World,"[5] and Houston Baker asserts that "fixity is a function of power. Those who maintain place, who decide what takes place and dictate what has taken place, are power brokers of the traditional. The 'placeless,' by contrast, are translators of the nontraditional."[6] If Baker's formulation too schematically frames place as power—consider the different relationship I have tried to articulate with respect to Mexicano narrative, for instance—his insistence that geography and identity are closely related in black texts, that dislocation, not a sense of permanence, characterizes black literature, is affirmed by a glance at even a very short list of autobiographical titles: Zora Neale Hurston's *Dust Tracks on a Road: An Autobiography* (1942), Maya Angelou's most recent autobiography, *All God's Children Wear Traveling Shoes* (1986), and Marita Golden's *Migrations of the Heart* (1983), for example.

Nor is the critique of the way in which culture is bought and sold articulated in the same way in the culinary autobiography of post-war black women and midcentury Hispanas. Cooking as a trope for the reproduction of culture has a long history in African American women's narratives. In an analysis of Victorian cookbooks of the American South, Alan Grubb cites a text by a white woman, Mary Stuart Smith's *The Virginia Cookery Book* (1885), for its recirculation of the "myth of the 'temperamental artist mammies.'" He goes on to cite this story of Smith's:

The most beautiful bread I ever saw was made by a poor creature only one degree removed from idiocy. . . . An old "aunty" in a Virginia homestead of the olden time made such exquisitely fair rolls, that a visitor asked leave to be permitted to have her recipe. . . . With a droll and puzzled air the cook answered, "La! missus, I just know I dar'n't make 'em no different." The old woman could give no other recipe; she knew what to do, and did it.[7]

When we read this anecdote against Nell Kane's recollections in *Between Women,* Judith Rollins's study of black domestic workers and their white employers, the cook's "puzzlement" looks more studied than accidental, and her vacant inability to reproduce her recipe reads as a covert effort to maintain control over the intellectual fruits of her cooking labor. If it is a full century removed from the "droll" antics catalogued in *The Virginia Cookery Book,* Kane's own withholding strategy nevertheless recalls the nineteenth-century cook's resistance:

I used to write up my own recipes. If I got an idea of something nice to serve, I would build a recipe up and try it. And if it was a success, I'd put it in this little book. I had created a lot of little decorations for their teas and dinners that I had written in there too. Whenever the ideas came, I'd write them down. And whenever you do, it's like a precious little thing that you do because you want to show your work.[8]

Like Sarah Rice, who remembers in her autobiography *He Included Me* (1989) that her mother "could take a cookbook and then use her own ingenuity and imagination and invent wonderful things,"[9] Kane's recollection dignifies a mundane labor by acknowledging its potential as an expressive art. For Kane, the cookbook is valuable because it testifies to her transformation of work in the service of another into a more dignified form of labor that creates and sustains self-respect. That her employer concurs in this perception of the domestic worker's literary labor is evident in the power struggle that ensues between the two women over control of this text, a struggle resolved less than happily when Kane laments the loss of her text, "borrowed" over her objections and never returned by her employer: "That was one of the most upsetting experiences I've had. That book was so valuable to me. I wanted my children to read it. . . . It was a history I would like to have kept" (231). "Precious" because it is the product of her own creativity, this "little book" is "valuable" as well as a "history" its author intended to pass down from generation to generation.[10]

Like Nell Kane's recollections, contemporary black women's culinary narratives clarify the larger cultural contest that underlies, for instance, the exchange of—or struggle over—a recipe. Books like *Princess Pamela's Soul Kitchen,* Helen Mendes's *African Heritage Cookbook,* Edna Lewis's *The Ebony Cookbook,* and Smart-Grosvenor's own *Vibration Cooking* celebrating "Afro-American cookery" (xviii) were published within the Black Arts Movement of the mid to late 1960s, a discursive context that takes for granted the need to formulate a separatist aesthetic and in which the development of an explicitly political art is mandated rather than censured. Whereas Cleofas Jaramillo has little precedent in establishing a Sociedad Folklórica that excludes nonnatives[11] and Fabiola Cabeza de Baca insists only obliquely on maintaining cultural proprietorship, Smart-Grosvenor's homage to " 'Afro-American' cookery" (xx) and Jessica Harris's Afrocentric guide to black American cooking are authorized by a well-established critical apparatus, a movement that has critiqued Martin Luther King Jr.'s advocacy of civil rights as "pandering to the fears and anxieties of the white middle class in the attempt to earn its 'goodwill' " (the words of Stokely Carmichael),[12] a movement that has watched the Black Panthers on national television and listened to Malcolm X in the streets, a movement that by the late 1960s had produced literary anthologies with names like *Black Fire* and volumes of poetry entitled *Think Black, Black Pride,* and *Black Boogaloo: Notes on Black Liberation.*[13]

"Things African have gained a new respect among black Americans," Houston Baker wrote in *Black Literature in America* (1971), one year after the publication of *Vibration Cooking:* "The writers of the twenties . . . were interested in shedding their chrysalises in order to merge into the mainstream of American life. Today's writers, however, are engaged in an attempt to construct a chrysalis of blackness, a distinctive covering which will set them apart and enable them to grasp the essence of the black American's reality."[14] Beginning as early as Ralph Ellison's *Invisible Man* (1947) and flourishing throughout the 1960s and early 1970s in books like James Baldwin's *Shadow and Act* (1955) and *The Fire Next Time* (1962) and Leroi Jones's *Blues People* (1963), recirculated in essays by James Stewart, James Boggs, and Larry Neal, reproduced in the critical literature two decades later with the publication of Houston Baker's important *Blues, Ideology, and Afro-American Literature* (1984), this aesthetic, for black men, at least, is best represented by music—most often, the blues.[15]

"Our music has always been the most dominant manifestation of what we are and feel," Neal writes in his "Afterword" to the anthology *Black Fire,* "The best of it has always operated at the core of our lives, forcing itself upon us as in a ritual."[16] So too Jones, although he later retracts this judgment, honors the vernacular, oral rhythms of the blues as the "essence of the black American's reality": "Blues and jazz have been the only consistent exhibitors of 'Negritude' in formal American culture simply because the bearers of its tradition maintained their essential identities as Negroes."[17]

Culinary Transnationalism:
Jessica Harris's *Iron Pots and Wooden Spoons*

If the music these writers and critics are listening to is performed as often by Billie Holiday as by John Lee Hooker, the literary and critical paean to it remains, as I have glanced at above, a formulation more often written in a masculine than a feminine hand. For women, by contrast, the "chrysalis of blackness"—or, to reframe Baker's statement, the affirmation of race in and through literature post–Brown vs. Board of Education—seems concentrated elsewhere. Once again, VertaMae Smart-Grosvenor provides a starting point when she comments, if obliquely, on the gendered inequity in representations of Black Art:

When *Vibration Cooking* came out in 1970, there were fewer than ten published cookbooks by Afro-Americans. There are not many more than that today. That's a scandal. . . . There should be a hundred more books on the subject. Afro-American cookery is like jazz—a genuine art form that deserves serious scholarship and more than a little space on the bookshelves. (xviii)

Jessica Harris's 1989 *Iron Pots and Wooden Spoons* is one such cookbook to have been produced since Smart-Grosvenor published her 1986 "Introduction" to *Vibration Cooking;* it is a coda to "The Travel Notes of a Geechee Girl," which provides readers with an argument about the formation and maintenance of African American cultural practice. Harris gives her book a format that emphasizes the similarities in food preparation across three continents in order to create a community that gains its authority not from rootedness, as I have argued about culinary autobiography by Hispanas, but from the experience of dislocation: "In truth, and in more ways than one, African cooking on the continent and in the New World can be summed up in one sentence: Same Boat, Different Stops" (xx).

As the historical focal point for this culinary autoethnographic narrative, the Atlantic slave trade provides Harris with a way to acknowledge oppression, not in order to bemoan the fate of the scattered survivors but, rather, to recuperate a notion of agency on behalf of her self and her people. Harris's retelling of the "largest forced migration in the history of mankind" enables her to develop a concept of cross-cultural contact that deemphasizes the capitulation of a subordinate to a dominant group in order to stress the ways in which, as Hertha Wong has indicated of Plains Indians pictography, "two cultures influence one another simultaneously."[18]

Granted, Harris describes cooking and culture within a colonial power structure. Consider the following phrase, where parallel syntax reinforces the sameness of oppressive circumstances across different countries: "In the Tara-like Casas Grandes of Brazil, the Great Houses of the Caribbean, and the antebellum mansions of the American South, black hands have turned wooden spoons in heavy cast-iron pots for centuries" (xv–xvi). The dreary consistency of exploitation, however, only makes the author's insistence on the cultural balance of power existing between slaves and slaveholders a more striking instance of the degree to which authority can be maintained under the most oppressive circumstances:

Reports of foods eaten during the slave centuries indicate that though planters may have attempted to reproduce the cuisine of their mother country on the other side of the Atlantic, a transformation was taking place. In African hands, the recipes were being changed according to local ingredients and African culinary techniques. . . . In time, their taste would win out over much of the South in what [Eugene] Genovese calls "the culinary despotism of the quarters over the Big House." (xvi–xvii)

The "culinary despotism" Genovese attributes to slave cultures is perhaps more easily discernible by the hindsight of history. Nevertheless, such attention to the cultural innovations of a population subject to the severest political and economic exploitation does reclaim agency. And, as I have noted above, its implications for refining theories that describe the politics of cross-cultural contact are significant, for it provides us with an alternative to what Arnold Krupat calls "dichotomous logic . . . inadequate to the actual complexities of cultural encounter in history."[19] The structural logic of Harris's book, in which a recipe for grits from the American South follows directions for preparing cornmeal mash from Barbados, reflects at the same time the geographical dislocations of the diaspora and its often productive cultural results. By providing different recipes with her auto-biographical ground as a point of origin, Harris can reproduce recipes from places as distinct as Antigua, Togo, and Martinique and yet empha-size the cultural parallels across borders. Her depiction of culinary cross-pollination thus directs us to see, as culture critic Kobena Mercer has argued about black aesthetics, that "what has taken place between the dominant (white) cultures and people of African descent . . . is a kind of mutual appropriation of artistic styles rather than a narrowly defined, blind imitation of white, Eurocentric standards."[20]

Yet the ethnographic assertion Harris develops in her intercontinental cookbook is articulated through an autobiographical narrative: the recollec-tion of one individual's journey re-collects as well those descendants of Africans who are now divided geographically. If her travels as a tourist inevitably locate her in the position of cultural Other and so threaten to place her in the decontextualized space a food writer like M. F. K. Fisher occupies, the familial reminiscences Harris intersperses between recipes return her to history and to "home."

Adapting a technique not unlike the weave of historical, familial, and personal narratives in N. Scott Momaday's automythography *The Way to Rainy Mountain*,[21] Harris uses her own journey to recover a sense of tribal history as a structural and thematic parallel to the journey of the slaves through the Middle Passage. Situating herself as "the most recent link in the chain, bringing international inspiration and a sense of history" (xxii), the author's collecting of recipes works to authorize African American cul-ture. "I hope that this book will fix the taste of cornbread, beans, collard greens, okra, chiles, molasses, and rum on our tongues for generations to come," she comments in her Introduction (xxii). Negotiating between per-sonal travels and historical voyage, to a description of the Middle Passage she appends an autobiographical statement which asserts community si-multaneously with the self:

Traditional foods trace a gossamer thin line as far back as I can remember or discover in my family. It is a tradition that I maintain and will pass on. Grandma Jones's banana fritters—born of the necessity of feeding a family of twelve during the Depression—cut the bad spots off the overripe bananas that no one wants and make fritters—have become a food that I now crave. (xx)

Significantly, the play of autobiographic and ethnographic discourses is predicated upon a maternal authority. Recollections of "Grandma Jones's" and "Grandma Harris's" cooking along with her own mother's dinners establish the narrator's autobiographical presence, locating her on a culinary family tree. "Fate has placed me at the juncture of two Black culinary traditions," she writes, "that of the Big House and that of the rural South" (xxi). Describing family reunions with a material plenitude of "groaning boards, of 'put up' preserved peaches, seckle pears, and watermelon rinds" (xxii), Harris evokes a sense of full family life, of the close ties which in turn produce the narrator herself.

Yet these childhood memories also gender culinary and cultural traditions. "Grandma Harris insisted on fresh produce," the author writes, "and some of my early memories are of her gardening in a small plot where she lived, tending foods that I would later come to know as African: okra, collard greens, black-eyed peas, and peanuts" (xxii). Harris thus suggests that her sense of ethnic identity is the product of conscious feminine labor, the result of Grandma Harris's careful tending of her garden. The maintenance of culture requires work, the author insists, and this responsibility is typically a female duty. The "heavy black cast-iron pots, caldrons, and skillets" which "are a leitmotif of Black cooking" (xxi) in Brazil, in Nigeria, in Barbados, in the United States, are typically the mother's gift to the daughter, and her own legacy is no exception: "My paternal grandmother, Grandma Harris, presented my mother with a caldron and skillet when she got married. These utensils, though at first disdained, have done over half a century's yeoman's duty in our kitchen. One day they will be mine" (xxi).

Peach Ice Cream and Plum Lightning Wine:
History and Nostalgia in
Spoonbread and Strawberry Wine

Its titular invocation of those homely substances "iron" and "wood" celebrating a distinctly working-class practice, Jessica Harris's Afrocentric narrative situates itself within the wake of the Black Arts Movement of two decades earlier. By contrast, Norma Jean and Carole Darden's *Spoonbread and Strawberry Wine,* although published in 1976, suggests an effort to escape the political momentum of this movement. On the cover, in a photograph colored cool rose and mint green, the two authors smile out at the reader. Their white smocks, straw hat, and patterned aprons do not invoke the iconography of the kaleidoscopic and relentlessly urban 1960s, but that of a rural, pre-war America holding the promise, through this backward glance, of abundance and tranquillity. Nor does the racially inflected reader-response of 1960s criticism get reinstated in this text. Smart-Grosvenor warns, "In *Vibration Cooking* I have told all I'm going to tell" (xx), to set limits on the voyeuristic demands of non-black readers, but, as the cover commentary from the *New York Post* advertises, the Dardens' book appears to invite everyone to share in their "lovingly compiled scrapbook . . . of recipes, memories, and family history."

The book's contents do not disappoint those nostalgic for a more ordered life. Delicate etchings of fruit and flowers alternate with sketches of turn-of-the-century bowler hats and upright pianos as recipe dividers, while the photos that accompany these "reminiscences and priceless family lore" (back cover) show a handsome, middle-class family, its members, to a person, displaying that quiet uprightness of bearing which promises not so much defiance as resolution in the face of obstacles. The recipes themselves, for such studiedly old-fashioned foods as hand-churned peach ice cream and homemade "plum lightening wine" further this illusion of grace under pressure.

Black critics and writers contemporaneous with its publication would likely accord the Dardens' rose-colored tributes to a genteel past about as much praise as they give to civil rights workers who "pander . . . to the fears and anxieties of the white middle class in the attempt to earn its 'goodwill.' " Nor would a great many contemporary readers shower it with accolades for its stubborn insistence on protecting the familial and personal past from violence. Consider, for instance, how little the final photograph of the Dardens' text, captioned "The Sampsons picnicking at roadside," reveals to readers unfamiliar with the context of black American history. The family look untroubled as they bow their heads over the laden table as if in thanksgiving for its abundance, and the table itself, stretching almost the length of the frame, refuses admittance to any disruption of its plenty. Yet, as Mamie Garvin Fields's granddaughter Karen acknowledges in her preface to *Lemon Swamp*, such open-air festivities were in actuality as often motivated by fears of racist harassment as by a desire to enjoy food *en plein air*. Remembering her own family's annual excursions across the Mason-Dixon line, Karen Fields's narrative provides readers with an alternate, historically coded figuration of the Dardens' laden table:

> The drive to South Carolina allowed us a transition from our own country to that one. My father always saw to it that we carried huge provisions—fried chicken, potato salad, roast ham, buttered bread, unbuttered bread, big Thermos jugs filled with lemonade, and anything else we could possibly want to eat or drink. We even carried bottles filled with plain water and a special container just for ice. As far as possible, the family car was to be self-sufficient. We carried detailed maps for the same reason that we carried so much food and drink: a determination to avoid insult, or worse.[22]

Yet if *Spoonbread and Strawberry Wine* is determinedly nostalgic and relentlessly backwards-looking, it does not obliterate history but, rather, substitutes for recent events an earlier series of chronotypes. The familial "seat" described in the opening pages of their recollections may advance their grandfather to the status of unofficial town ruler, but if the Dardens are intent on providing their own middle-class status with an historical precedent, they are equally interested in providing ignorant readers with lessons in nineteenth-century American history more generally. In the middle 1870s, Wilson was a "small, slow-paced, rather quiet tobacco town with about 4,000 citizens, 40 percent of whom were black, so things looked encouraging for black political progress," they write. "But by 1875, Reconstruction had given way to terrorism. In Wilson as well as the rest of the South, the Ku Klux Klan had spread its sheets. Voting was over" (17). In the context of this nineteenth-century terror, Charles Henry Darden signifies black resistance: "He was convinced that economic self-reliance now held the key to the survival of the black community" (17), the authors argue, coding their narrative as a rereading of the nineteenth-century goals of racial uplift and Washingtonian self-reliance.[23]

Spoonbread and Strawberry Wine, then, provides readers with an alternative model for a race-inflected authority. And a gendered authority as well: the celebration of maternal power which in Jessica Harris's book remains the constant amidst geographical change is characteristic of Norma Jean and Carole Darden's culinary reminiscences too. As in *Iron Pots and*

Wooden Spoons, in the Dardens' book the close relation between the struggles of the family and the work of the writer is captured in the formal structure of the memoir. Biographical reminiscences introduce the recipes of each family member, the collection as a whole composing, as in Jessica Harris's book, a culinary family tree. In fact, it is in the act of (re)collection that the sisters locate their autobiographical subject. Writing the cookbook was motivated by a desire to "strengthen family ties, and [to] learn more about our ancestors' history and tradition" (10). In so doing, the authors deliver "a testimonial to those who lovingly fed us" and simultaneously provide themselves with "a better sense of ourselves" (11).[24] Consistent with this jointly authored text's tribute to a familial collective, most of the confessional moments here are not so much produced by the sisters as reproduced by them. There are few memories intimately connected to the authorial "we," more that provide representations of family members, recollections which distill for us a sense of "character"—the loving reassurances of Uncle John to his fiancée Jean before their wedding day, for instance, or Uncle Clyde's insistence on maintaining control over his own narrative sketch and his resistance to the sisters' efforts to draw him out.

Sisterly portraiture in *Spoonbread and Strawberry Wine,* then, does not so much recall the constantly developing identity of Jessica Harris's travelogue as remain fixed in a likeness of childhood. The celebration of maternal authority with which the authors preface their recipes reflects such a notion of the self as graspable through a series of quintessential, unchanging characteristics. The authors recall watching their female relatives "as they moved about in their kitchens . . . preparing meals. Each one worked in a distinct rhythm, and from the essence of who they were came unique culinary expressions" (9). The "essence" of each individual, readers learn, can be apprehended by the collection of recipes that represent them: enterprising Papa Darden is well regarded for the strawberry, blackberry, and dandelion wines he concocted annually and sold in his store, but which he never drank himself, while sentimental Aunt Maude, "a great believer in the power and joy of love" (55), is known for her caramel kisses and candied rose petals. Like Maya Angelou's parallel between cuisine and culture in *I Know Why the Caged Bird Sings* ("Through food we learned that there were other people in the world" [175]), representation in the Dardens' text is synecdochic rather than metonymic. These are culinary snapshots, with recipes providing an almost one-to-one index to personality.

As is consonant with the text's nineteenth-century historical focus, the autobiographical axis remains retrospective. Both the autobiographical interventions in the sketches of family members and the personal voice of the book's introduction recount memories from a fixed point of view in childhood. In their literary researches, the authors explain, "we encouraged people to talk about the times of their youth—their hopes, dreams, highs, lows, and of course thoughts on food" (10). The effect, like that of the sentimental memories of earlier days in Cleofas Jaramillo's and Fabiola Cabeza de Baca's work, is nostalgic. Like those passages in midcentury Hispana narrative where ethnographic studies of fading "custom" close with invocations to a cultural and/or familial community, such affiliating texts run the risk of dividing a past graspable only in memory from a sense of history as continuous, subject to the interventions of writing. What stops this reification of history as History is that it is spoken in the first person. Produced as autobiography, historical revision need not need have a termination point but can be reproduced and revised again in the present:

It is a simple act of thoughtfulness to the living, but it takes the form of a feast. Turkeys, hams, roasts, and casseroles are given, but as children, we had a natural interest in the sweets and hot breads that were offered, and to this day we find it particularly appropriate to take a cake, a pie, or bread to the family of the departed. (241)

Soul Food and Self-Provisioning: VertaMae Smart-Grosvenor's *Vibration Cooking*

Although it was first published in 1970, only eight years before *Spoonbread and Strawberry Wine*, VertaMae Smart-Grosvenor's *Vibration Cooking: Or, The Travel Notes of a Geechee Girl* seems a half-century distant: irreverent where the Dardens are worshipful, exuberant where the Dardens are restrained, flippant where the sisters are in earnest, and—most important with respect to autobiography—elusive, presenting readers with a multiplicity of seemingly incompatible self-representations. To the extent that Smart-Grosvenor makes use of the metaphor of travel to describe a self in process, *Vibration Cooking* is reminiscent of Jessica Harris's *Iron Pots and Wooden Spoons*. And, as with Harris's book, the model of the self in Smart-Grosvenor's autobiography is historicized by being developed in the context of colonialism. In this passage invoking the Underground Railroad, however, cooking is not so much the metonym enabling political critique as it is itself quite literally a political act:

Sometimes they would be in the middle of their dinner when the stops [homes that hid slaves en route to freedom] got word that a slave or slaves were coming through that night. They might even have some neighbors or even members of the family there who were not cool . . . so they had to have signals to let each other know that tonight it would happen. Uncle Costen said they had a special dish they would serve called "Harriet Tubman Ragout." (29)

While this description locates the resistance to slavery inside the homes of African Americans rather than in the offices of William Lloyd Garrison, it does not oversimplify the dynamics of intraracial relations in order to do so. Community here is not a function of race but an active political choice; the picture of familial harmony around the kitchen table is deceptive, the affirmation of African American solidarity only apparent. Those readers who insist on racial uniformity put themselves in the position of the hoodwinked individuals of more than one race, who unsuspectingly help themselves to second portions of a ragout that is to the circle of politically minded diners a vehicle for more than corporeal support.

This commentary provides a much-needed revision of a history of slavery and slave insurrections that is all too often framed in the plodding critical terms of binary opposition—those who "resist" set against those who "accede" to oppression. It provides, as well, a critique of that very aesthetic apparatus, the Black Arts movement, to which Smart-Grosvenor's epigraph to Amiri Baraka suggests her narrative owes a substantial debt. With Hurstonian resistance to being catalogued, the critical "community" *Vibration Cooking*'s title advertises as its own is simultaneously welcomed and held at arm's length by Smart-Grosvenor. Just as her commentary on the history of slave resistance invokes a position only to keep to its margins, so her use of the artistic credos of Black Power acknowledges her reliance upon such formulations and yet keeps them at a critical remove. On the one hand, then, she carries out Stokely Carmichael's manifesto on maintaining culture ("The racial and cultural personality of the black community must be preserved and the community must win its freedom while preserving its cultural integrity")[25] when she argues for a reappraisal of black English:

You know people got to dig that "nigger dialect" is really beautiful. The slaves were just adapting to a language that wasn't their own. They were from many tribes, and plus the masters didn't talk too tough themselves. So they took the English language and did what they could with it and it was beautiful. Black people are the only people in this country who speak English and make it sound musical. (67–68)

On the other hand, she glories in parodies of Geechee tall tales that are designed not only to hoodwink unsuspecting white folks (this being almost too easy) but also to mock the sometimes pompous, often humorless prose of "Negro artists" whose black-and-white cultural models cannot do justice to the ragged contours of real life.

The "real life" of Smart-Grosvenor's *Travel Notes* has more switchbacks than Black Arts Movement critic James Stewart's formulations can safely negotiate.[26] "In Paris I used to eat what they called crepes," Smart-Grosvenor recalls. "They are very good but I don't make them. . . . Crepes are delicate to make and you have to have an expensive and fancy pan to make them. I prefer hoe cake of bread like Grandmama Sula used to make" (20). Like white bread with a French accent, the crepe, sniffs Smart-Grosvenor, is too high-toned for any hard-working black girl from South Carolina to enjoy properly. Smart-Grosvenor's prose may be sassier than Stewart's essay, but her argument reproduces his own aesthetic agenda: "The dilemma of the 'negro' artist is that he makes assumptions based on the wrong models. He makes assumptions based on white models. These assumptions are not only wrong, they are even antithetical to his existence. . . . Our models must be consistent with a black style, our natural aesthetic styles, and our moral and spiritual styles" (3). Only a chapter later, however, Smart-Grosvenor doubles back to insist that "Salade Niçoise is a French name but just like with anything else when soul folks get it they take it out into another thing" (62). Recalling a series of wily female predecessors, this kind of contretemps flies in the face of Stewart's insistence that "we must even, ultimately, be estranged from the dominant culture. . . . Our black artists . . . can not be 'successful' in any sense that has meaning in white critical evaluations" (6). Like the author of *Incidents in the Life of a Slave Girl* and her grandmother, who "use language as a weapon" to "suggest a feminine reflection of the trickster figure,"[27] Smart-Grosvenor contravenes any attempt at systematizing and thus simplifying the complicated negotiations that make up both intra- and intercultural contact, or, as her chapter titles articulate this division, "Home" and "Away from Home."

Throughout her culinary travelogue, in fact, Smart-Grosvenor invokes truisms of race relations in order to suggest their ultimate unreliability as a gauge of her subjectivity. As a kind of trickster chef, she serves dishes that look like the genuine article but actually have unsuspecting readers consuming humble pie. The text begins as a cross between a Daniel Boone narrative of the Wild West—translated to the swamps of South Carolina as the story of "Birth, Hunting and Gator Tails"—and an account of miraculous birth reminiscent of Hurston's *Dust Tracks on a Road*. Just as Hurston focused on the originality of her introduction to the world, with her mother assisted by a midwife who was not only white but male, in order to ensure her success as marked from the cradle, Smart-Grosvenor describes her own birth as a remarkable event, complete with fortuitous intercessor:

I was so weak they put me in a shoe box and put the box on the wood-stove oven door. That was a kind of incubator. My mother says it was a case of touch and go for a while, cause she got the childbirth fever. She said, "I'm sorry child you'll have to fend for yourself" and started to throw me in the fireplace but all praises due to the gods Aunt Rose caught me. When I go down south now they treat me so good, cause they know that I wasn't but three pounds when I was born. Everyone always says, "Well do Jesus. To think that you wasn't no bigger than a minute when you was born and now you six feet tall and strong and healthy and you got two fine children of your own. The Lord works in mysterious ways His praises to behold." (7–8)

From this singular beginning the author goes on to describe the equally unusual food she was raised on, more straightforward recipes for "Smothered Rabbit" and venison giving way to progressively campier concoctions like "Stewed Coon" and "Peacocks" (too beautiful to be eaten, the cook advises, in the event that a reader seriously considered the possibility), ending with a flourish of "African" standards like "Kangaroo Tail Stew" and "Elephant Tails" and the American version of them, "Betty's Barbecued Gator Tails." Even the most gullible of readers, one assumes, would find this culinary history of African American culture a trifle disingenuous, especially upon learning that the kangaroo tail must be obtained at the local gourmet food store. In case the more earnest fail to learn their lesson, such directives are followed by more explicit critiques which call attention to the tall tale the autobiographer plays out. Recalling a Thanksgiving spent in France, Smart-Grosvenor describes her search for "genuine" American food: "I ran around to find an exotic food store that sold American canned goods and finally found one near the Madeleine where I bought cranberry sauce and Maxwell House coffee" (59). The juxtaposition of the "exotic" with the mundane disappoints readers determined to find in "soul food" access to the cultural Other.

Placed in the context of the Black Arts Movement, Smart-Grosvenor's critique of (white) cultural voyeurism appears at once less startling—many of her contemporaries were writing to protest the commodification of African American culture—and more specifically coded as a gendered response, its argument and form invoking a feminine literary tradition. The flyleaf of the second edition of *Vibration Cooking* genders Smart-Grosvenor's argument from the outset; just as Janie ostensibly tells her story to Phoeby in Zora Neale Hurston's novel *Their Eyes Were Watching God*, VertaMae writes to Stella, framing her reevaluation of cooking with a traditionally feminine series of appeals. Smart-Grosvenor counsels Stella and, by implication, all her women readers, "If you cook with love and feed people, you got two forces cooled out already. . . . Food can cause happiness or unhappiness, health or sickness and make or break marriages." The beginning of the narrative proper genders such culinary labors even more clearly: "I like men who enjoy food," Smart-Grosvenor asserts in a pointed razzing of one of the tenets of late 1960s Anglo-American feminism. "Cooking for a man is a very feminine thing" (3). Marialisa Calta sees the recipes in Ntozake Shange's 1982 novel *Sassafras, Cypress and Indigo* as "a way to acknowledge all the time women spend cooking for and feeding other people" (time, Shange argues, that " 'the world at large often doesn't see as significant' ").[28] Similarly, Smart-Grosvenor reevaluates cooking: if it is quotidian, it can also "make or break life."

Still, the immediate precursor to Smart-Grosvenor's book is unarguably Amiri Baraka's 1962 essay "Soul Food."[29] Replaying Ellison's debt to Proustian memory ("I yam what I yam," the narrator of *Invisible Man* acknowledges, as the fragrance of roasting sweet potatoes recalls him to all of black Southern history), Baraka's sweet potato pies "taste . . . like memory." Anticipating Smart-Grosvenor's attention to the class inflections of the culinary metaphor, Baraka uses "collards and turnips and kale and mustards" to critique the pretensions of the black bourgeoisie; since greens are "not fit for anybody but the woogies ... they found a way to make them taste like something somebody would want to freeze and sell to a Negro going to Harvard as exotic European spinach" (86).

Thematically Smart-Grosvenor's riff on greens, as we see below, owes much to Baraka's, but its tone and form recall a distinguished series of female autobiographical precursors: canny like Harriet Jacobs, feisty as Harriet Wilson in *Our Nig*. But again it is Hurston as anthropologist and autobiographer that *Vibration Cooking*'s complicated, jokey self-situating most closely duplicates. Other Black Arts writers condemn not only whites, particularly those who Stokely Carmichael calls the "Pepsi generation" ("young middle-class Americans" who "have wanted to come alive through the black community"),[30] but also blacks who have internalized the hegemonic standard. Larry Neal, for instance, indicts black literature for "providing exotic entertainment for white America" (650). But, like Baldwin's blues, "tart and ironic, authoritative and double-edged" (41–42), Smart-Grosvenor's assessments are self-conscious and street-smart, sharp-eyed hits that implicate herself, with Hurstonian bravura, as both buyer and seller of culture: "I exploit Afro-American dishes every chance I get ... for instance, collard greens" (xv–xvi), she brags with a devil-may-care-but-all-the-time-looking-back-over-your-shoulder duplicity. Reliable narrator? Hardly. From the outset, Smart-Grosvenor represents herself as a trickster figure, pointing readers in one direction while she walks off in the other. Consider this grocery store exchange:

So there I was, in line, holding my collard greens. A white woman asked me, "How do you people fix these?" Now, more than likely if I had not been in such a Purple Funk, I might have let the "you people" go by, but this particular morning I didn't. "Salad," I said. . . . I have often wondered if that white woman went home and actually made a collard green salad with Italian dressing. (xvi)

Like Cabeza de Baca's emphasis on the impossibility of complete translation, Smart-Grosvenor's willful mistranslation provides a check on readers—at least white readers—eager to make African American culture their own. As a comment on the pitfalls of cross-cultural exchange, the story provides a gloss on the book itself, suggesting that cooks think twice before reproducing its recipes.

There are other cautionary tales. Take the coda to the story of how hush puppies got their name, for instance: "You can believe this," she says, "if you believe all the other American folk tales" (94). Besides providing the writer with a degree of interpretive control, such tongue-in-cheek gestures at the expense of the credulous also affirm black pride as they critique the paucity of white culture. The word-play in recipes for "Steak with Beautiful Black Sauce" and "Stuffed Heart Honky Style" (114, 115) requires no further commentary. While African American tradition is celebrated via culinary custom, Anglo-American culture is denounced through its edibles as a contradiction in terms. The directions for "Cracker Stew" advise cooks to "take a can of any kind of soup and add 1 box of any kind of frozen vegetables and then add 1 cup of Minute Rice. Heat and serve with toasted crackers on top" (79). The implicit contrast drawn between Anglo cultural poverty and the richness of African American life is later made explicit when Smart-Grosvenor describes the dinner preparations of a white colleague in the theater. "No smells of food cooking or having been cooked" (101) issue from the kitchen. The meal, when it arrives, is prepackaged: frozen peas, instant potatoes, canned chicken. Returning to her own kitchen, the author promptly "fried a piece of liver and put on a little bit of grits and in a short time I had an epicurean delight" (102). Echoing analyses by Killen, who characterizes white culture as the "pallid mainstream of American life," and Addison Gayle, who critiques gringo "cultural deprivation,"[31] the Anglo-American cultural repast, according to Smart-Grosvenor, is scant: show without substance, containing little real nourishment—let alone flavor.[32]

While such indictments provide readers with an appreciation of the fullness of Afro-American tradition, they tend to a certain extent to occlude the autobiographical subject herself. That is, although such anecdotes are often framed as personal narrative, the cross-cultural comparison they develop positions the subject as an ethnographic "we," a collective identity rigidly framed in opposition to "them." Consider, for instance, how the following critique of "white bread culture" positions pronouns, constructing an "I" contingent upon its affiliation with an aggregate that is unable to accommodate difference: "You white folks just keep on eating that white foam rubber bread that sticks to the roof of your mouth, and keep on eating Minute Rice and instant potatoes, instant cereals and drinking instant milk and stick to your instant culture. And I will stick to the short-lived fad that brought my ancestors through four hundred years of oppression" (177).[33]

The "I" who eloquently protests racism and affirms African American survival expresses herself as a spokesperson more than she asserts singularity here. Yet at the opening of the text Smart-Grosvenor as vigorously affirms her specificity as a black woman writer who can maintain a cultural vision while she simultaneously practices cultural pluralism. She refuses to fix her identity as a "soul food" writer:

It seemed to me while certain foods have been labelled "soul food" and associated with Afro-Americans, Afro-Americans could be associated with all foods. . . . My kitchen was the world. . . . I don't have culinary limitations because I'm "black." On the other hand, I choose to write about "Afro-American" cookery because I'm "black" and know the wonderful, fascinating culinary history there is. (xv)

Unlike the concordance of autobiographic and ethnographic discourses which in Jessica Harris's *Iron Pots and Wooden Spoons* and the Darden sisters' *Spoonbread and Strawberry Wine* situates the subject in cultural context, in VertaMae Smart-Grosvenor's *Vibration Cooking* the languages of self and culture often appear at odds: contradictory, discontinuous, working against one another. Impulses toward black collectivity counterpoint an emphasis—reminiscent of that in Hurston's autobiography—on the miracle of the self's uniqueness. Yet this self-assertion is itself abruptly exchanged for an affirmation of "my people."

On the one hand, then, Smart-Grosvenor uses role-playing to insist on identity as multiple and contingent upon circumstance. "In *Vibration Cooking* I have told all I'm going to tell" (xx), she announces in the book's introduction, distinguishing between the narrative's "I" and the identity of the author who has produced the book. On the other hand, in a statement reminiscent of Jessica Harris's tribute in *Iron Pots and Wooden Spoons*, she uses the trope of culinary succession to suggest an identity fixed as woman-centered. "Throw out all of [the cooking pots] except the black ones" she advises. "The cast-iron ones like your mother used to use" (2). By dedicating the book to "my mama and my grandmothers and my sisters in appreciation of the years that they worked in miss ann's kitchen and then came home to TCB in spite of slavery and oppression and the moynihan report," she establishes gender as a central factor in her self-conception, one that provides the book's multiple self-representations with a single reference point.

Smart-Grosvenor uses a variety of languages in this book in order to emphasize the shifting and multiple nature of self-representation and to document the historical struggles that have contributed to its formation. Lack of discursive harmony need not be read as a structural weakness, however. What enables the smoothly modulated articulation of both Harris's and the Darden sisters' culinary autobiographies, after all, is a conception of the subject as essentially fixed. Norma Jean and Carole Darden locate the first-person plural in childhood; Jessica Harris explores the development of an adult "I" through the detached observations of the tourist. Smart-Grosvenor's speaking voice, in contrast, does not remain rooted at any one vantage point. Travel produces neither an "I" emphatically rooted at home nor a subject whose visits to foreign places wholly defy efforts at self-situating; instead, it suggests the contingency of identity.

On the level of the (culinary) signifier, Smart-Grosvenor expresses this doubled vision in explaining her appearance on an ethnic cooking series: "I wanted to use the opportunity to prove that Afro-American cookery was more than chitlins and pigs' feet, and at the same time I wanted to acknowledge the traditional dishes" (xvi–xvii). The author also articulates the problematics of autoethnography more directly. In fact, the difficulty involved in affirming culture without being perceived as its one-dimensional emissary occupies the autobiographer throughout her narrative. In "The Demystification of Food," she addresses the problem by presenting two alternative selves. The first is celebrative, sentimental, nostalgic. Recalling past New Year's Day parties with friends, she exclaims:

What times! Times, oh, times! I often get nostalgia for the old days and old friends. Like those New Year's open houses I used to have and everyone I loved would come. Even Millie came from Germany one year. She arrived just in time for the black-eyes and rice. (3)

But the reader's understanding is promptly undercut:

And that year I cooked the peas with beef neck bones instead of swine cause so many brothers and sisters have given up swine. . . . You supposed to cook the whole hog head but I couldn't. I saw it hanging in the butcher store on Avenue D and I didn't dig it. I left the swine hanging right where he was. (3)

In this attention-getting shift, the first-person pronoun insists on self-determination. Here the idiosyncratic is affirmed; difference, not similarity, finally constitutes the "plot" of the passage.

This tactic—describing expected behavior only to flout expectation—is the rule rather than the exception in this narrative. I argued earlier that Smart-Grosvenor often presents herself in a manner reminiscent of Hurston's capricious narrators, and I would suggest that such teasing shifts in self-representation provide for both writers a means of circumventing readers' attempts to fix the speaker as an ethnic "type." Both Hurston and Smart-Grosvenor indict such type-casting, using their emphatically eccentric self-imaging as a means of insisting on their own agency. Constructing an ethnic identity is a difficult maneuver; it requires careful negotiation between the demands of cultural affirmation on the one hand and the requirements of self-determination on the other. And, like Hurston, Smart-Grosvenor does not disdain acclaim for her technical facility. Rather, she delights in the performance.

In "Home," the first section of Smart-Grosvenor's book, readers are treated to a particularly eye-catching display of autobiographical gymnastics when the author describes her brief stint in England as "Princess Verta from Tabanguila, an island near Madagascar" (26). As an African princess the author enjoys the attention of the Dover Press, who publish an account of her interview as "Princess Verta Studies Our Way of Life" (27). The 1970s equivalent of in-your-face attitude, this eye-catching posturing flouts racism's invisibility syndrome, what James Baldwin describes as, "Black people, mainly, look down or look up but do not look at each other, not at you, and white people, mainly, look away" (30). Besides critiquing racist type-casting through parody, this literary disguise acknowledges the complicated nature of cultural representation by playing upon the series of self/other oppositions any autobiographical description creates. As ethnographic investigator, Princess Verta is Other, not only with respect to her English "audience" but with reference to "Home" and readers as well. (Note, however, that the author insists on her subjectivity by placing herself in the position of actor: Princess Verta examines her audience; they do not study her.) In counterpoint to later chapters of *Vibration Cooking* that situate Smart-Grosvenor's "I" within a cultural community, this portion of the text acknowledges the divisive mechanics of ethnographic description. The admission of complicity in this kind of type-casting ("A lot

of people like to say they are the descendants of African chiefs. I have
been through that stage" [26]) checks complacent readers by suggesting
that such eccentric behavior is itself "typical." Yet the confession also
maintains Smart-Grosvenor's difference; the act of telling is itself an idiosyncratic maneuver that acknowledges, even as it critiques, the Afrocen-
trism of the Black Arts movement.

I would like to look closely at another passage that uses role-playing to
call attention to the dynamics of self-representation. Aspiring to become
an actress, the author initially settles for working as a cook for the Hedgerow Theatre. She mocks her efforts to fashion a self that is independent
of the tyrannical structuring principles of race, class, and gender:

I used to get the Chester bus to Rose Valley from Media and it was only full
of black women who worked out there. They couldn't figure how come I was
wearing jeans and sweaters to work. In my most Chekhovian voice I would
say, "I'm an actress, not a domestic. I'm on my way to the theatre." They
would look at me like I was out of my mind. One day I got on and the driver
said, "Too hot to scrub floors today, right sweetie?" (98–99)

This stereotyping becomes literalized further on. Her first "big chance"
(99) at acting comes in *A Streetcar Named Desire*. She is not to play
Blanche, however, but one of the women who observes this grande dame
from her doorstep. Mocking at once her own idealism, the naïveté of her
readers, and the closemindedness of the theater crew, she continues:

I had one line. "Dis is it, honey-o" or something like that. . . . I was a nervous
wreck. Maybe they wouldn't like my projection. Maybe they wouldn't like my
delivery. Maybe they wouldn't like my technique. Maybe they wouldn't like
me. But they didn't pay me no mind. My little part was so insignificant. (99–
100)

In a coup reminiscent of Hurston and the Brer Rabbit stories of African
American folklore, it is the "lady on the stoop" (99) who enjoys the last
laugh. By the end of the week she has caused a scandal:

Everyone had warned me what a bitch Diana Barrymore was, but she was
the only person I talked to during the whole week I was there. As a matter
of fact, we became friends. We talked about voodoo and vibrations and stuff
like that. The scandal I caused was because some apprentice said he saw me
in my dressing room on my hands and knees talking in unknown tongues. It

was a lie. I was on the floor looking for my shoes and cussing to myself. See, that's what I mean, white and black folks speak a different tongue. (100)

I have quoted this passage at some length because it so aptly illustrates the interplay of autobiographic and ethnographic discourses in the text, those "different tongues" Smart-Grosvenor speaks to forestall readers from reducing a complicated subject to a one-dimensional silhouette. Consider, for instance, the abrupt shift in posture from the self-castigating sarcasm of "My little part" to the subdued triumph the actress enjoys in her more significant role as friend to Diana Barrymore. The disjunction in self-representation is striking: from anxiety and belittlement as she labors over her part only to discover its complete "insignificance," to satisfaction at creating a performance that turns heads throughout the theater, if only backstage. Seizing the limelight, the author enjoys undeniable social prestige in a gratifying reversal of power over members of the cast who previously had found her too unimportant to acknowledge.

More significantly, however, it allows her to assert interpretive authority over readers who, like the audience of actors and theatergoers at the Hedgerow, are in a position to "pay no mind" to her literary performance in *Vibration Cooking*. Just as she takes the upper hand with Diana Barrymore—with respect to "voodoo and vibrations" the starring actress plays apprentice to the apparently more authoritative Smart-Grosvenor—so she advances upon the interpretive domain of readers by creating a situation of sufficient ambiguity to cause them to question their own proficiency at reading. "Home remedies" given earlier, such as, for a nosebleed, "Catch the blood on a piece of brown paper and burn the paper" (138), constitute a sympathetic-medicine practice not dissimilar to "voodoo and vibrations and stuff like that." Voodoo further resonates with Baraka's 1969 *Black Magic* and recalls Larry Neal's edict in *Black Fire* that the black writer must be a "magician, working juju with the word" (655).[34] The disjunction between mundane actuality (looking for shoes) and exotic fantasy (speaking in tongues) needles readers with a penchant for primitivism, but it nevertheless calls attention to a race-inflected reading of a different order. To the apprentice (and to those unwilling to allow for a more generous reading of the subject as a black woman), she *is* in fact speaking in an unknown tongue.

Smart-Grosvenor's dramatic costume changes demonstrate that it is racism that produces, if only momentarily, a fixed identity. Stepping onto a bus after the driver has put up prolonged resistance ("Who do you people think you are?" he asks rhetorically), she responds: "We are" (89). The struggle for existence robs the "I" of singularity: faced with a hostile "them," eccentric individuality is exchanged for the security of a common "we." If it is generated in response to oppression, however, this means of grounding the subject is nevertheless framed in the affirmative. A cousin living in the West Indies provides the author with recipes for sweet potatoes and a tribute to Ellison: "Did you know there are all kinds of yams? These are only a few. There are many different types here. . . . Then there is a yam called nigger yam. I won't even deal with that because after all a yam is a yam is a yam" (46). An accusation that she is "misrepresenting" herself as African because she wears the clothes of her ancestors prompts another affirmation of the essential rootedness of the "I" who can dress up as Princess Verta and down as the woman on the stoop:

Now I have done a lot of research on food and found out that Long Island ducks are not from Long Island at all. They are the descendants of ducks imported from Peking around 1870. . . . Potatoes are native to South America and were taken to Europe by the Spanish explorers "when they discovered South America." . . . Now, if a squash and a potato and a duck and a pepper can grow and look like their ancestors, I know damn well that I can walk around dressed like mine. (120)

The acknowledgment that oppression checks self-assertion could potentially undercut the confidence with which Smart-Grosvenor insists she is free to define herself. Yet the down-to-earth quality she evokes here domesticates this scene and deprives it of the power to terrorize. Through culinary comedy, assault becomes the vehicle for a quite unforgettable kind of self-affirmation.

Culinary Labor, Cultural Work, and the Autobiographical Subject

Ethnicity is not something that is simply passed on from generation to generation, taught and learned. . . . Insofar as ethnicity is a deeply rooted emotional component of identity, it is often transmitted less through cognitive language or learning . . . than

through a process analogous to the dreaming and transference
of psychoanalytic encounters.

> Michael M. J. Fischer, "Ethnicity
> and the Arts of Memory," in James
> Clifford and George E. Marcus,
> *Writing Culture*

So, you see, this book is the reflection of our pilgrimage "home,"
which revealed to us not only good food but the origins, early
struggles, and life-styles of our family . . . it is therefore a testi-
monial to those who lovingly fed us and at the same time gave
us a better sense of ourselves by sharing themselves.

> Norma Jean and Carole Darden,
> *Spoonbread and Strawberry Wine*

Certainly the development of ethnic identity, as anthropologist Michael Fischer suggests, is neither simple nor straightforward.[35] The autobiographers of the culinary memoirs I have discussed in this chapter, however, despite their ideological, thematic, and formal differences, all share a strong sense of the conscious and careful rhetorical work that is needed if they are to reproduce cultural practices while at the same time asserting their own authority. They expend a great deal of narrative energy in order to affirm that the cultural work their female predecessors have undertaken is a difficult labor. In this sense, the disdained but serviceable "caldron and skillet" passed down from mother to daughter in Jessica Harris's *Iron Pots and Wooden Spoons* provides an appropriate metaphor for ethnic autobiography by women more generally. If they are humble, they are nevertheless instrumental in providing (material) nourishment, just as women autobiographers describe the mundane work of women, pointing to the common labors of their grandmothers, mothers, and daughters as ultimately the most significant in providing the emotional and spiritual sustenance necessary for self-assertion. Merely because it is conscious does not, after all, ensure that a labor is uncomplicated—if that were the case, civil rights struggles would have been resolved before now.[36]

This insistence on the conscious labor involved in the reproduction of cultural practice provides, I would suggest, a means of affirming the work of female antecedents who often are given little attention in texts by male autobiographers. Hence the choice of gender-inflected metaphors of cultural practice and its maintenance: the culinary metaphor, distinctly feminine, and the reproductive model of cultural development and identity, specifically maternal. Such a recuperation of a female legacy of course enables women's textual self-assertion at the same time as it celebrates the lives of women family members as role models. The eulogy Norma Jean and Carole Darden provide for their grandmother Dianah Scarborough Darden, for instance, implicitly stresses the self-assurance of the authors as it affirms their grandmother's strength of character: "She was not one to merely accept second-class citizenship, and instilled in each child what was then called 'race pride;' insisting that they hold their heads high and assert their equality before God and among men" (28).

But there is a second, equally important reason impelling women writers to represent the relation between subjectivity and ethnicity as a conscious, practiced one. Over and over again, these authors emphasize the struggle that self-assertion demands, a struggle that is as much the task of family and community as of the subject herself. Using the metaphor of culinary labor to develop an ethnic identity thus associates endeavors in the cultural sphere with struggle in the political domain. In the sense that it replays political conflict as a struggle for cultural ownership, the autoethnographic discourse of Jaramillo's and Cabeza de Baca's culinary memoirs is characteristic of the personal narratives of American women of color more generally.

Cultural struggle, I would argue, is not incidental to political conflict but essential to it, the ideological signifier of shifts in political power, constituting itself, as John Brenkman asserts, "*within* and *against* the forms of domination that organize the society in which [it] is produced and the one in which it is received."[37] It thus encompasses discourses of resistance as well as those languages of oppression that are used to justify the forcible possession of land and labor and to reconstruct the social monopoly as in the best interests of the cultural Others who provide the work necessary to accumulate such capital. Because it calls attention to the work involved in cultural reproduction, then, the culinary metaphor provides writers with a means of reexamining power. Figures like Eugene Genovese's "culinary despotism of the quarters" suggest that a kind of cultural authority may operate simultaneously with—and against—political sway. Such examinations of cultural work reconceptualize the fixed model of oppressor-oppressed power relations. Without sacrificing an acknowledgment of the physical and emotional burdens imposed by imperialism, these writers recuperate a sense of agency for people who in traditional political and literary theory have often been subjects in name only.

Part Two

Negotiating Authority:
Edited Personal Narrative

Chapter Three

Is That What She Said?

The Politics of Collaborative Autobiography

The Politics of Collaborative Autobiography

Sometimes the woman go to the doctor and ask them if they are pregnant. They are only one or two months. The doctor checks them and says, "No, I don't think so." So they come back to me, and they say, "Jesusita, I came to see you, I think I'm pregnant." So I check them, and I can tell them when they are one month. Two is easy. And I can tell them when it's a tumor. Sometimes they're going to the doctor . . . and say, "I don't know what's the matter with me; I have a hard pain," but the doctor can't say. So they come to me, and I check them, and I call the doctor that is taking care of them, and I tell him, "Did you know what's the matter with this?" "No." I say, "I know, she's going back to you and give her some X-rays. She's got a tumor." And they take my word, the doctors.

> [Jesusita Aragón as told to] Fran Leeper Buss, *La Partera: Story of a Midwife*

I found Jesusita Aragón's voice compelling from the start: here was someone who recounted her difficulties in order to emphasize her success in overcoming them. Her self-affirming narrative only made the introduction, appendices, notes, and glossary that framed this edited autobiography appear more jarring. Where, to point up the value of her own practice, Aragón criticized the intervention of the American Medical Association (AMA) into New Mexican birthing techniques, editor Fran Leeper Buss commended this system's regulatory intercession.[1] Flourishing statistics in her introductory comments and concluding remarks, Buss represented the doctor as a benevolent patriarch, kindly condescending to instruct the natives in the miracles of modern medicine. Buss's interpretive intercession was distressing, but such clear narrative conflict did force me to reappraise Aragón's position in an autobiography which omitted her name and to consider the relations between speakers and editors in collaborative texts more generally. To what extent could the speaker work against the interpretive rubric imposed—so firmly in the case of *La Partera*—by the editor?

If I found the directness of Aragón's voice recounting her work on behalf of others compelling, I had to question what might be motivating such an interest when, returning to the library to find other such voices, I encountered quite a number of edited personal narratives, seemingly made to order, on the shelves. Looking more closely at these life histories in order to consider not only the power of the speaker's words but also the power relations structuring such speaker-editor collaborations, I found a number of patterns.[2] Typically, these books were published by university presses. Usually there was a clear class distinction between the editor, a professional woman with an interest in furthering feminist work, and the speaker, a working-class woman with a commitment to serving her community. Often these texts inscribed racial or ethnic difference as well, with a woman of color recounting the story of her life and work to a white woman who transcribed, edited, and published it, often with little or no discussion of the complicated process of turning oral history into text.

Jesusita Aragón's recollections in *La Partera: Story of a Midwife* and Onnie Lee Logan's autobiography *Motherwit: An Alabama Midwife's Story* are cases in point.[3] Published as part of the University of Michigan Press's Women and Culture Series, *La Partera* is clearly an outgrowth of recent feminist interest in working-class women and women of color, groups previously ignored by Anglo-American literary scholarship. *Motherwit* is less obviously the product of the academy's discovery of "other voices," but E. P. Dutton has marketed the book with an eye to the commercial confluence of gender and cultural studies, as the back-cover endorsements by James Mellon (editor of *Bullwhip Days: The Slaves Remember*), Susan Tucker (author of *Telling Memories Among Southern Women: Domestic Workers and Their Employers in the Segregated South*), and Alice

Childress (author of *Like One of the Family*) demonstrate. Prefatory and concluding material in both books directs readers to see the life histories as valuable insofar as they illustrate the "hard and useful lives" of rural, working-class women of color.[4]

More specifically, both life histories focus on the relationship between gender and the practice of "alternative" medicine as defined by the medical establishment in the United States. Through the stories of Jesusita Aragón and Onnie Lee Logan, editors Fran Leeper Buss and Katherine Clark demonstrate how women committed to serving their communities maintain this commitment in the face of strong pressures denying the validity of their healing practices. Both Aragón's and Logan's life histories document such pressures at length, describing physicians as, at best, grudging partners; at worst, obstructive of their own work as midwives. But over and against the midwives' own pictures of a resistant and defensive AMA, their editors celebrate medical intervention in, regulation of, and control over rural midwifery. It is this triangulated relationship of medical conflict, editorial opposition, and the speakers' critiques of both that I wish to consider more closely here.

Obstructive Obstetrics: The AMA and Traditional Midwifery

> Our midwives . . . have a wholesome fear of the law and the "State Doctor." In the beginning some of them were disposed to criticize the doctors. I have tried to make them understand that they should attend only normal labors, and that the doctors were their best friends and their last court of appeal in time of trouble. . . . I am also persuaded that the great body of midwives in the county have a more wholesome respect for the doctors than they had five years ago.
>
> J. Clifton Edgar, "The Education, Licensing and Supervision of the Midwife," *American Journal of Obstetrics*

Even if Dr. J. Clifton Edgar's medical restaging of the taming of the shrew were exceptional—which it is not—I would not be venturing very far out on a critical limb to argue that the embattled history of midwifery provides a less than sustaining environment for autobiographical assertion. As both

Jesusita Aragón and Onnie Lee Logan attest, obstetric practice as developed under the administrative wing of the AMA has been hostile to the practitioners of traditional birth methods ever since its own accouchement before the turn of the century. Edgar's counsel may be framed particularly baldly, but it provides a clear statement of the AMA's political principles: scores of early twentieth-century medical records insist on the need for teaching midwives a "wholesome" fear of and respect for medical authority. The power struggle between doctors and midwives reflects both the efforts of federal and state agencies to exert tighter control over local practice through regulatory measures and the racial conflict underlying such surveillance.

Attempts to bring local practices under a national medical umbrella began at the turn of the century, when physicians concerned about the status of obstetrics began to find in the critique of midwifery a convenient means of raising esteem for their own profession. An influential study conducted by Dr. J. Whitridge Williams on behalf of obstetric medicine and published in the *Journal of the American Medical Association* in January 1912 was forced to acknowledge both that medical schools were "inadequately equipped for teaching obstetrics properly" and that the majority of medical professors believed that "general practitioners lose as many and possibly more women from puerperal infection than do midwives."[5]

In addition to concerns about status, financial questions also preoccupied the doctors. According to Judy Barrett Litoff, who has chronicled the history of American midwifery in two studies: "A frequent complaint expressed by physicians was that they were poorly reimbursed for their obstetric services. Many doctors feared that this trend would continue as long as midwives persisted in attending fifty percent of all the births for less than one half the fee charged by medical practitioners."[6] Because they presented an economic threat to American physicians, midwives became a chief target for the medical lobby, which succeeded in having the Sheppard-Towner Maternity and Infancy Protection Act passed in 1921. That act provided for "instruction in the hygiene of maternity and infancy through public-health nurses, visiting nurses, consultation centers, child-care conferences and literary distribution."[7] Not surprisingly, this and other forms of federal regulation, and particularly the intervention of state bureaus of child hygiene created in the wake of this federal "protection," led to a significant decline in midwife-attended births: in 1900 about 50 percent of births were directed by midwives; thirty years later, the percentage had dropped to about 15 percent.[8] Contemporary regulations vary from state to state; in New Mexico, where Jesusita Aragón practices, once midwives have passed "stiff requirements for certification," they are legally authorized to practice home births; they are also "entitled to mandatory third-party reimbursement by health insurance plans." By contrast, Texas permits lay midwifery only provided the practitioner informs her client of the "limitations of her skills and practices."[9] In other states, as editor Pat Ellis Taylor confirms in her Introduction to Jewel Babb's personal narrative *Border Healing Woman,* midwifery has been either phased out gradually or prohibited completely.[10]

Anxiety over midwifery, articulated by the state as a threat to "public safety" and by doctors as endangering their own financial health, speaks to a number of larger political preoccupations as well. Quoting T. J. Hill, a New York physician, Litoff suggests that many physicians preferred midwives to women doctors; the midwife, after all, could be taught to " 'listen eagerly' " to the male physician: " 'She will sit at the feet of her Gamaliel . . . and hearken to his admonitions on things pertaining to the art of obstetrics.' "[11] But the medical condescension exerted toward both Aragón and Logan is racist as well. "The midwife of Robeson County is rather typical of the midwife of the rural South," pronounced a North Carolina physician. "She is far below the European midwife in intelligence and no training under the sun could make her a competent obstetric attendant."[12] Not to be outdone by his Carolina colleague, Dr. Felix J. Underwood, director of the Bureau of Child Hygiene for Mississippi during the early 1920s, lambasted the practice of midwifery with the rhetorical zeal of a latter-day Jonathan Edwards: "What could be a more pitiable picture than that of a prospective mother housed in an unsanitary home and attended in this most critical period by an accoucheur, filthy and ignorant, and not far removed from the jungles of Africa, laden with its atmosphere of weird superstition and voodooism?"[13]

Such overwhelmingly hostile language remained a mainstay of medical discourse on midwifery through at least the first half of the century. In 1938, some eight years after Onnie Lee Logan began practicing midwifery in Alabama, the director of that state's Bureau of Hygiene and Nursing characterized midwives as "ignorant . . . many of them highly superstitious, some of them very slovenly in their personal habits."[14] Concluding his address in language that echoes Nazi propaganda on the "Master Race" with unnerving precision, Dr. Austin insisted, "We have a tremendous task on our hands to teach these midwives how to do the things that we want them to do. . . . They are required to get permits each year. Of course, it is needless to say that they are given a physical examination, including a Wassermann test, and in that way we attempt to eliminate the most unfit physically" (95).

Nor did midwives like Jesusita Aragón escape similar judgment working in New Mexico. Condemning "the poorer class of Mexican people" for "almost invariably employ[ing] a midwife at the time of confinement," Dr. H. Garst efficiently vilified midwives in general and working-class Hispanos in particular. The people who chose to rely on a midwife rather than a physician were labeled "primitive," but the full force of righteous vituperation was reserved for the midwife herself.[15] A "Report on the Midwife Survey in Texas, January 2, 1925" represents rural midwives as "illiterate, usually dirty and in rags, gesticulating, oftentimes not able to talk or understand the English language, superstitious and suspicious." Hispanas are singled out as particularly resistant to the doctor's orders: "The Mexican midwife is more difficult [than the black midwife] to manage. Her ideas and traditions seem more fixed. She is more high-strung and more suspicious of the Americans." What underlies the hostility of the Texas report with its repeated jeers about "superstition" and Spanish speakers, I would argue, is anger over the reaffirmation of cultural practice: the refusal of Mexicanas to stop practicing birthing techniques "handed down to them by their mothers who usually had been midwives themselves," practices perceived as "inherited customs and beliefs . . . seldom, if ever in accord with modern science."[16] It is precisely this lack of "accord" with Anglo-American medical dictates that most provokes physicians of the AMA.

The Ethnographic Subject
of Collaborative Autobiography

If the narratives of Jesusita Aragón and Onnie Lee Logan provide readers with an alternative set of glosses on the *medical* establishment's "management" of midwives, they also indicate that *editorial* management of their words often undermines rather than confirms their own critical positions.

Titles and courtesies notwithstanding, editorial advocacy in both *La Partera* and *Motherwit* is directed toward the AMA rather than toward American midwives. The editorial exegesis Clark and Buss practice, that is, puts into the mouths of Logan and Aragón words the speakers themselves work to refute at every turn: that doctors save lives midwives put at risk.

This overriding—overwriting—demonstrates the pressure editorial ethnographic inquiry exerts on autobiographical voicing. Their authority eroded, Logan and Aragón serve merely as representatives of a contested practice. Significantly, the titles of these edited autobiographies omit the names of their subjects, introducing the speakers as illustrations of an occupational type.[17] Occlusion of the name defines the subject as historical source rather than agent of history; for their editors, Aragón and Logan tell the same story of the relation between a "traditional" medical discipline and the "marginal" women who practice it.

This transmutation of the "I" into type is far from a recent phenomenon. Hamilton Holt's prefatory note to the 1906 publication of *Undistinguished Americans* speaks to editorial agenda in contemporary collaborations as well: "The aim of each autobiography was to typify the life of the average worker in some particular vocation, and to make each story the genuine experience of a real person."[18] The equation (note the coordination of phrases with "and") between what is "average" (representative of a "they") and what is a "genuine experience" (spoken by an "I") demonstrates that editorial interest in constructing an "authentic" speaking voice works here not to enable a particular storyteller to discuss her views on what is important to her—family conflicts? political opinions? reflections on personal achievements, however defined?—but, rather, to authenticate a given statement as telling the historical "truth" about—again—a type of work ("some particular vocation").

Ethnic autobiography itself—not only the "lifelet" but any number of contemporary, more sustained collaborative narratives—labors in the service of sociology. The subtitles *A Pioneer Korean Woman in America* and *An Indian Woman in Guatemala* (the latter especially strikingly, given the title, *I . . . Rigoberta,* which dramatizes the individual, idiosyncratic voice) illustrate how this process works.[19] To her credit, Lee's editor Sucheng Chan articulates her own agenda as an historian: "By trying to 'locate' Mrs. Lee's account in its proper historical context, and by discussing the research that went into validating it, I have sought to turn one woman's memoir into a credible and representative historical record" (138). Still, the conflation of "I" with "we"/"they"—the fact that work by writers of color is more often than not shelved under "Sociology" or "Anthropology" or "Culture(s)" rather than "Literature" or "Fiction" or "Autobiography"— deprives these writers of attention as *writers*.[20] Benjamin Franklin's *Autobiography* could just as well be filed under "Early American History," but the fact that it is considered by many critics as one of the first American autobiographies accords its author respect as a "Distinguished American" whose life in and of itself demands attention and whose work as a stylist and rhetorician merits scrutiny.

As Philippe Lejeune indicates in "The Autobiography of Those Who Do Not Write," the relation between ethnography and autobiography suggests that we should pay closer attention not only to the dynamics of speaker-editor relations in particular texts but also to the context of the production of collaborative narratives more generally.[21] And, clearly, the inequities of power implicit in the process of speaking, collecting, writing, editing, and publishing life histories implicate the consumers of this literary work as well.

Not to mention the critics. Granting that editorial prerogative often works counter to the narrative goals of the speaker herself, where am I to situate my own commentary on these texts? I argue that editorial agenda can mask but not obliterate the imperatives of the speakers; if we attend more closely to the discursive patterns in specific women's narratives, we can begin to pick up the necessarily oblique theorizing about race and gender politics—as well as about many other issues—that is encoded in them. Such listening demands attention to the complicated intersection of any number of factors operating simultaneously: racial exploitation, generational tensions, inequities between urban and rural populations, class differences, gender conflict, the shifting particulars of state politics and social relations at specific points in time.

Yet while I am interested in refocusing attention on what tends to be filtered out by the editorial lens, my own preoccupations impose patterns upon the narratives I discuss as firmly as does any other editorial gloss. Certainly my arguments here and in the following chapter are designed to demonstrate how speakers maintain interpretive authority over their own words. But the danger of taking the words right out of people's mouths— even if "well-meant," if "for their own good"—is painfully obvious. Southwestern historian Joan Jensen argues that "our ultimate goal . . . in doing working class oral history . . . as with all work in Women's Studies, must be to help empower women."[22] But from the point of view of our "research interests"—people, remember, here!—our own differences as scholars may be at times less significant than our shared position as academics. The affirmative and assertive histories recounted in these narratives are compelling for critics and readers who insist that the academy begin to listen to other voices. Nevertheless, working in the service of politically responsible criticism requires that we consider a number of issues. Among them is the fact that, in academia, the celebration of "empowerment" can easily slide into a kind of philanthropic activity with all the self-interest this implies.

Yet if an acknowledgment of what we—I—stand to gain can locate the writer and forewarn readers, it nonetheless should not, I think, discourage the critical work of appraising such narratives. Recognizing power differences is not the same as either wishing them away or apologizing for them, but instead means outlining what is sometimes made to appear invisible. Daphne Patai has argued convincingly that "the current emphasis on 'empowering' or 'dialogic' research" is incapable of resolving the "fundamental contradiction" between academic research and "social transformation." The academic equivalent of the Emperor Who Wore No Clothes, it often speciously promises what it does not expect to deliver. Nevertheless, I would not frame this relation between theory and practice as invariably tainted from the outset, as Patai suggests: "Our enjoyment of research and its rewards constantly compromises the ardor with which we promote social transformation. At the very least, it dilutes our energy; at the most, it negates our ability to work for change."[23] If writing for an academic audience is writing for a relatively small audience, it is not always preaching to the converted (only the extreme right wing characterizes college students as an indistinguishable mass of "rabble-rousers"), nor is it always speaking for a uniformly privileged group; consider, for instance, those professors and students who are among the first in their families to have attended college.

It may be useful, too, to distinguish between professionalization and political acumen. The way our writing gets shaped for publication may have to be translated for people outside the academy, but once words like "subject position" get rewritten as "point of view" and words like "hege-

mony" get spoken as the "haves" united in opposition to the "have-nots,"
almost anyone who has been around for any length of time will no doubt
have plenty to say about them. Furthermore, specifically political work
may go hand in hand with its apparently more attenuated academic equivalent. Appraising published collaborative narratives and preparing legal appeals out of the personal narratives of people requesting asylum, for example, could be mutually informing.

To return to the question of collaboration with which I began: why is
this particular textual formation currently so popular with scholarly presses
and institutions? What functions do such books serve for readers and critics? Any scholar of Native American literature could respond that textual
collaboration is not a recent phenomenon in the United States, nor is it
limited to the production of personal narrative per se. As Dexter Fisher
points out, Mourning Dove's novel *Cogewea, the Half Blood* (1927) is a
different book for the intervention of its "mentor," Lucullus Virgil
McWhorter: "Had McWhorter not passionately encouraged her to record
the tales of her tribe," her fiction would not have been framed as a folkloristic narrative.[24] F. H. Matthews accounts for this ethnographic interest in
the 1920s by describing the "revulsion from Americanism" then current in
Anglo intellectual circles. While some writers asserted "their identity with
some minority" or "raised folk arts to self-conscious status," others "who
lacked a vital region or ethnic minority with which to identify turned instead . . . to quarrying the national past in search of lost virtue."[25] If we
consider the history of immigration in this country and the social and legal
responses to it over the years, this kind of identification begins to look less
nostalgic and more anxiety-ridden. Hamilton Holt (himself "New England–descended and Yale educated") wrote a Foreword to *The Life Stories of (Undistinguished) Americans* that advances one rationale for the
substitution of multiple brief lives in place of sustained autobiography:
"The place of the full single life story that Louis Wirth, himself an immigrant from Germany, had contemplated as a source of insight, may then
rightfully belong to a collection of short lifelets by undistinguished authors
of diverse ethnic backgrounds" (xiii). If celebrated Americans earn life stories, the "poor huddled masses" can reasonably ("rightfully") demand only
the "lifelet." Form here anticipates ideological function; the collective,
amalgamated structure of Holt's compilation, together with his emphasis
on ethnicity, suggests that this book of lifelets is designed to mimic the

melting pot in which those of "diverse ethnic backgrounds" are supposed to meld.

Recent collaborative compilations may, like Holt's autobiographical encyclopedia, provide one means of managing ethnicity. But the sustained life histories that jointly-authored texts provide for readers suggests that this more direct form of control is frequently exchanged for ostensibly less invasive mediums. In his study of Chicano literature, Ramón Saldívar argues that Shakespeare's Caliban "performs a positive function; he is a good example, in other words, of our own savage natures, which we must control."[26] For that part of ethnic autobiography's readership who distinguish themselves as beyond ethnicity, the speakers of collaborative narrative may hold up a mirror to the reading self and the (editorial) writing self—a mirror, as Virginia Woolf comments wryly in *A Room of One's Own*, twice life-size.

Undoubtedly there are other reasons for the recent proliferation of mediated texts. The consistent emphasis on "hard and useful lives" advertised in such books points to their appeal for scholarly readers and writers who may frame their own work in opposition to "real" labor. Reading and writing about the "hard" work of women like Aragón and Logan may offer a voyeuristic connection to academics anxious about the class status of their own activity. But Philippe Lejeune's focus on "Those Who Do Not Write" directs us to still another service such books perform. "What one tries to capture in writing," he argues,

is the voice, the autobiographical discourse *of those who do not write.* . . . Their story takes its value, in the eyes of the reader, from the fact that they belong (that they *are perceived* as belonging) to a culture other than his own, a culture defined by the exclusion of writing. The bookstore exploits an *ethnological* type of curiosity. . . . The admission of collaboration . . . becomes here an essential piece of the system: it is a matter of guaranteeing that the model has written *nothing!* (196)

If academic culture, in apparent contradistinction to working-class culture, is a culture that values writing, the world which frames the college campus does not. Just as television supplanted radio, video makes the printed word look as old-fashioned as the illuminated manuscript; the rapid shift and spin of images in recent novels like Jessica Hagedorn's *The Dogeaters* (1990) mimes the visual tease of MTV, while video stores begin to crowd out McDonald's. Thus the repeated insistence on distinguishing between the literate and the nonliterate begins to look like the preoccupations of a professorate memorializing "orality" in order, paradoxically, to maintain the authority of script in a climate that no longer reveres the written word as a form of magic.

The Still Vanishing Subject:
Some Cautions on Revising "Authority"

If questions of form are contingent upon format, as Arnold Krupat has concisely stated of Native American narrative, we cannot isolate either the content or the presentation of any life history from the methods used to obtain it.[27] Consistently, however, literary, sociological, and anthropological studies position the subject of discourse—even when she is speaking in the first person—as a textualized object, malleable according to the researcher's interests and academic uses. And in the interests of more faithfully rendering quality of voice, such studies are inclined to ignore, even to conceal, the intersubjective context out of which such narratives are generated. In a discussion of the status of field work in anthropological research, Kevin Dwyer takes the work of Clifford Geertz as symptomatic of the way in which this professional blind spot has been sustained, arguing that while Geertz recognizes field work as "constructive activity," he denies the dialectical relation of speaker and editor at the moment it is in play, seeing it only at the level of "theoretical activity":

At the most basic level of the "small fact," of the informant's interpretation, Geertz systematically refuses to see the anthropologist in his or her human relation to the informant or to accept the inevitable interdependence of Self and Other at the very origin of the search for "information." . . . The dialectical confrontation, for Geertz, does not take place during the field encounter with the Other, but is restricted to the privacy of the anthropologist's study.[28]

This inability to acknowledge how a participatory relationship governs the production of the anthropological text (and here we could substitute the term "literary" text, given the flexible discursive parameters any postmodern critical theory presumes) tends to objectify one of the participants in this process and to ignore the history of imperialism which informs such interracial "collaborations." Yet, as Dwyer very acutely points out, a recognition of this history is crucial to any analysis of first-person narratives: "Mere participation . . . inevitably locates the Self culturally as the 'outsider' intruding on the Other's terrain, and historically as a representative of a society that has a prior history of intrusion" (274). Nor, as this chapter will suggest, should we assume that an *intra*racial collaboration will necessarily avoid the abuses of a coercive discursive and political history: differences of class, gender, and region (not to mention of political agenda) also inflect speaker-editor relations. The subject of an intraracial inquiry, then, is not necessarily immune from definition as ethnographic object.[29]

I would like to focus for the moment, however, on mediated texts that inscribe racial difference. Even a quick glance at the following excerpts from *La Partera: Story of a Midwife* and *Motherwit: An Alabama Midwife's Story* tends to confirm the way in which autobiographical voicing is contained and muted by the assumptions of ethnographic discourse:

I met Jesusita Aragón, the last of the traditional, Hispanic midwives in the area, through several women who had babies with her. . . . I knew immediately she had a story worth telling, and Jesusita was eager to tell it. (*La Partera*, vii)

She was the last granny midwife in Mobile and one of the last in Alabama. . . . Caught in the flux of a changing culture, Onnie is an unusual victim of historical "progress." (*Motherwit*, xiii)

Brief as they are, such editorial comments indicate how narratives produced out of an interracial collaboration may reproduce in some measure the disabling history of race relations in the United States. Their commitment to representing Jesusita Aragón and Onnie Lee Logan as speaking subjects places the editors within social science methodological traditions in which, as Genaro Padilla argues of recent life histories of Mexican immigrants, the "I-speaking voice" is "simultaneously privileged and dismissed."[30] Although both editors attempt to replicate their subjects' verbal presence, they work against autobiographical presentation by situating the speakers as a kind of cultural litmus paper. Aragón and Logan, that is, are introduced to us as "the last" of a kind of "traditional" practitioner. Their distinction—that singularity which should justify their autobiographical stature—is to be a type, the single survivor of a deteriorating culture. Buss's preface recalls the nineteenth-century literary iconography of the "noble savage" in that it positions Aragón as the last of a dying breed, archetype of a "broken" culture (13). Similarly, Onnie Lee Logan's distinction is to be a "victim," "the last granny midwife in Mobile and one of the last in Alabama." It is only because she is a rare specimen, the editor's description implies, that Logan's story is valued at all.

This conflict between presencing and preservation suggests in microcosm the problematic relation between autobiographical and ethnographic impulses in life histories more generally. Echoed by editor Katherine Clark's elegy depicting Logan as having "faithfully and successfully served one world only to be told by the next that she was no longer needed" (xiii–xiv), such texts frame the complicated question of cultural identity within a system of binary absolutes where one means of signifying identity has been "vanquished" by its successor. In a politically oppressive environment urging homogenization to a cultural-political "mainstream," it is perhaps all too easy to envision the means of assigning cultural value as a process controlled by an ideological monopoly. But cultures are not created and recreated in accordance with a Darwinian teleology, imposing a new world's rituals over a now-anachronistic tradition. Produced from the historical context of imperialism, ethnographic discourse defines what is in fact a synchronic process between multiple, continually flexible cultural relations as a diachronic history, a story of cultural rise and fall.[31] Ethnography often forgets, moreover, that this "history" is itself produced in response to anxiety about an inability to subdue the articulations of people who define themselves in contradistinction to dominating models.

Lejeune's definition of collaborative writing as a negotiation "between the model's supply and the public's demand" (189) very acutely situates the narrative as the product of a complicated and often conflicting series of intentions. This sophisticated political analysis, however, although it deconstructs the concept of authority as "a relative and conventional thing" (193) and the speaker as one who "is reduced to the state of source" (189), nevertheless positions that very speaker's authority as the museum piece Buss and Logan make it out to be. Here is where much of the "dialogic" discourse celebrated by postmodernism speaks to and for only those sitting in the box seats. According to anthropology scholar James Clifford, such "plural authorship" is "a form of authority . . . [that] must still be considered utopian," because the very notion of joint authorship "challenges a deep Western identification of any text's order with the intention of a single author."[32] But in whose interests, finally, is this kind of "subversion?"

Proclaiming the death of the author at the very moment when writers of color are beginning to enjoy wider commercial success seems, as a number of scholars have pointed out, a little suspect.[33] And if authority is so unappealing, why do most editors keep scrambling to emblazon their own names, not the speakers', on the spines and covers and title pages of collaborative book projects? Just so in Lejeune's critique of the way power relations objectify the subject does the subject serve as object lesson. His use of the word *model* is particularly curious: the product of a mixed metaphor, not to mention mixed media, it suggests the still silence of the painter's model, the subject who best fulfills her function when she is least an agent.[34]

It seems to me that this is the danger of deconstructing the subject, an operation Lejeune carries out too well. To assert that the narrative of the mediated text "is not the writing of an identifiable and personal 'other,' but a kind of floating writing, an autobiographical form with no subject to ground it" (189) is to reproduce the coercive context in which such writing is produced, to ignore the material product of such literary effort (and specifically its title page, which assigns authority, however arbitrarily, to *someone*), and to forget that the "other" may exercise the ability (even if it must be carried out in an oblique fashion) to speak against editorial appropriation. If, as Lejeune has stated, the collaborative text "blurs in a disturbing way the question of responsibility" (192), then just who should be assigned responsibility remains a question rather than a given. Similarly, the formulation "the one to whom the responsibility is given" assumes an agency (albeit one which is either acceding to or dispensing with authority) that we need to examine, not dismiss.[35]

I would suggest that if we look closely at the narratives of mediated texts, we will find the traces—sometimes explicit in the interpretive conflicts and argumentative tensions between editorial preface and speaker's text, often articulated more obliquely in the speaker's preemption of or resistance to the process of textualizing her life history—of her insistence on maintaining her status as author. In spite of inequities of class, race, generation, and education, collaboration does not necessarily mean capitulation. Mary Paik Lee's resistance to full "disclosure" in the edited version of her autobiography, *Quiet Odyssey: A Pioneer Korean Woman in America,* demonstrates, as editor Sucheng Chan acknowledges, not so much modesty as a dogged, if "quiet," insistence on controlling the textual boundaries of her story.[36] Claudia Salazar cites the final sentence of *I . . . Rigoberta Menchú: An Indian Woman in Guatemala* as illustrating Menchú's refusal to satisfy anthropological desire to "know The Indian": " 'I'm still keeping my Indian identity a secret. I'm still keeping secret what I think no-one should know. Not even anthropologists or intellectuals, no matter how many books they have, can find out all our secrets.' "[37]

Nor is withholding speech the only strategy autobiographers use to circumvent editorial management or provide readers with lessons in how to interpret their stories. As chapter 4 argues in greater detail, textual politics in *La Partera* and *Motherwit* do not, for instance, prevent either Aragón or Logan from critiquing practices they see as racist. Given the combined onslaught of medical hostility and editorial inattention or, often, resistance to the speakers' race-inflected critiques, however, it is not surprising that both women resort to rhetorical camouflage in order to make their points. To that end, they frequently employ modes that are not consistent with feminine self-affirmation. They may theorize race politics using an apparently conciliatory rhetoric that maintains a posture of humility and nonaggressiveness.[38] A particularly telling criticism may be prefaced by a concession that makes it more palatable to an otherwise defensive listener. Often comments condemning racial oppression are developed circuitously, in a series of sentences that may seem contradictory.

Acknowledging how autobiographical desire and ethnographic necessity often set speaker and editor at odds should not lead us to assume that every editor is oblivious to the historical and literary pressures that position transcriber and subject in an unequal relationship, however. Close analysis of edited life histories suggests that "those who do not write" often do just that; editorial acknowledgment and prefatory comments frequently admit the extent to which the speaking subject is a writing subject, sharing the work of transmuting spoken word into print. Rather than assuming that the title-page division of responsibility between authority and life history represents the final word on the relation between speaker and editor, we need instead to consider the evidence of the edited text as a whole.

Editorial Agency in the Mediated Text

Just who is constituted as the author for any given collaborative text remains a complicated question. The literary authority vested in the signature provides one account of the relation between subject and editor, but, as Lejeune indicates,

> authorial status has different aspects, which can be dissociated and possibly also shared: the juridical responsibility, the moral and intellectual right, literary ownership (with the financial rights related to it), and the signature, which, at the same time that it refers to the juridical problem, is part of a *textual* device (cover, title, preface, etc.) through which the reading contract is established. (193)

To acknowledge that authority is not a divine or natural right but, rather, a historical, legal, and textual privilege does not obliterate its power, however, nor does it mean that readers can simply forego their responsibility to question its relation to the narratives of mediated texts. Deconstructing "the 'life' " by indicating that it "belongs to both of them—but perhaps also, for the same reason, belongs neither to one nor to the other," as Lejeune asserts (192), is a potentially dangerous evasion of the practical ramifications of publishing a collaborative text, for it provides a justification for the very appropriation the critic condemns. Nor should we assume that it is the writer who "is entrusted with all the duties of structuring, of control, of communication with the outside. . . . Condensing, summarizing, eliminating the inferior parts, choosing the lines of relevance, establishing an order, a progression" (189).[39] The absence of description about the textual process does not necessarily imply that this labor has not been a joint endeavor; it may, in fact, only point to an editor's desire to maintain interpretive control over the narrative.

Although such studied editorial inattention is not uncommon, some editors do acknowledge how their organizing and structuring techniques contribute to the form of the narrative and provide a rationale for glossing its contents. Bob Blauner's argument about sociology's use of first-person narrative, where "the editing process virtually is the analysis" (47) is confirmed by editor Pat Ellis Taylor's afterword to *Border Healing Woman: The Story of Jewel Babb* (1981): "I am afraid that my confessed interest in her ability to heal led her into certain emphases on the material that she might not have chosen herself. . . . The information she gave me on other facets of her life was at least as extensive as the information she gave me on healing" (104).

Nor is Taylor alone in acknowledging the extent to which the narrative "present" is constructed by the editor, "coming to the healer with pad and pencil in hand" (104). In *Lemon Swamp and Other Places: A Carolina Memoir,* Karen Fields positions herself as "collaborating author" alongside her grandmother, Mamie Garvin Fields. The younger Fields does not offer her prefatory and concluding statements as interpretive index or "scientific" apparatus, framing devices which would inevitably situate her grandmother's narrative as a form of ethnographic data inaccessible to the reader without editorial assistance.[40] Rather, she asserts that the text is the "outcome" of "an extended conversation" which "involves our two subjectivities, not hers alone" (xiii). By emphasizing her familial relation to the autobiographical subject, Fields runs the risk of justifying her editorial work as appropriate because it is in some way "natural." If this familial authorization avoids positioning the subject of the narrative as ethnographic other, then, it may unself-consciously affirm the relation between two collaborating but nonetheless distinct subjects and, in so doing, obscure the labor of textual production. Karen Fields's perception that the book works in part to reconstruct a genealogy between granddaughter and grandmother inclines in this direction: "We both came to feel that even if *Lemon Swamp* never saw the light of day, our enterprise would have justified itself. After all, how many grandmothers and granddaughters have the opportunity of befriending one another as adults?" (xii). Yet her acknowledgment of conflicts between the two reminds readers that the text is the product of a dialogue between people "who find their way through the disagreements that arise inevitably and who work to spell out for themselves the agreements that must be conveyed to others" (xii). Fields is quick to articulate the nature of these conflicts, as when she distinguishes between her own need "to relegate childhood shocks about Dixie to their proper place" and her grandmother's determination "to pass on a heritage" (xx). Even the recognition of difference can be useful, however, for it opens room for the speaker by acknowledging that there are two ways of reading any particular utterance or situation. Thus just as the insistence on compromise asserts the text as constructive activity, Karen Fields's admission of editorial fallibility reauthorizes her grandmother as speaker and prevents her from being objectified as textual evidence for an editorial thesis.

Karen Fields's acknowledgment of the narrative conflict generated by any collaborative project remains the exception rather than the rule, however. More often than not, editor-speaker entente is asserted so vigorously as to look more like a mask for editorial intent than an explanation of joint interpretive effort. Frequently, initiative for the collaborative project is not assigned jointly but is represented as wholeheartedly the speaker's impulse. I would like now to look more closely at a number of mediated life histories that demonstrate this pattern.

"The initiative for the project was hers": Owning Up to Joint Textual Production

Jesusita was anxious to share her story with someone, and we eventually met together a number of times. . . . The following, then, is the story of Jesusita Aragón. The story is told in her own words and contains glimpses into the lives of many others. Many of the names have been changed to protect people's privacy, but the facts of their hard, and useful, lives remain the same.

Fran Leeper Buss, Introduction to
La Partera: Story of a Midwife

Onnie has always regarded midwifery as her real life's work, however, and the inspiration for this project came not from me, but from her overwhelming desire "not to die with it," as she said—not to die without sharing the "wisdom and knowledge" but especially the stories from her lifetime of experience. Onnie, a semiliterate woman with little formal education, told me she was "gonna write this book" if she "had to scratch it out" herself. "I got so much experience in here that I just want to explode," she told me.

Onnie Lee Logan, *Motherwit:
An Alabama Midwife's Story*

Mentioning only that in producing *La Partera* she and Doña Aragón "shared countless long distance phone calls" (vii), Fran Leeper Buss refrains from describing the division of responsibility the transcription from spoken to written word entails, emphasizing instead the collaborative nature of the project: "We tape recorded our many conversations and from the tapes I have organized the story of her life and work" (8). The actual process of producing the text is left obscure. Did the two meet to discuss the way that these conversations would be "organized" by the editor? What principles of selection did Buss use to transform untold hours of taped recollections and dialogue into seventy-two pages of text?

While, as Blauner indicates, "editing personal narratives is a creative process which actively shapes materials by reducing them" (51), what takes the place of any such admission in *La Partera* is a substitution of gesture for word, a picture of rapport between editor and speaker so complete it need not be communicated through speech. Buss foregrounds her memories of Aragón's "touch, the touch of her arms as she embraced me, the memory of her hands stroking mine, holding them in times of greeting and parting, and touching them for reassurance or emphasis" (8), while leaving unrecorded the inevitable conflicts that arise in any effort at communication: disagreements, misunderstandings, differences in emphasis, corrections, amplifications, questions. As anthropologist Patricia Zavella indicates:

Rapport is not automatic. . . . It is a continual process to achieve intimacy not only with the same informant through successive interviews, but also throughout each encounter. . . . We also need to anticipate that our status as insiders will only allow an entrance. From there, because we are also outsiders, we must be prepared for reticence, political differences and various social distances.[41]

Ignoring the difficulties dialogue involves, Buss's insistence on elemental harmony avoids emphasizing what should be a crucial admission in this interracial collaboration: the question of difference.

In fact, this editorial version of harmonic convergence is typical of recent collaborative narrative more generally. Lejeune characterizes "identification" rather than "distance" as the dominant relation in mediated narrative: the editor, "imbued with his story . . . is going to try to imagine himself as the model in order to be able to write in his place" (190–91). Judith Stacey argues that this kind of affiliation is particularly appealing for "feminist researchers," who are "apt to suffer the delusion of alliance more than the delusion of separateness."[42] What both critical formulations point to is the tendency of recent editors to style themselves as literary "mediums," endeavoring like Virgil to guide other souls through the difficult passage from speech to writing. When editor Pat Ellis Taylor describes healers like Jewel Babb as "conduit[s], seeing themselves as bringing supernatural forces to bear on the patient" (116), she more accurately describes a kind of *editorial* desire, an (impossible) wish to remain characterless in order to take on the character of another. In the case of *La Partera*, editorial "channelling" creates a very compelling speaking voice. But whose voice is it? If the Buss and Aragón venture results in a kind of writing that looks alive on the page, it is built on concealment, on the pretense of speaking as one, an Other, rather than as both doubled and divided.

This erasure of difference is troubling, as feminist scholar Elizabeth Jameson reveals when she discusses concerns about her own interviewing process: "I asked a friend who is an anthropologist with much more field work experience in other cultures than I have, if she felt that I sounded as if I were leading my informants. Her reply relieved me, and I hope vindicated the complex relationships represented on the tape. 'Yes,' she said. 'You led them right where they wanted to go.' "[43] Given the potential for misreading—("How . . . did we, who had a close confidential, long-standing relationship, manage to misunderstand each other so completely?" Katherine Borland recollects of her relationship with her own "informant," her grandmother Beatrice Hanson)[44]—how can any researcher be assured that she has correctly, consistently, and fully determined "where they wanted to go?"

As is the case in Borland and Hanson's collaboration, in *La Partera* the assumption of a shared point of view erodes Aragón's authority while bolstering the editor's. Buss's introduction, for example, provides an interpretive rubric for Aragón's narrative that directs readers to perceive this text as contiguous to—more precisely, as illustrating—an editorial thesis. Yet Aragón's own arguments, the subject of the next chapter, are ideologically at odds with this imperative. Suffice to say here, however, that what is foregrounded in Buss's introduction is not really Aragón's life history, but, instead, a sketch of a culture in decline: a New Mexican landscape drawn both from postcard vistas and from the modernist interest in primitivism, where skies are perennially "turquoise," the sun constantly "brilliant," the desert always "vast," "stark," and "immense" (2–3). The language of ethnography shows itself in other ways as well: in consistent images of deserted adobes crumbling in Parthenon-like silent grandeur, of "deteriorating buildings" (12) and "broken" windmills (13), of churches "fallen into disarray" (14) and "the graves of relatives and friends" (14)—in sum, a description not of people but of their "remains" (13).

Notwithstanding a commitment to convey the nuances of Aragón's speech, invoking the discourse of what I can only call "romantic ethnography" (consider its elegiac tone and lament for lone survivors) inevitably reduces the speaker to artifact. And, as I have already indicated, this ethnographic imperative is not specific to *La Partera*. Like Buss's figuring of Aragón as midwife, Katherine Clark's titling of Onnie Lee Logan's narrative as *Motherwit: An Alabama Midwife's Story* constructs the speaker as representative subject. This story of a midwife—doubly glossed as such by Clark's preface—is as poorly documented as is *La Partera*. Clark provides no acknowledgment of the way in which the narrative has been constructed, other than to affirm that Logan provided the "inspiration" for the project. She is about to "explode" with the desire to "write this book," Clark writes, if, despite her status as "a semiliterate woman with little formal education, she 'had to scratch it out' herself" (ix). Such a statement, as Sandra Gunning reminds me, can as easily be read as a veiled threat— Logan's defiance of editorial efforts to manage her speech—as it can as evidence in support of Clark's editorial venture.[45] In any case, such strenuous advocating of Logan's agency here seems suspect, for it insists simultaneously on the urgency of the speaker's need to textualize her life history and the urgency of editorial intercession: since Logan barely writes, someone else must be persuaded to assist her.

This scrutinizing of editorial motive is severe, yet it seems to me a necessary corrective for Clark's own lack of self-scrutiny. The following quotation will make the point more clear, for it constructs the impetus for the project as contingent upon the speaker's anticipation of her own death, as the shift in verb tense indicates: " 'I got so much experience in here that I just want to explode,' she told me. 'I *want* to show that I *knew* what I *knew*—I *want* somebody to realize what I *am*' " (ix–x, emphasis added). Succeeding upon the definition of "midwifery as her real life's work," a work she wants to describe in order " 'not to die with it' " (ix), this description of the text's inspiration suggests that the narrative motive is one of sanctification, of enshrining a person/practice that is passing.

Like *La Partera* and *Motherwit, He Included Me: The Autobiography of Sarah Rice* at once obscures editorial motive and styles the speaker as cultural anachronism.[46] According to editor Louise Westling, it is Rice who calls upon *her* to provide the necessary technological apparatus. "The initiative for the project was hers," Westling affirms, echoing the editors of interracial textual collaborations as a whole, "in response to the urging of family members and friends that she record the story of her life. Through my sisters and brother in Jacksonville, she let me know that she would like my help" (xi). Yet, clearly, whether it is speaker or editor who initially prompts the telling of the life story, the process of collaboration constructs a subject quite distinct from the authority who writes her history without the assistance of another; as Carole Boyce Davies argues, "The phrases 'I edited,' 'I arranged' and 'selected' camouflage a whole host of detailed ordering and creating operations."[47] To insist, then, that "control of the narrative's shape and progress was always Mrs. Rice's. My job was simply to turn on the tape recorder and occasionally interject a question for clarification" (xi) is to ignore the entire context of the story's production. Since one presumes that Mrs. Rice could have performed this mechanical operation by herself, this positioning of the editor cannot help but look disingenuous, an editorial sleight of hand to mask the mediated nature of the speaker's story and to obscure the narrative frame of what is, as the title page reminds us, a joint labor.

Perhaps most significantly, Westling's refusal to invoke the context of textual production means she must deny as well the structure of power that informs this Southern relationship. Ignoring how unequal political authority must inevitably inflect a collaboration between a white professional and a black domestic, the editor instead relies upon a picture of intimacy: "We have known each other for 30 years, ever since she began working for my mother once a week when I was 14" (xi). That this "close relationship," which she affirms is "typical of Mrs. Rice's associations with families in which she has worked," may be defined differently by employer and employee does not figure here. Nor does she distinguish between the intimacy of friends and that maternalism which Judith Rollins documents as characteristic of the relations between domestics and their employers in the American South.[48] Westling does acknowledge that the relationship between editor and speaker has some bearing upon the text: "When we began the project, we had a rapport which made the collaboration relaxed, even as it must certainly also have limited some elements of the narration" (xi). Yet she does not recognize that her vantage point as the child of a household in which Mrs. Rice was an employee may give her a perspective very different from that of Mrs. Rice herself.

Toward a Methodology of the Local:
Life History as History

*To isolate Mrs. Babb's role as a faith healer is a distortion not
only of the way she perceives herself but also of the way in
which she is perceived by the outside observer, who in this case
was myself. . . . To me, she is primarily a strong, yet compas-
sionate, woman, able to be at home in a desert environment that
most of us would consider at best unfriendly, at worst unlivable.
In recounting her story, she gave at least as much emphasis to
her trials and tribulations as a young bride and mother as to
the manifestations of healing abilities and spirit helpers. . . .
However, Mrs. Babb's role as faith healer held a great degree
of interest for me, and for that reason I urged her on in that
area while I might not have urged her in others.*

Pat Ellis Taylor, Afterword to Jewel
Babb, *Border Healing Woman*

*Notwithstanding the respects in which I am a Southerner, I
tended to operate with a Northerner's "sociologism" about the
South, that is, with an abstract schema lacking the texture of
lived lives. By contrast, my grandmother dealt in actual people
and places, in the choices that she or her neighbor confronted,
in what a man or woman did given a particular circumstance.
Aggregated, much of this could become the events and processes
so dear to social scientists, but my grandmother was telling me
about experience before it became either.*

Karen Fields, Introduction to Mamie
Garvin Fields with Karen Fields,
Lemon Swamp and Other Places

I have critiqued the tendency of some recent life histories to exploit an
individual life in order to dramatize an editorial thesis about culture.[49] Yet
politically sophisticated life histories do exist, texts that acknowledge the
autobiographical subject as the product of a relationship among the various
people involved in the transformation of spoken memory into written reminiscence. Arnold Krupat praises Lucullus Virgil McWhorter's work in *Yellow Wolf: His Own Story* (1940) for consistently noting "shifts in tone,
pauses, or changes in diction on Yellow Wolf's part, refusing to erase the
inevitable gaps and fissures of the actual narrative event to produce the
illusion of the unified, seamless textual object" (158). Further, he notes,

McWhorter "interrupts Yellow Wolf's monologues within the various chapters, to speak directly in his own voice . . . to explain that Yellow Wolf is speaking in direct response to a question McWhorter has posed, or in acknowledgment of a request to follow up some earlier matter" (157–58).

This self-conscious textual practice identifying the speaker's narrative as constructed out of what anthropologists call "field dialogue" is used by Pat Ellis Taylor in *Border Healing Woman* as well, allowing us insight into the way the relationship between speaker and editor is narratively inscribed. The Babb/Taylor book is from the point of view of the critic of collaborative work both interesting and frustrating: interesting for Taylor's detailed and self-conscious discussion of her own editorial concerns and her recognition of the ways that they sometimes come into conflict with Babb's own; frustrating because despite her integrity as a scholar and her sharp-eyed acknowledgment of narrative difference, the editorial apparatus she provides nevertheless works to reposition the speaker as icon rather than individual. While Taylor places a high value on "preserv[ing] . . . Mrs. Babb's unique 'voice,' editing as little as possible, other than to arrange the spoken and written segments in orderly sequence" (xvi), she intersperses between portions of the speaker's narrative her own "impressions of the time I spent with her and of the environment which, in my opinion, has contributed to the formation of her personality and her beliefs" (xvi).

Such editorial intercession tends to position the speaker not as coauthority but as specimen subject, upon which a scholarly apparatus of preface, afterword, and endnotes will be brought to bear.[50] Endnotes are especially crucial to this process: as the final word, they provide an authoritative reading of Mrs. Babb's narrative, establishing two levels of interpretation in the text. The speaker's explanations, many organized under the ethnological rubric of folk tales (see in particular the "stories," bracketed with such titles as "The Light That Saved the Beggar's Life" and "The Man Who Could See into Another Life," at the close of chapter 6, "Changing Circumstances") become "raw data" to be glossed by the editor's notes in a series of "scientific" affirmations, elaborations, and negations. In addition, the notes mark specific passages of the text as direct transcription from tape but fail to indicate which portions of the narrative are in fact reproduced—with or without editorial intervention—from Mrs. Babb's written recollections, making it difficult to determine to what extent Taylor has reconstructed Mrs. Babb's reminiscences. Nevertheless, Taylor's insistence on the text as the product of dialogue clearly affirms the life history as collaborative process. Furthermore, if such interjections tend to dispel the quality of voice the editor works to (re)produce, her decision to alternate chapters of Mrs. Babb's narratives with her own perceptions of the speaker calls attention to the fact that Mrs. Babb is situated by this process as a kind of textual *character*. If the final product appears more Taylor's than the speaker's, such an effect at least honestly directs readers to consider the relation between editorial author(ity) and autobiographical subject in this book.

In fact, thanks to Taylor's very extensive accounting of editorial practice, *Border Healing Woman* foregrounds the narrative tensions between the speaker's own ordering—and thus, interpretation—of her history and the reconstruction of her memories by an editor. Taylor's "Afterword," which distinguishes specific events as particularly formative of the speaker's character, suggests how such editorial reevaluation effectively disguises the speaker's own impulses toward self-formation. For instance, Taylor assigns Jewel Babb's move from Langtry, Texas, to the hot springs near Sierra Blanca a value at odds with Mrs. Babb's own gloss. The editor identifies the shift from urban to rural environment as "undoubtedly . . . the major turning point in Mrs. Babb's life" (112) for its contribution to her knowledge of healing. Yet her previous admission that her own "interest in her ability to heal" has no doubt led Mrs. Babb "into certain emphases on the material that she might not have chosen herself" (104) allows us to evaluate Taylor's later judgment more critically. Character descriptions such as the following provide a perfect example, in addition, of how autobiographical presence can be overwritten by editorial ethnography: "And when she left the hot springs, she was very different from the simple ranching woman who had first arrived. In the course of time, Mrs. Babb had learned as much as anyone who had ever been associated with the hot springs about how to use the mud, mosses, and waters" (115). The autobiographical subject is trivialized here, yet Jewel Babb's own recollections of her ranching work—her relationship with her mother-in-law; her feelings about the physical and emotional trials this work involves; her assessment of the relation between this kind of labor, traditionally perceived as masculine, and her sense of herself as a woman—all suggest that this "simple ranching woman" would not necessarily agree with the "healing woman" model Taylor ascribes to her.

The frankness with which Taylor acknowledges her own interests in the text is as commendable as it is exceptional. What her comments indicate, however, is that the process of selecting a given person's life story as worthy of note is contingent on a conservative model of history, one that situates the personal record as valuable only insofar as it is monumental. Or, as Cletus E. Daniel reframes this in his introduction to Victoria Byerly's collection of oral histories, it requires a model of history as "somehow larger than the individual lives that populate it."[51] Either you are a distinguished citizen whose self-formation becomes conflated with political formation more generally (thus Benjamin Franklin's *Autobiography* is read as defining the American-made self, while, conversely, Jefferson's *Notes on the State of Virginia* is glossed for the insight it affords readers into the character of its author), or you attain distinction by the extent to which your particular history works as a synecdoche to invoke a monumental historical force—of class formation, of racial politics, of gender conflict. This "typographical" theory precludes, of course, precisely what a more accretive version of history would guarantee as valuable: the study of particular lives as significant through their very particularity.

In distinguishing between two quite different interpretive modes, the excerpt from *Lemon Swamp* with which this section opened provides a useful outline of this alternative historical model. "I began my part of *Lemon Swamp* with a mental map showing historical events and processes, a map strongly colored with discrimination, violence, economic pressure, and deprivation of civil rights," Karen Fields begins, identifying her own perspective as "sociological." Her grandmother, she realizes, by contrast, "was not trying to convey 'how black people fared in Charleston over the first half of this century,' but 'how we led our lives, how we led *good* lives' " (xix–xx). The distinctions Fields is drawing here between ethnographic or "sociological" discourse and autobiographic utterance—what she defines as articulating the "texture of lived lives"—identify the conflicting narrative impulses of collaborative texts with compelling clarity. Because she does not privilege abstract modes of analysis over more concrete conceptual systems, Fields avoids reducing autobiographic discourse to "data" upon which editorial analysis must be imposed. Instead, she points to the very significant theoretical work such recollections may produce. In remembering how people lived "good lives," Mamie Garvin Fields is in fact organizing the details of experience just as the ethnographer would, that is, within the rubric of an evaluative (in this case, ethical) system. Focusing on the particular, then, does not indicate the absence of an interpretive framework and thus does not require the imposition of ethnographic analysis in order to be granted value. Rather, it provides readers with a means to argue the political and moral usefulness of detailing "the texture of lived lives."

By contrast, the way the "monumental" theory of historical value operates can be seen quite clearly in Taylor's comments about the production of *Border Healing Woman*:

> This book represents Mrs. Babb's life story and her views on her healing powers in her own words. The account which emerges of her developing consciousness as a faith healer is an exciting one, not only because of the insight it can provide on healers in general but also because of the model it presents of a strong, individualistic woman coming into her own powers without benefit of the support either husband or community would usually provide. (xvi)

Ranching and goatherding and farming and healing work: memories as a daughter, granddaughter, sister, wife, daughter-in-law, and mother are filtered through an editorial lens that focuses on the exposition of two "abstract schemas." The editor directs us to see Mrs. Babb as a "model" of self-reliant femininity and—a prescient choice, given its current popularity in academic circles—as an icon of "border culture"; as a healer, that is, Babb functions as a kind of "cultural medium" or "cultural bridge" (105). While Taylor is clearly interested in the implications of Mrs. Babb's story for feminist autobiography, it is the second argument that ultimately defines the speaker. And define her this argument does: by the close of the text, any self-presencing impulses the editor has gestured toward in her prefatory and concluding comments, as well as the speaker's own oblique contentiousness (her resistance to "reminiscing" [54]—the ostensible project of this text!) and explicit directions for interpretation, both strategies that I will trace in the next chapter, have been completely obliterated. Taylor explicitly anthropologizes Babb as "an example of the survival and revitalization of a . . . border culture" (105). The final sentence of the book clamps down on interpretation as it effectively reduces the speaker to type: "But this is sure: Mrs. Babb is a true representative of a border culture which has provided a climate for bringing traditions together. . . . Mrs.

Jewel Babb: border healing woman—a special breed of woman in a very special part of the world" (122).

This wholehearted reassertion of editorial interpretive control accords with romantic ethnography's formation of the subject-as-anachronism. A "special breed," Jewel Babb is a throwback to a (fantasied) earlier age where the land and its inhabitants conversed in a prelapsarian tongue very different from what the academic establishment—tired of the successive linguistic estrangements of modernism and postmodernism?—mourns as its own bloodless circulation of words. "Yuccas eight and ten feet high" nod to each other in anthropomorphic splendor, "as if they were the incarnations of desert people friendly with each other and watchful of strangers" (4). Meanwhile, Mrs. Babb becomes at once animal, vegetable, and mineral, her quavery voice not the result, as she herself suggests to Taylor, of "a broken blood vessel in her esophagus," but, rather, at one with "the melodic waver the goats speak with to each other" (23). Still later she takes on the serenity of a desert plant: a picture of still tranquillity, she "sat in her big armchair by the window with her palms held up toward Chuck, who was sitting, relaxed, on the couch" (24). With "hay in her hair from the last feeding time of the goats at sunset" (24), she becomes the Earth Mother incarnate.

My somewhat fanciful interpretive imposition here may look as overdirective as Taylor's own. Hyperbole aside, however, it is impossible to ignore the nostalgic yearning for an apparently more "primitive" past that colors the narrative, a yearning that is invariably produced when the discourse of ethnography is invoked to explain autobiographical utterance. Arnold Krupat has suggested that the primary goal of twentieth-century collaborative Indian autobiography is to allow "the scientist to express his objectivity. The first-person pronoun demonstrates his absence from the text, and so, too, demonstrates the 'objective ... authenticity' of his account."[52] This may be an overstatement if applied to the kinds of life histories discussed here, but Krupat's description of "academically based anthropology" as ethnographic "salvage" (155) nevertheless points to the use of this kind of literary production as a cultural epitaph. In *Border Healing Woman*, this narrative impulse is never more clear than at its close. "I would think about death, that is always just a breath away," the final paragraph begins. "Then I would turn around, and there would be the sunset. Beautiful beyond description. And I think there will be a time I can step right off my hill and walk right up through it. And maybe I will just go away that way" (103). Here the speaking "I" and the textualized "I" find closure at the same moment, to make the flesh-and-blood subject of the narrative its scripted object.[53]

That collaborative autobiographies that position the editor and speaker in ethnographic relation appear so consistently to undermine the speaker's attempts at self-presencing is distressing, but hardly surprising. The etymological link between the words *representation* and *representative* suggests that observation, regardless of context, must always rely to some extent on categorization. But if the textual apprehension of another always involves a negotiation between levels of description, the ethnographic project uniformly favors one end of this sliding scale of perception. Contemporary criticism often conflates theorizing with generalizing, according "abstraction" a higher value than "specification." This impulse to provide a typology of the subject is especially fraught in ethnographic representation. All too often, the privilege of both activities is assigned to the editor, "collaboration" becoming monopolization of intellectual resources.

Recognizing that an oral history is produced from a context of political inequality does not mean that we should dismiss it, a priori, as a form of ventriloquism for the Voice of Authority, however. Clearly the conjunction of editorial and publishing interests works to impose its own interpretive rubric upon the mediated text. We can acknowledge that such autobiographies operate in a kind of Bakhtinian world of linguistic struggle, however, without conceding that the victory is foreordained. That people will use the languages available to them—whatever their ideological self-positioning—should come as no surprise to anyone who has ever tried to get published. What we need to listen for, then, are those inflections that mark even what may look like the most rigidly controlled text as a place of contending forces.[54]

Chapter Four

"You might not like this what I'm fixin to say now"

The Speaker as Author(ity) in the Edited Text

"I found space to be alone": Making Room for the Subject in *Singing for My Echo*

When I take my patient to the hospital I tell the doctor, "Don't give her any X-rays. Take her in there; she's this way and that way." The doctors found out; they trust me. . . . I go and examine that girl, and it's a tube baby. . . . I call the obstetrician right away and tell him I have a girl like this. . . . He operate on her that night, and tells me, "Jesusita, how did you know this?" I tell him "I don't know, I just use my hands, no instruments, and my hands can tell."

Jesusita Aragón, *La Partera: Story of a Midwife*

I coached her right on through that along with him. And I hadn't had my own baby yet. I was just coachin her what to do and what not to do. I didn't give him a chance to do it. That's how come he was givin me the eye. I know he was wonderin "Where is that comin from?" And that's when he asked me he wanted to know where'd I get trainin. . . . As soon as he finished he sit down and have a long conversation with me and he said, "You would make a good midwife. Not only make a good midwife. I think you'll make a good doctor."

Onnie Lee Logan, *Motherwit: An Alabama Midwife's Story*

In this chapter I wish to consider the forms self-possession takes in collaborative narrative. Chapter 3 argued that self-authorization is generally sustained against editorial dictum; here I would like to engage the speakers themselves. What is it that authors, not editors, wish to say? Given that they are often impeded from speaking their mind and corrected (in editorial introductions, prefaces, afterwords, and conclusions) when they do so, what kinds of representational strategies do different speakers exploit to further their own arguments? This chapter considers a number of edited texts as autobiography and critique, looking closely at the relation between self-representations and representations of work. Editors Buss and Clark read the lives of Aragón and Logan wholly to examine their labor; the speakers themselves, I would argue, develop more variegated self-portraits in which their lives as working adults compose one narrative strand rather than the whole cloth.

What speakers have to say cannot be summed up with the ease and brevity of editorial theses. I shudder to think of my own curriculum vitae reproduced as an index for an autobiography, of my sense of my profession used to explain and stand in for my sense of self. Yet this kind of interpretive imposition is the rule rather than the exception in edited personal narrative. Leaning for support on the textual frame the editors provide may allow academic readers like myself quick interpretive access to the memoirs of rural women. This dependency on editorial gloss may also mean, however, that we fail to hear those phrasings, hesitancies, and accents that give each voice its distinctive inflection.

Following editorial direction in Gregorita Rodríguez's transcribed memoir *Singing for My Echo: Memories of Gregorita Rodríguez, a Native Healer of Santa Fe*, for instance, would lead readers to see Rodríguez's script not as a sustained personal history—which it is—but as shorthand for the cultural history of Santa Fe.[1] The cover photo literalizes this metaphor: two santos, their faces level with the Señora's portrait, compete with her for attention. On the back is a photo of "author" (that is, editor) Edith Powers, who "with the publication of this book . . . continues a long-time interest in the healing ways of the Spanish and Indian traditions of the Southwest." Rodríguez's own epigraph merely reinforces this transformation of autobiography into ethnographic case study: "All my life," she is quoted as saying, "was preparation for the healing I would do someday." As if these prompts were not enough, Powers's Introduction explicitly transforms the recollection of memories into the gathering of herbs for healing. Señora Rodríguez's childhood home, El Quelites, a place the speaker herself locates as the repository of autobiographical rather than cultural memory ("I love it here. I found space to be alone" [7]) is significant for the *editor* because it is the place where the Señora "learned the secrets of the herbs and the balance that exists in the natural order of things. She held these treasures close, and she shared them with those she helped. Gregorita is a healer, a *curandera*" (8).

But editorial orchestration is undone a few pages into the "curandera's" recollections. Notwithstanding its memorializing Introduction and the illustrations of herbs and healing practices which interrupt the narrative in a series of visual non sequiturs, this book has very little to say about curanderismo. Instead, Rodríguez speaks of herself: of the imperious two-year-old demanding bread from the archbishop; of her childhood at El Quelites, picking wildflowers and dressing up as royalty; of mourning the inauguration of New Mexico into statehood (which enables her to provide readers with a revised, critical representation of the state's history); of growing up hoping to be discovered as a singer, and, later, of wishing to enter the convent or work as an army nurse; of her sense of betrayal and loneliness when her mother urged that she marry; of her father's and sister's deaths from typhoid and the ensuing loss of the family rancho; of her married life, her children, and the difficulty of finding time for herself; and finally, after some seventy pages have elapsed with only the briefest mentions of herbs and massage, stomach problems and backaches, of her work as a curandera.

Even here, however, Rodríguez's self-description is curiously at odds with the editor's romanticization of curanderismo as her life's work rather than as a means of helping neighbors and putting food on the table. A "reluctant" healer (70), Señora Rodríguez, according to her own recollections, was led to learn and practice through external coercion, not by some inner voice:

Both Tía Valentina and I were busy with our own lives. I wasn't able to go visit the sick as often as she asked me to go. There were times when she insisted that I go with her. . . . When she became forceful in teaching me, she began to expect me to massage her patients. . . . This was hard for me to do. In my family we did not touch each other very much. I was not used to touching the flesh of other people, especially people that I was not related to. . . . My natural response was to throw up my hands and turn away. (66–67)

Describing her healing as distinct from rather than synonymous with her self ("busy with our own lives"), as a practice unnatural rather than innate ("I was not used to touching. . . . My natural response was to . . . turn away"), allows Señora Rodríguez to relate stories of healing without sacrificing herself to these miracles. What we are left with in her narrative (an account supplemented by the editors of *Medicine Women, Curanderas, and Women Doctors*, who interview Mrs. Rodríguez along with Jesusita Aragón and Sabinita Herrera)[2] is a tribute not so much to native folkways as to stubborn self-possession. Even when she accepts recognition as "Mrs. Senior Citizen of New Mexico" for her work on behalf of older people like herself, she frames this honor as an official legitimization of her own private authority: "I did not realize that anyone important had noticed who I was and what I was doing. I had just done what I thought I should" (83).

Midwifery as Mothering:
Maternal Desire in *La Partera* and *Motherwit*

A bunch of us riders was together when this here lady come up and begins askin questions 'bout the buffaloes; and Injun names of flyin,' walkin' and swimmin' things and a lot of bunk. Well, you know how the boys are. They sure locoed that there gal to a finish; and while she was a dashin' the information down in her little tablet, we was a thinkin' up more lies to tell her.

> Mourning Dove, *Cogewea, the Half-Blood: A Depiction of the Great Montana Cattle Range*

Notwithstanding its heavy-handed editorial apparatus, *Singing for My Echo* sustains a vocal quality unhampered by Edith Powers's voice-over. Rodríguez's rich patterning of memories provides the autobiographical "I" with more than one vantage point to speak from, so that her narrative develops a sense of full family life without endangering individual integrity. The other collaborative narratives I consider more closely in this chapter, Aragón and Buss's *La Partera: Story of a Midwife,* Logan and Clark's *Motherwit: An Alabama Midwife's Story,* and Babb and Taylor's *Border*

Healing Woman: The Story of Jewel Babb also describe women who maintain distinctive speaking voices while giving detailed portraits of familial
networks and community service.[3] But where Rodríguez's recollections
open outwards at a leisurely pace, meandering from childhood through
adult life to old age with ample time to pause for full-scale portraits along
the way, Jesusita Aragón's history and the memoirs of Onnie Lee Logan
and Jewel Babb seem at once more directed and more directive, con-
strained by editorial interference, pushed to dwell at length on patient
histories and doctors' offices, so that stories of childhood play or of relations with spouses and kin surface only momentarily, to be as quickly reabsorbed into the dominant autobiographical schema established by editorial
shaping.

Such unaccommodating textual politics, as I have argued at length in
chapter 3, cannot help but leave their mark. We can trace criticisms of
masculine medical practitioners with relative ease, for instance, because
they accord with editorial interest in providing readers with models of
"heroic" women (as Alice Walker put it on the cover of *Motherwit*) and in
depicting independent, self-reliant womanhood. Nor is such attention to
sexual politics unwarranted. To say that recollections which encourage us
to read a life history with attention to its gendered configurations may in
interracial textual collaborations between women be marked more clearly
than other memories is neither to discredit a speaker's consciousness of
herself as feminine nor to devalue her observations about oppression suffered on the basis of sex. An emphasis on indictments of gender inequities,
however, occludes other memories—generational conflicts, familial relations, racial politics, detailed evocations of landscapes, personal rituals,
community events—all of which must work together to define the emotional high tides and low water marks of any particular life.

But speakers do find ways to speak around editorial overdubbing. The
editors of *Medicine Women, Curanderas, and Women Doctors* implicitly
document resistance to their own interpretive impositions:

Carte blanche from informants was not easily forthcoming, and we were not
automatically granted permission for publication. In most cases, stipulations
were required. For example, Dhyani Ywahoo objected strongly to a brief history of the Cherokee people written with the use of academic sources as references. She insisted that the portrayal of her people's history was not accurate and was biased from a white, Anglo educational system's point of view.
Accordingly, the segment about Cherokee history has been deleted from this

text. . . . Although more interpretation of the information might be wished
for, it could not be achieved without substantial risk of losing permissions.
(xiii)

Pat Taylor more self-consciously acknowledges the way Jewel Babb corrected interpretive "imbalances" in *Border Healing Woman* by sending
"additional segments whenever she would recall some incident which
seemed to her to be of value to the story" (xvi)—supplementing and revising editorial interpretation, that is—and by "beginning a manuscript devoted to her goats . . . because, to her, goats are at least as large in her life
as is faith healing" (104–5). Nor is it difficult to read in Babb's refusal to
affirm a rose-colored vision of the past a critique of those who dredge it
up; as Taylor notes, she "does not think it is healthy to be drawn into
reminiscing" (54). At the least, this discrediting of the autobiographical
project by the autobiographer suggests that readers should listen to the
personal record with an ear open to hearing those observations made sotto
voce as well as comments accorded amplification by editorial technologies.

Consider the gendered readings supplied by editorial prompt in *La
Partera* and *Motherwit*, feminine bildungsromans which interpret the
mother-daughter relationship as the origin for Jesusita Aragón's and Onnie
Lee Logan's obstetric careers. In *La Partera*, Aragón's initial self-situating
as her mother's daughter provides the narrative with a frame of reference
that will remain one of its structuring principles: "My mother got pregnant
again, her eighth baby. All girls. Eight girls, trying to have a boy. Only
three girls lived. I was the first that lived" (17). Here Aragón describes
herself not by virtue of her singularity but, rather, as the issue of a maternal labor. In that the missing subject of the phrase "trying to have a boy"
is "mother," this syntactical positioning of the "I" reproduces the maternal
absence which structures the story as a whole.

Maternal lack is thus posited, as early as the second paragraph of the
text, as the shaping principle of self-formation. Nor is this focus on denied
maternal desire confined to the early pages of the narrative; it continues
to make itself felt throughout Aragón's recollections. The memory of her
mother's death provides one particularly telling illustration, as it follows
closely upon the description of Aragón's birth and thus radically disrupts
chronological sequence. The middle portion of *La Partera*, which records
Jesusita's difficult years as a single mother, also interpolates a maternal
presence, privileging her own mother as a figure of enormous symbolic

value: "There is nothing in the world like your mother. That's your best friend. I never forget her or forget how she looks or how she holds me. If I'd had my mother I would never have been put out of the house later. Never. She would have been good to me" (19).

While this textual "motive" accords with Buss's editorial design, the syntactical and stylistic construction of such allusions suggests that it is an impulse shared by Aragón herself. The speaker's assertion that "there is nothing in the world like your mother," for instance, by ungrammatically slipping into the present tense, underscores the intensity of Aragón's desire to foreground maternal absence as integral to the shaping of her identity as an adult. Likewise, Aragón's insistence on the curative power of her own touch ("when I touch people they feel better 'cause they trust me" [78]) reflects her faith in the redeeming quality of her mother's touch.

Although the combined weight of editorial interests and the speaker's own agenda directs readers to see this maternal deprivation as the single most important event leading to Aragón's calling as a midwife, consideration of the nuanced recollections of her early life suggests that this thesis fails to describe the complicated mesh of intimacies and distances which characterize familial bonds for her. Aragón may frame her work as a midwife in order to represence her mother, yet she suggests early in her narrative that this impulse is itself rooted in her relation to her father, or, more precisely, in her father's denial of her status as a daughter. She affirms feminine relationships not by distinguishing woman-to-woman ties from human relations in general but, on the contrary, by contextualizing them; her autobiographical revision of femininity, that is, is predicated upon an assessment of the ways in which masculinity is defined as well. She explains, for instance, "You know how my daddy used to call me? Amigo. Because when my mother was pregnant he was thinking that I'm going to be a boy. So that's why he called me amigo. 'Mi amigo, mi amigo, mi amigo' " (19–20). The tripled repetition is suggestive here—of a certain weariness on the part of Aragón; of stubbornness on the part of her father. That such a misnomer has complex effects on the daughter is indicated by Aragón quite explicitly. If she acknowledges that being called "amigo" "made me feel good," she asserts in the same sentence that "I wish I was a boy, but I wasn't" (20). The respect and authority of her position as her father's compañero comes at a cost which the articulation of unfulfilled desire in the second half of the sentence spells out. Despite eighteen years of being raised "like a boy" (20), that is, Aragón places the greater emphasis on the disjunctive shift from daughter to fellow itself. Ultimately, the constructive aspects of playing the masculine part are outweighed by the dislocation of the self such a shift in gender roles produces.

In fact, Aragón makes it clear that her peculiar upbringing was designed so that she might more adequately fill the role of the missing son—not to "liberate" her from traditional sex roles, but precisely because of the necessity of keeping such roles intact. She is taught "to ride like a boy" (23), for instance, so that she will be able to do the work reserved for sons. A contemporary reader might be inclined—on editorial cue—to read her description as an affirmation of the enlarged possibilities open to women freed from constraining gender roles. But Aragón stresses the restricted options of a feminine upbringing, not to stigmatize women as hopelessly crippled by their circumstances but, rather, to praise their greater strength. "It's easy to be raised for a boy" (22); it is far more of a challenge to grow up female. Whereas Aragón is taught to ride like a boy, her grandmother sits a horse sidesaddle: "She can run and do how she wants on horseback, and she didn't fall. Every woman used to ride like her. But they didn't teach me to ride that way" (23). Far from impeding her progress, her grandmother's riding sidesaddle demonstrates her superior control, for she can maneuver on horseback as well as anyone riding astride.

Ultimately, the assumption of masculine chores is physically isolating and psychically estranging: "And when we have big fiestas over there, and I have to take care of the sheeps and everybody was at the fiesta, I have to come by myself on horseback, like a boy. Not like a girl, like a boy" (23). In her guise as vaquero, Aragón invokes her geographical liminality at the border of *campo* (country) and *hogar* (hearth) as a metaphor for the spiritual frontier she sees herself occupying as female "amigo." Her acknowledgment that her outdoor work fosters an independence and resilience that will help her survive her later difficulties contrasts with the fond nostalgia other Hispana writers express for their rare excursions "outside the walls."[4] Yet she perceives her roaming as divorcing her from the love and care of the feminine domestic sphere from which she derives strength. Masculine work, it turns out, does not so much signify paternal respect as indicate familial disregard. Not surprisingly, her solitude on the land evokes longing for her mother:

When it rained and I was out far with the sheeps I have to stay there, taking care of them. I get under a rock or under a good tree. Sometimes I'm scared. . . . I cry for my mother. You know what I said? "Oh, dear mother. If I have you I wouldn't be here." She wouldn't make me work outside like that. I would be able to stay home, but the others don't care for me like my mother. (24)

Yet with this recollection we come full circle, for Aragón's unusual direct appeal ("You know what I said?") focuses our attention not so much on her recollected past as on her present relation with the editor who is calling up this series of memories. Is the address to Buss a way for Aragón to stress the significance of maternal absence? Or is it a response to a question of the editor's directing her to frame her history in terms that satisfy Buss's own interest in gendered readings?

The representation of maternal identity in Onnie Lee Logan's edited autobiography, *Motherwit: An Alabama Midwife's Story,* provides another instance both of the temporary accord of autobiographic impulse with editorial design and of the ways the speaker's gloss of familial and professional affiliations escapes editorial assignment of value. Like Jesusita Aragón, whose work as a midwife suggests the need to recreate the mother-daughter bond, Logan posits maternal loss as formative of her own career. Some fifty-five years past her eighteenth year, Logan recalls the death of her mother as a severe trauma to her adolescent self. The reiterative exclamations of loss testify to the intensity of the shock: "When I lost her I was at a loss. I didn't have nobody to go to ask. . . . I was lost. That's the very reason I didn't go on to school. I was lost. I couldn't find myself" (73). Like Aragón, Logan describes her own birth in the third person, but where Jesusita's opening paragraphs sustain this self-distancing reference point, Logan's provides readers with two locations for narrative self-insertion: "The next sister, Evie Louise, raised the seven-month-old baby along with her baby. He was older than Lily Mae's baby. Evie taken Lily Mae's baby and raised it. Then Onnie was next to Evie Louise. I was the fo'teenth child. Next to Onnie is Bernice" (34).

With the advantage of hindsight, the speaker marks her interest in her vocation as originating in her mother's teaching: "Mother tried to give us the best thing to grow up on. She loved to get us around her sittin on the flo' around her and she start tellin us these things that would he'p us. She

would just sit us around and she'd start tellin us these stories about her
mother-in-law that was such a good midwife" (47). A glance at the editori-
ally selected title of this oral history suggests that acknowledgment of maternal influence does as much to develop Clark's agenda as to articulate
Logan's own interests. On the one hand, the privileged location of this
tribute as the opening paragraph of "Tradition" (a section and heading
presumably designed by Clark) indicates that we should situate the emphasis on the maternal as an editorial interpretation. On the other hand, Logan's patterns of repetition suggest that this gloss is shared by the speaker:

Whatever they needed and whatever had to be done I did it. I could just see
Mother in me doin those kinda things. I could just see Mother all over and
I still can see her. When I get to doin somethin that's constructive like that
for somebody else that's what Mother would've done herself. That's what she
wanted me to do. That's the way she taught me to do. So I enjoy doin it.
(96)

Such reiterative patterning is not unique to this paragraph but operates
throughout the text. Over and over, Logan's work identity is framed as an
outgrowth of a maternal legacy. "My mother did the same work. My
mother delivered a many babies. She had the same record" (49), Logan
affirms early in her story. Then, later:

My mother would send me down to tend and bathe my sisters' and brothers'
babies. I got my good experience by bathin. That's where I got my start.
That gave me experience in my early days—teenage. That just grew at me.
That's what I want to be. It really did. It just expand in me that that's the
job I want and I tried so hard. Mother told me, she said, "You've got to
study to be gettin it. You've got to study to do nurse work." (71)

That this impulse cuts across section divisions suggests that Logan is articulating her own narrative goal here.
    Like Aragón's affirmations of maternal influence, Logan's frequent allu-
sions to her mother effect a rapprochement between editorial agenda and
autobiographical impulse, as the speaker's emphasis on maternal influence
coincides with the editor's desire to equate midwifery with feminine authority. This confluence of goals conveniently overlooks the collaborators'
racial differences and thus helps to suppress questions about the role of
race in the making of the book. In reality, this conditional narrative accord

raises more questions than it solves. Yet it also allows Logan to develop her most sustained critique, a critique directed explicitly at the medical profession and more obliquely at editorial resistance to Logan's reassessments of obstetric "progress." Not surprisingly, given its publishing context, the clearest indictments of medical practice are developed around the question of women's reproductive rights. In one of the most assertively voiced theses of the text, Logan insists that decisions about birthing methods must be made by the mother. "Childbirth is not a sickness," she argues:

I declare a woman gonna have a baby if she out there in the middle of the street. She gonna have it. All she needs is somebody to wrap it up and take care and put some clothes on it. Fact of business, she can get up and do that herself. . . . Nobody supposed to pull that baby unless there is an emergency that she cannot have her baby normal. The contractions and the pressure brings the baby. . . . She can get up and do it herself. (130–31)

The statement provides a pointed critique of medical dependence on forceps. Coupled with the vigor and willfulness of her rhetoric here, Logan's attention to maternal resourcefulness, capacity, and will (read: "defiance") suggests that her comment is directed not only to a specific invasive technique and the abuses of (largely white and male) medical practitioners nor even to obstetric resistance to lay midwifery as a whole, but also to Clark's unwillingness to support her own critique of the medical system.

Consider, for instance, the editor's initial representation of lay midwives, "[In 1910] one-half of all births in America were attended by unlicensed, untrained midwives" (x), a statement that confuses an unlicensed practice with a lack of practice. Lay midwives are not by definition inexperienced. They are unlicensed simply because they work outside the aegis of the American Medical Association, which confers certification only upon midwives who are also nurses; people trained, that is, within the AMA's own educational system. Throughout her Introduction Clark discredits Logan even as she is apparently affirming her narrative. "[Logan's] story is not only the story of midwifery, but of her personal odyssey as a rural black woman determined to lead a life of meaning and fulfillment," she states (x); apparently women are exceptional if their lives have "meaning and fulfillment." She then proceeds to describe the story of midwifery by derogating the skill involved in labor coaching and assistance: "Midwifery

. . . persevered through time as *little more* than the practice of childbearing women calling upon other women in their community to serve as birth attendants" (x, emphasis added). As if this were not enough to pull the rug from under Logan's feet, Clark continues to undermine midwifery: Massachusetts is a "progressive state" because it "had been able to outlaw midwifery altogether," whereas, "on the other hand, in 1919, Alabama"—Logan's home state—"was just passing its first law to regulate midwifery" (xi).

A focus on *editorial* as well as *medical* opposition to Logan's work reveals a first-person defense embedded in the following third-party description of labor coaching: "Durin labor I kep' em on their feet where in the hospital they buckle em down. . . . They don't like bein buckled down to have their baby. They don't likes it when they have the baby, they buckles em down and the nurse and the doctor leaves em. They get so uncomfortable being there and nobody sayin nothin to em" (141). Direct as is this critique of the medicalization of childbirth, what is perhaps most compelling here is Logan's affirmation of the subject, maternal and literary. What is really insufferable about hospital childbirth, the comment suggests, is the way physicians, through their use of invasive labor procedures, objectify the person who is giving birth. Similarly, what is most damaging about editorial-assisted autobiography is the way invasive scholarly representation deprives the autobiographer of authority over her own story.

Desanctifying the Clinic:
Racializing Medical "Progress"

The ear accustomed to Onnie Lee Logan's clear-voiced defiance of the obstetric standard may not initially hear Jesusita Aragón's censure of physicians. Where Logan's narrative frequently stages opposition, Aragón's text as often uses the rhetoric of affirmation to further her critique. Presenting her relationship to the medical establishment by locating the doctor within her own frame of reference, for example, allows Aragón to recuperate her apparently subordinate clinical role. When a physician from Santa Fe comes to observe her work (presumably to ensure her "competency" under his own standard of measurement), Aragón retells the visit with the doctor as pupil-supplicant rather than teacher-examiner: "He asked me many questions and watched me. He's a midwife. What do you call it? An obstetrician. He wanted to know how I used the olive oil and how I held the baby. . . . Other doctors come too. It makes me feel so good to have them come and watch me and talk with me" (72). Rather than distinguishing between their positions, Aragón emphasizes their professional similarity. By renaming the doctor as a midwife, she levels differences in authority.[5]

In spite of Buss's resistance to this reading—which she articulates in her prefatory and concluding remarks—Aragón not only succeeds in criticizing the regulatory methods of the medical establishment, but manages to use that criticism as an effective vehicle for censuring the invasive tactics of Anglo-American political dominance more generally. Medicine, in her narrative, becomes simultaneously the referent and the metaphor for race relations.[6] The confidence she demonstrates in the face of a potentially critical physician not only shores up her own authority as a midwife but allows her to resist medical and editorial censure.[7] Recall that she repositions her "supervision" by the obstetrician as an exchange between colleagues; this kind of revision is pervasive throughout the narrative. By reauthorizing the techniques of midwifery, Aragón indicts medical blunders without sacrificing the affirmative rhetoric which sustains the narrative. In her story, it is Aragón who educates physicians about proper health procedures. " 'Don't give her any X-rays. Take her in there; she's this way and that way,' " she explains (72), the repeated imperatives made imperious by the arbitrary generality of "this and that." The doctors are forced to recognize the accuracy of the midwife's diagnosis and to comply with her directives.

In contradistinction to medical wisdom, which as late as 1968 saw rural midwives as "untrained individual[s]" in no way to be compared with the "modern, well-trained . . . obstetrical assistant,"[8] Aragón defines AMA techniques as generally inferior substitutes for Hispano practices: "I go and examine that girl, and it's a tube baby. . . . I call the obstetrician right away and tell him I have a girl like this. . . . He operate on her that night, and tells me, 'Jesusita, how did you know this?' I tell him, 'I don't know, I just use my hands, no instruments, and my hands can tell' " (77). "Hands of flesh" have been displaced by "hands of iron," putting into question the extent of this medical "advance."[9] Whereas the doctor is at the mercy of his instruments, Aragón can control the diagnostic process herself, using her hands and a knowledge of childbearing acquired through personal experience and the familial expertise that has been passed down to her. The expression of uncertainty ("I don't know") is a deft rhetorical maneuver; apparently noncontentious, it in fact sustains the critique.

This discursive strategy of apparent acquiescence is characteristic of the text as a whole; where it is found, readers can expect to see Aragón at her most argumentative. The speaker uses a similar rhetoric when she describes the way she renegotiates her work schedule at a Las Vegas parachute factory. What looks like acceptance of the boss's demands for overtime—"When my boss asks me to stay two or three hours after work, overtime, I never say no" (57)—actually defines her as indispensable. " 'I can't send you home because I like your work; you do everything I tell you,' " her supervisor acknowledges (58). Recollecting a bet the two made, she describes herself as working above and beyond his demands. Yet, just as Joanne Braxton cites Charlotte Forten Grimké's constant apologies "as a literary strategy" to avoid appearing "presumptuous or self-serving" (92), so we can see that Aragón's more contemporary accommodation masks her appropriation of authority. Although the boss's gamble is an exploitative strategy, her recollections focus not on the way he extracts her labor but, rather, on the means by which she establishes rules for working.

What begins as conciliation concludes unapologetically. By the close of her account, the balance of power between employee and employer is reversed. When Aragón lets her boss know that she also works as a midwife, he asks: " 'Why didn't you tell me? I was ready to fire you, to send you back three times,' " to which she responds, " 'Well, if you send me home I can look for another job.' 'No, that's OK, and you can go out when they need you' " (58). Not only does her defiance reveal her boss's threat as signifying nothing, it forces him to acquiesce in her restructuring of the work environment. Rather than endangering her job at the factory, her insistence on the priority of her work as a midwife consolidates her position there. It also improves conditions for other women workers:

So, he never bothers me again. When somebody goes to the office and asks for me, my boss goes and stands by me and says, "Somebody needs you better; you have another baby." And they let the ladies who are pregnant work to the last minute, and you know what he says, "You don't have to quit; here is Jesusita." And when they're to lift a heavy box or something, he says, "No, don't do it" and he looks for something easier for them to do. (58)

Aragón uses a similar disarming rhetoric whenever she passes judgment on the AMA. Consider the reiterated gesture of humility that prefaces each of her most significant rebuttals to Anglo health practices in the following passage:

> So many things have changed over the years. Many things change in how we deliver babies. When I first be a midwife, some mothers give birth the old way; the way that's gone now. . . . I deliver two that way, and one of them was my sister-in-law. *I don't know why,* but with her first baby, she kneels down, and she says, "I feel better that way." So kneeling down is not too hard. And another lady, she does the same thing. It helps. *I don't know why* they stop doing that way, why they start laying on their backs. I think because to squat down is an old-fashioned way. (63, emphasis added)

A cursory reading might frame this comparison as noncommittal, a lament for tradition more quizzical than critical. A more attentive reading, however, suggests that the comment develops a sustained argument on a number of levels. Aragón's emphasis on the "help" that squatting provides in easing labor pains implicitly censures physicians for their cavalier neglect of the mother's welfare by suggesting that the change in methods has more to do with their out-of-hand dismissal of the "old-fashioned way" than with any considered opinion about the advantages and disadvantages of a specific technique.[10] In addition, by initially invoking change to signify difference in the abstract ("So many things have changed over the years") she frames the specific change in birth method as argumentative support for a more general thesis about cultural change. The charge against "modern" medical practice encodes a racial inflection as well, for "the old way" is implicitly defined as Hispano here, while "change" is enforced by an Anglo-American system that disregards established practices without regard to their merit.

When the speaker does concede a certain efficacy to hospital birth practices, she frequently describes these techniques in the context of her own methods, a discursive strategy which reaffirms Hispano practice as it demystifies the "inventions" of the AMA. Such a strategy is particularly significant when one considers that arbitrary seizure of political power is often justified as a scientific "advance."[11] For example, Aragón presents hospital incubation of premature infants as an alternative to an already existing practice rather than a miraculous innovation of AMA-sponsored medical science: "Now if there are tiny babies, premature babies, they take them to the hospital and into the incubator, but long ago I had two babies, two-pound babies, and they grow; they're alive" (65).

This strategy of desanctifying the clinic by deconstructing the peremptory association of "change" with "progress" operates throughout Aragón's description of the Anglo health-care system. Recalling her sister's death and the doctors' inability to care for her, she focuses on the humble origins of Anglo medical techniques. Modern medical knowledge does not spring fully formed from the doctor's head; rather, it is painfully compiled from past mistakes—mistakes paid for by a community which had heretofore practiced its own methods of healing without the intercession of Anglo-American patron saints. Notwithstanding the apologetic disclaimer designed to disarm editorial resistance, Aragón's story indicts physicians for their ignorance, as her concluding remarks emphasize: "Now that I see too many things, I don't want to say the doctors don't know anything in those years, but the doctors know more now, have more experience, and they study too much, and they found how people get sick. Then the doctors didn't know what happened with my sister, and she got worse" (48).

Nor is medical ignorance solely a function of the past. Aragón discusses her experience with one young woman who almost dies because she is mistakenly assumed by both her physicians and her father to be pregnant. This anecdote upholds her own medical authority by documenting her correct diagnosis of the girl as sick with a tumor, but the story also focuses attention on her restoration of the daughter over and against patriarchal injunction. By juxtaposing medical disregard with paternal insensitivity, she demonstrates how gendered articulations of power intersect with racist hierarchies. If Anglo physicians are thus implicated in a violation of the woman's body—"the doctors do anything they want to with me" (77)—the father is also censured for his willingness to sacrifice the daughter as sexualized scapegoat for what is "bad" in the family's situation: "Her daddy says, 'No, I know she's going to die because you know what's the matter with her? She's pregnant, that's why she is bleeding and swelling. She's a bad girl, that's why' " (78).

In this consistently self-affirming narrative, Aragón explicitly voices the tension between speaker and editor only once: two pages after this unusually direct theorizing about the intersection of racial and gender oppression, she addresses Buss in a gesture that records the strain of maintaining a consistently confident stance with respect to medical and editorial authorities. Like the young woman whose own word she defends against paternal indictment, Aragón insists, "I do many things for the patients and I'm not lying; I'm telling the truth. I'm working hard, working so hard" (81).[12]

Like Aragón's strategies for self-affirmation, contested both within the narrative by Anglo-American medical authorities and metatextually in the conflict between Buss's editorial agenda and Aragón's own, the critique of medical authority in Onnie Lee Logan's account of her work as a midwife is self-authorizing. Whereas Aragón often introduces her severest critiques with disclaiming modifiers, Logan, like Sarah Rice, generally calls attention to conflict directly. When she discusses race relations, for instance, she frequently invokes the racial politics encoded in her own mediated reminiscences. Thus in an argument about white-on-black rape she critiques the privileged status of white women in a gesture which includes her editor, Katherine Clark:

Now I tell you what they would mostly do. If they thought a black man was after a white woman, was likin into a white woman, off go his head and his foots too. . . . That happened, honey. That's just the way it was. But now let me tell you one thing. In those days—you might not like this what I'm fixin to say now. In those days when the white woman was involved, the white woman mostly involved herself. (38)

Such gestures toward the narrative frame—and to the conversations between editor and autobiographer that eventuate in the narrative—compel readers to recognize how these inequities of power structure the speaker's ideas about race relations. They ask us to consider to what extent Clark's probable disapproval ("you might not like this what I'm fixin to say now") shapes Logan's speech. Here is a particularly explicit account: "*They* didn't have to accuse *em* in those days. *They* didn't have to have no reason. Or *they'll* make up a reason. Because *we* was Negroes, that's all *I* can say. *We* had to keep to *ourselves. I* could say a slight word to *you* and *you* could say anything in this world to *me you* wanted to. If *I* would answer *you* back *I* was go'n get it" (40, emphasis added). The manipulation of personal pronouns requires readers both to question their own responses (how does ethnicity inform my/our/ their reading practice?) and to consider how racial dynamics structure the speaker's sense of her audience. Significantly, Logan establishes ethnic identity without losing the distinction of autobiographical voicing. Negotiating between the languages of ethnography and autobiography, she connects notions of the self with ideas of community by linking them syntactically in the relation between "they/[th]em" and "we/I/you."

This focus on the mechanics of textual production almost always accompanies the speaker's more direct critiques of racism, even when such open denunciation is modified by being filtered through an appraisal of specific obstetric practice. The most severe condemnations, then, are framed in such a way as to discourage both a resistant editor and any defensive listeners from argument. Explaining why blacks preferred a midwife to a physician, Logan indicts racism and corrects Clark's representation of "'grann[y]'" midwives as poor substitutes for obstetric medicine: "The white doctors at this time—*let me tell you* about the white doctors at this time. . . . They didn't care. . . . *One thing, honey,* two-thirds of em didn't use the black at that time as a human being. They thought that we was—as they used to call us—animals" (56, emphasis added). The same open appeal characterizes this later discussion of the subject: "But now *I'll tell you the truth.* The black people would always prefer a midwife. . . . The general run of em was white that was runnin that clinic. The black have always avoided the white. Why? *I can tell you* why black people was afraid of white doctors. They was afraid for the way they know they was gonna be treated" (101, emphasis added).

Logan's censure of racism is not always so explicit, however. When the speaker shifts from discussing "those days" (the irretrievable past, that is) to recollecting her own history, her language becomes more circuitous: "The white girls they start readin mo' about havin their babies and they learn mo' about what they do in the hospital. Now this is what they say. 'In the hospital they acts mo' like it's their baby than it's my baby.' I'm tellin you what they tells me. I ain't talkin bout what I said. This is what they say" (129). Despite the fact that her point about the doctors' preemption of maternal prerogative coincides with Clark's agenda here, the sources Logan uses to authorize her reading of the situation compel her to state this thesis less directly. That affirmative voice with which Logan asserts her critique of medical practice begins to falter when her comments address racial politics. Note how she describes the turn from home remedies to over-the-counter drugs:

Open up the chest from the smell of the turpentine. No doctor—had to have some kinda medicine. It worked. But now since the world gets weaker and wiser the doctors has gotten to the place and science has gotten to the place they makes all these other medicines to take the place of those old Indian remedies. You don't have to have so much of it now. Befo' it wasn't to be bought. (62)

Initially Logan appears to be describing turpentine as a medical anachronism, a rough approximation of "some kinda medicine" to be discarded with the advent of physicians' pharmaceuticals. Certainly the discourse of progress is here; insisting "You don't have to have so much of it now" locates the earlier remedy as a historical necessity rather than a preferred cure. But a closer reading suggests how Logan subverts the very language of medical progress the passage appears to be supporting. The emphatic assertion of the third sentence, for instance, insists that we not discredit practical solutions merely because they are less glamorous than medical substitutes. The following sentence builds on the implicit critique in this phrase, the alliterative conjunction of "weaker" with "wiser" calling into question the nature of this medical "advance." All of this quiet irony works to destabilize the discourse of progress, allowing us to read into the final assertion, "It wasn't to be bought," a marked feeling of loss, a sense of a kind of knowledge beyond the dictates of the medical marketplace.

The discrepancy between received notions of obstetric advance and Logan's critical reappraisal of them is even more acute in the discussion of "those old remedies" which follows this passage. Asserting that she does not depend on home cures as much as her mother did, Logan discusses the apparent merits of newer drugs:

Along about my time they was plenty of medicine that you could go buy. Vicks salve for fever and for colds but I always have said it's made outa the same stuff that lil weed is. See all a that start comin in that you could go to the drugsto' or you could go to the sto' and buy it durin my time. So I didn't have to deal with those home cures but I've heard of it so much so until I know they used it in those days. I'm glad I wasn't here to have to in those times. I knew better. Everything had improved since those times. With all of that science I didn't have to come in contact with so much of that other stuff. (64)

I have quoted this passage at some length in order to demonstrate its circuitous discursive strategy, a strategy which ultimately reauthorizes "that other stuff" censured by medical advance. Logan frames her critique by invoking the discourse of progress, gesturing toward the improvements of science. The most extensive argument of this passage, however, flies in the face of the assertions that introduce and conclude it. Rather than deriding home cures as a tradition of the past, the middle section insists on their continued efficacy by establishing a link between "old remedies" and "science." Drugs like "Vicks salve," Logan maintains, are derived from the herb midwives use to cure colds and fever. Subversive use of the language of technological innovation thus allows Logan to praise her own methods of care without appearing overly contentious and without seeming to contradict that assumed wisdom which any midwife practicing under the rubric of the AMA would necessarily be expected to appreciate.

Granted, this kind of rhetorical see-saw is not always the rule in Logan's narrative. Nevertheless, we very rarely see theorizing about race relations outside some kind of modifying discursive frame. Where she is more explicit, as I have suggested, she calls attention to the narrative frame by appealing to her editor.[13] In the absence of direct address, however, Logan frames her critical remarks within a rubric like the one discussed above, one ostensibly affirmative of the medical norm.

Her reaffirmation of midwifery against obstetric judgment (65) provides a final illustration of this oblique form of argumentation. On the one hand, she appears to accept the medical judgment of midwives as unskilled: "They were doin . . . a job well done as fur as their knowledge would lead em." On the other, her insistence that "those old midwives in those days was black womens not doin it for a job but doin it as a person knowin there was need for it" pointedly suggests that the obstetrician's driving concern is not so much his patient's welfare as his own financial health. Having censured physicians both for their lack of concern for mothers— "The person with all the knowledge and all the sense didn't come around and didn't make no effort and didn't do nothin"—and lack of support for midwives—"They were doing the best they can . . . I don't call that ignorant"—Logan then disarms potential resistance by a rhetorically dramatic concession which, if it distressingly mimics racist discourse, constitutes a form of critique in and of itself: "I don't say she wasn't filthy. I don't say she wasn't uncompetent. Those old Negroes in those days needed trainin."

Like Aragón's comparative critique, Logan's arguments not only restore status to midwifery but insist upon her own authority. Assertions like "I got a permit quicker than any midwife that was in Mobile" (88) articulate what is distinctive about this autobiographical subject and thus work against the editorial tendency to define the speaker as significant because she is somehow "representative."[14]

Many of her most vigorous affirmations of self-worth depend on a religious discourse. Where either a literary or a political context would discourage such expressions of self-worth, defining her medical successes and personal triumphs as God-given enables her to focus attention on her strengths without appearing contentious or overly prideful. Thus Logan follows a particularly pointed story of medical triumph by ascribing her success to God. When the physician in charge counsels her not to attend the birth of a breech baby, it is the Lord who provides her with the means of contravening this superior (medical) authority, and the Lord who blesses her with success: "The Lord said, 'Now you don't need Dr. Muskat. You can handle this'. . . . About three or four minutes later I had delivered that breech birth and that was my first baby and I did it all by myself" (91). Thus the rhetoric of divine power authorizes self-congratulation in a historical climate that demands from the midwife humility above all else (recall J. Clifton Edgar's smug assertion in the preceding chapter that "the great body of midwives . . . have a . . . wholesome respect for the doctors"). It also provides a way to reaffirm cultural practice (given that spirituality is a racially coded discourse) and to sanctify personal triumph with an unarguably potent stamp of approval. Consider, for instance, the following claim in *Motherwit*:

The classes taught me how to tie the cord. The classes taught me how to put the silver nitrate in the babies' eyes. . . . But so many things that I have run into that the classes did not teach me. . . . I can only put it this way and I can be for sho that I'm right. Two-thirds of what I know about deliverin, carin for mother and baby, what to expect, what was happenin and was goin on, I didn't get it from the class. God gave it to me. So many things I got from my own plain motherwit. (90)

Logan's invocation reiterates an "I" defiant of the medical establishment and affirms the authority of "my own mind" (91) as superior to the teachings of that establishment. The need to justify her power as derived from God, then, enables rather than mitigates self-possession.[15]

Aragón, too, represents her healing and divining powers, as well as her fortitude in caring for two young children alone, as of divine origin when she insists that "I never get too tired when I was young. Never, and nothing hurts me. . . . I don't know why, but never, and that's a good gift. God gave me that" (50). God's grace, Aragón suggests, renders familial neglect and economic hardship insubstantial, making her impervious to hurt.

Such self-validating comments do not only allow Aragón and Logan to speak pointedly about familial and medical neglect. Perhaps more important, they provide a language for theorizing about racial and sexual politics in discursive contexts that discourage plain speaking. Thus Aragón follows up her comparison of medical systems by gesturing toward the cultural conflict that underlies it:

Now kids don't pay no attention to your eyes. It's hard to make them understand. I don't know why. Once I asked a doctor about this, about these modern kids who don't mind. . . . "Because they are drinking milk instead of nursing when they're babies." . . . And I believe that. But I think it's harder now for kids to grow. They don't know so much what to do with themselves. Things have changed a lot, and there's no more land. (86)

The question of feminine—here, a specifically maternal authority—cannot be disengaged from the facts of racial exploitation. It is the seizure of Hispano property, Aragón argues, and the poverty, unemployment, and frustration that attend it that lead to familial abuse: "I think of why people are so poor, so many poor ladies all along. I think that . . . people don't have their land and that people are unhappy and drink. I think of single mothers who are afraid to ask their parents for money, and I think of ladies whose husbands don't want to work or they're getting drunk all the time, and that's why they don't have money" (84).

Similarly, Logan's critique of medical practice acts as a metonym for a discussion of racist practice more generally, as in the following substitution of "white doctors" for "whites": "You know why the blacks avoided the white doctors? Because, honey, they avoided the whites period" (58). Or consider this story about a mother in labor. Just as the mother must learn patience—"You will have a much easier, shorter time if you get in yo' mind, it's my baby and God's gonna let me have him in due time" (176)—so "I would say to black people that are bitter to take yo' time. You cain't hurry God. That was my point. . . . A midwife like me, they just take their time and let God work the plan" (176). Marking the segue from maternal labor to a measured racial advancement as "the point" of her story does not displace autobiographical distinctiveness, however. In the final assertion the speaker reinserts herself (albeit as midwife) as the pivot upon which the entire theory of race relations turns.

An Object Lesson from Resisting Subjects

The analysis of such rhetorical strategies suggests that current critical models are inadequate for explaining discursive practice in the apparently non-oppositional text. In demonstrating the capacity for resistive, even radicalizing utterance in *La Partera* and *Motherwit*, Jesusita Aragón and Onnie Lee Logan demand that we reevaluate Philippe Lejeune's thesis about "Those Who Do Not Write."[16] Clearly, the demands of collaborative publishing make plain speaking difficult; it would be politically naive to expect otherwise. Yet the mere presence of linguistic constraints does not preclude resistance. Both Aragón's critique and Logan's methods of argumentation, for example, are no less pointed for being framed indirectly. In fact, in the process of learning to recognize their discursive patterns—contentions developed "on a bias" across gestures of accommodation, criticisms articulated by invoking the "master's" language only to read against it, emphases developed through patterns of repetition, arguments that do not bulldoze the opposition but proceed circuitously or through a process of accretion—I have begun to recognize the degree to which such sophisticated critical maneuvering, by inflecting the scripted discourse, allows the speakers to direct the text. Jesusita Aragón and Onnie Lee Logan, then, do not so much, as Lejeune assumes, "accede to" those "images of themselves that have already been formed" (199–200) as work around such representations. Rather than assuming that working-class speakers are inevitably either "spoken for" or "spoken about," we need instead to pay closer attention to what they are actually saying and to recognize that rhetorical resourcefulness which allows the subject of a collaborative text to use someone else's literary script to speak her own mind.

Part Three

Rethinking the Feminine Subject:
Labor History

Chapter Five

"Such a lady"

Class-Consciousness and Cultural Practice in Jewish Women's Autobiography

"Slum Dwellers," Not "Sturdy Pioneers": The Anti-Semitic Context of Jewish American Autobiography

In the audience sat a Wisconsin farmer who followed the recital [of the Battle with the Slum] with keen interest.... It turned out that he and his sister had borne a hand in the attack.... Soon after he had come west and taken homestead land; but ... after fifty years his interest in his brothers in the great city was as keen as ever, his sympathies as quick. He had driven twenty miles across the frozen prairie to hear my story. It is his kind who win such battles, and a few of them go a long way.

Jacob A. Riis,
The Battle with the Slum

However hard one may work, he can only exercise the gifts with which nature has endowed him.... The thrifty, hard-working and intelligent American or Teutonic farmer is able to economize and purchase his own small farm and compete successfully.... But the backward, thriftless, and unintelligent races succeed best when employed in gangs on large estates. The cotton and sugar fields of the South with their negro workers have their counterpart in the plantations of Hawaii with their Chinese and Japanese, and in the newly developed sugar-beet fields of Nebraska, Colorado, and California, with their Russians,

> *Bohemians, Japanese, and Mexicans.... The Jewish immigrant,*
> *particularly, is unfitted for the life of a pioneer.... The factory*
> *system, with its discipline and regular hours, is distasteful to*
> *the Jew's individualism. He prefers the sweatshop, with its going*
> *and coming.*
>
> John R. Commons, *Races and*
> *Immigrants in America*

> *Bleak American names, New England names frosty as a winter*
> *morning, written out in Yiddish, becoming strange, un-New-*
> *Englandish things, smacking somehow of witches' numerals.*
>
> Pauline Leader, *And No Birds Sing*

Whether anti-Semitic or sympathetic, early twentieth-century representations of Jewish life in America resonate with the same doubtfulness about
the possibility of domesticating Jewish "strangeness." In John Commons's
smug catalogue of American types, Jews—like Mexicans, like blacks, like
everyone whose darkness or smallness or less-than-Teutonic bone structure betrays origins outside the pale of Bismarckian settlement—are
clearly "unfit" to be pioneers, a people who by nature prefer the close
atmosphere of the sweatshop to the open expanse of homes on the range.[1]
And if reformer Jacob Riis is more hopeful about the prospect of cleaning
up the slum, his identification of the Crèvecourian farmer with the savior
of Hester Street (why not its own peddlers and cobblers, knife sharpeners
and garment workers, after all?), and his admission that "there is yet an
element of doubt about the Jew as a colonist" suggest that the Danish
immigrant also subscribes to a theory of racial development that identifies
assimilation of the Jew as little short of miraculous, a distinctively American alchemy.[2]

    In fact, Riis's attention to the squalor of the slums, their absence of
light and air, their dirty streets, their teeming populations, situates his
championing of the Jews within a long-standing tradition of liberalism in
America, a tradition that has been as preoccupied with the healthy birth
rates of "blighted" communities as with the degraded quality of their living
standards. Like Jefferson's focus on black/white population ratios in *Notes*
on the State of Virginia (1787) or California senator Barbara Boxer's appeal to the National Guard to beat back the "floods" of undocumented
workers from Mexico over two centuries later, Riis's urgent call for the
annihilation of the slum is predicated not only upon the misery its people

endure but on nervousness over the sheer numbers of ethnic "others" living there. Although his work demonstrates genuine sympathy, its rhetoric worries over what is unassimilable in the immigrant condition: the absence of light signifies darkness (a darkness not to be relieved, despite roomier housing, until Jewish children cease running away from "Santa Claus as from a 'bogey man'" and begin "embracing" the "spirit of the Christian Church" [436–37]); the filthy streets denote a sexual and moral excessiveness (Italians are more "manageable" and "inclined to cleanliness" [101]); the press of people living over and alongside one another signal an intimacy that threatens to overwhelm the onlooker. "A little while longer," Riis begins his famous *Battle with the Slum*, "and we should hardly have escaped being dragged down with him" (2).

Yet if even the apologist for "Jew-town" (364) sees the slum as "the enemy of the home" (7), what of Jewish representations of the ghetto? Where immigrants from Mexico generally insist in print on their *mexicanidad*, the autobiographical literature of the Jewish *grine* (greenhorns) appears to dispense with Passover traditions and bar-mitzvah celebrations as quickly as with Yiddish. Sociologist Manuel Gamio's *The Mexican Immigrant: His Life-Story* gives us portraits of immigrants who respond to racism by denying the impress of American manners and mores and reaffirming their ties with Mexico: "I can't adapt myself to certain customs of this country. To tell the truth I am even opposed to its tendencies of dominion and of power. It wouldn't bother me much to attack it hard," one woman interviewed by Gamio insists.[3] Not all such critiques of American life rehearse Soledad Sandoval's shift from indifference to hostility with such alacrity, but many people interviewed are equally quick to acknowledge injustice at the hands of "gringo thieves" (167) and few immigrants claim any substantial benefit from life on this side of the border.

Like the contemporary anti-immigrant rhetoric that targets Mexicans, the discursive context within which early twentieth-century Jewish autobiographers were forced to insert themselves was equally hostile to their "alien" presence upon the American scene. In historian Moses Rischin's account of the lower East Side, populist and literary formulations of Jewish Americans sound the same note: "A 'Hebrew Conquest,' mused Henry James, 'swarming Israel,' echoed Herbert Casson, 'the Great Jewish Invasion,' insisted Burton J. Hendrick."[4] As with racist language more generally, anti-Semitism does not discriminate in terms of class distinctions or regional differences, preferring instead to define its objects en masse. "The prevailing stereotype of the Jew, foreign, mysterious, associated with trade and a world financial cabal," Rischin notes, "embraced counting house and sweatshop, Fifth Avenue mansion and Rivington Street slum" (259). Even Riis falls back on a familiar litany of racist slurs in his apology for the slum dwellers:

Their very coming was to escape from their last inhuman captivity in a Christian state. They lied, they were greedy, they were charged with bad faith. . . . One might have pointed out that they had been trained to lie, for their safety; had been forbidden to work at trades, to own land; had been taught for a thousand years, with the scourge and the stake, that only gold could buy them freedom from torture. But what was the use? The charges were true. The Jew was—he still is—a problem of our slum. (192)

Framed as the apotheosis of the American farmer with his love for the soil, the Jewish "problem" is in Riis's account urban, a culture of crowds, (klezmer) bands, kosher butcher shops, fake auction stores, and synagogues (214). While some early twentieth-century Mexicano autobiography indicts Anglo-American hostility to immigrant culture, however, most Jewish testimonies at the turn of the century stress the wrenching nature of geographical dislocation only to end by insisting (despite and to spite the non-Jewish fixation with what is unalterable in the Jewish character) on its transformative power. Notwithstanding condescension on the part of the goyim, Jewish texts seem reluctant to stand upon their own difference. Instead, their narratives sacrifice the integrity of long-standing cultural practice with the zealousness of the converted, embracing the New World as the cradle of personal and collective renaissance. "I was born, I have lived, and I have been made over," Mary Antin asserts in *The Promised Land,* a text that was to become the standard for early twentieth-century Jewish immigrant autobiography.[5]

Sheer distance from the homeland accounts in part for this response: Mexicanos can, if at personal risk, cross and recross from *este lado al otro;* Jews from Eastern Europe were irreversibly cut off from their countries of origin. A more vexed relation to "home" also underlies the readiness with which many Jewish immigrants undertook to make themselves Americans. Emma Goldman's insightful appraisal of immigrant consciousness resonates here: "They were Jews who had suffered much," she indicates of a group of Russian settlers; "some of them had even been in pogroms. Life in the new country, they said, was hard; they were all still possessed by nostalgia for their home that had never been a home."[6] Across space and time, Jewish citizenship in Europe was never more than partial and always tentative: from Spain to the Ukraine, from the Inquisition through the pogroms, as European economies faltered people's rights were suspended, then, with the onset of civil conflicts, abrogated entirely. Given this historically continuous deracination, economic and psychic when it was not geographic (the Dreyfus Affair was one reminder to bourgeois Jewish subjects that their personae as French nationals was no more than a disguise), the Statue of Liberty's emblazoned call to full participation in American life must have appeared a welcome release.

If in casting off their European garments Jews could begin to recover from the effects of centuries of estrangement, their relatively high chance of passing underscores the willingness of Jewish American authors to bracket the "ethnic" portion of their doubled identity. Given this tendency to efface Jewish culture, John Common's uncompromising anti-Semitism, despite its dismissiveness, usefully supplies a historical context many Jewish autobiographers gloss over or leave out altogether. The University of Wisconsin economics professor's disparaging commentary also calls attention to the complicated relation between class and culture played out in the personal narratives of Jewish immigrants—both those who romanticized their climb out of the ghetto and those who chose instead to relive their struggles in the garment factories of the East Side.

Louis Levine begins his 1924 history of the International Ladies Garment Workers Union by investing Emma Lazarus's "tired and huddled masses" with the dignity socialism accords the world's workers: in his refiguring of the greenhorns, the Jewish rank and file become the new American heroes as "the sweatshop worker is transformed into an industrial citizen who begins a new and constructive struggle for the democratization of his work-shop and for the Americanization of his home."[7] In its curious conflation of class-consciousness and cultural accommodation, Levine's formulation reiterates the discursive gestures of much Jewish American autobiography. The question of ethnicity reverberates in the work of such writers, even—or, more precisely, all the more—when it is explicitly disparaged as irrelevant or figured as an anachronism. Analyzing the variety of textual moves such books display by reading the historically troubled relation between acculturation and ethnicity back into them reveals not only how representation is informed by cultural practice but how it is formed by the pressures of American anti-Semitism upon it. Once again, Commons provides a cogent restatement of this relation, one in which Jewishness becomes inextricably linked with its negation: "That which makes the Jew a peculiar people is not altogether the purity of his blood, but persecution" (93). Despite protestations to the contrary or summary dismissal of its unimportance, then, anti-Semitism serves as the narrative pivot of Jewish American autobiography.

Because it uses the language of class to address the issue of culture, Levine's formulation provides a way of glossing the problematic representation of ethnic identity in immigrant narrative. Like Chicanos, Jewish Americans have historically been a working-class people. If czarist decree promised only poverty to the Jews of the Pale, the path their immigrant descendants walked to sweatshop and factory was hardly a smooth one. To demonstrate Jewish class-consciousness, labor historian Alice Kessler-Harris quotes a lullaby popular in immigrant households at the turn of the century: "When my little baby's grown / You'll soon see which is which. / Like the rest of us, you'll know / The difference between poor and rich. / The largest mansions, finest homes / The poor man builds them on the hill. / But do you know who'll live in them? / Why of course the rich man will!" As the title of Anzia Yezierska's 1925 novel *Breadgivers* suggests, Jewish life in both the fictional renderings and the autobiographical accounts of immigrant authors is commonly described as a series of struggles for bread.[8]

If the language of class speaks for the practice of culture, then what at first appears to be an inability to address the question of ethnicity begins to look more like a problem of translation. Across a wide range of personal narratives from the turn of the century through the 1960s, cultural affiliations remain present but unspoken, mapped by proxy as class ties. Consider the autobiographies of Rose Pesotta (1944) and Rose Schneiderman (1967), for instance, whose records of labor organizing, with their studied inattention to American Jewish identity, seem to favor assimilation.[9] Yet while Judaism as religious ritual is invoked only sparingly in both books and experience of anti-Semitism in America is articulated even less often,[10] Pesotta's and Schneiderman's determination to maintain a working-class consciousness despite the discursive pressures pushing the immigrant to reiterate the rags-to-riches American success story bespeaks a secular Jewish cultural practice. Because of the preponderance of Jewish labor leaders in Russia and the influence of the Bund on radical politics there, to agitate for labor reform at the turn of the century was inevitably to be associated with the progressive sector of Jewish thought and culture. In the unstable political atmosphere of the Pale, labor organizing became a form of filial piety, a secular translation of the previous generation's religious rituals. When she recollects the zeal with which her radical Russian parents maintained their political commitments in California, American-born Shura Eastman illustrates how class substituted for culture and the extent to which this equation was driven by anti-Semitism: "Our parents believed in politics. They came from orthodox religious backgrounds in the Old Country, but they were totally disillusioned with a God that would allow pogroms and sweatshops. So they replaced religion with socialism. It was a total commitment to socialism, just like their parents had followed religion back in the *shtetl.*"[11]

By contrast with Eastman and other first- and second-generation American Jews who speak in Kenneth Kann's oral history of Petaluma, accounts of the transition from the Old World to the New published before the First World War more often invent American selves by renouncing Jewish culture. In books like these, the Americanization of the self is overtly framed as a story of class rise. Even when they deny working-class affiliations, however, assimilationist restagings of Jewish American identity, like those that celebrate labor struggles, remain resolutely class-conscious.[12]

"I can never forget": The Mixed Message of Assimilationist Narrative

> *"The husband sweats from early morning till late at night, stitching his life away for every penny he earns. And she is such a lady, when she goes to the market, she don't bargain herself to get things cheaper like the rest of us. She takes it wrapped up, don't even look at the change. Just like a Gentile."*
> Anzia Yezierska, "Wild Winter Love"

Critics often rehearse conventional distinctions between Old World and New when they describe early twentieth-century narratives that focus on the transition from the Russian Pale to the streets of New York's lower

East Side: orthodoxy versus apostasy, slavery versus freedom, poverty versus the chance to accumulate riches. The facile generalizations this kind
of bipolar figuring encourages deny what is in many narratives a very
nuanced depiction of the tensions between cultural practice and Americanization. And, too often, early twentieth-century autobiographies that
celebrate assimilation have been summarily dismissed as a critical embar-
rassment. Yet a close analysis may uncover ideological equivocation in even
the most determinedly bright recollections of successful conversion: Mary
Antin's *The Promised Land* and Elizabeth Stern's *My Mother and I*, for
instance.[13]

In her wide-reaching historical study of Jewish women, Susan Glenn
provides a much-needed complication of the relation between what is often called Americanization in these reminiscences and more contemporary
definitions of *assimilation* by suggesting that

Jews were neither the "uprooted," culturally dislocated immigrants portrayed
by Oscar Handlin and other historians writing in the 1950's nor the stubborn
traditionalists romanticized by more recent studies of immigrant and labor
historians.... We should think of the cultural negotiations that took place
among eastern European Jews in the decades after 1880 as part of a trans-
Atlantic phenomenon, a process that began in the Old World but accelerated
and took on new dimensions for immigrants in the U.S.[14]

The 1972 findings of the Pittsburgh section of the National Council of
Jewish Women underwrite Glenn's revision of traditional Jewish historians.
Suggesting that a desire to be identified as American is not mutually exclusive with the need to maintain a sense of Jewish identity, the authors decided that "only one or two [of the people interviewed] tended toward the
'melting pot' or 'assimilation' theories of adjustment. Most expressed their
strong identification with the Jewish people and their desire to continue
that identification in either religious or cultural terms."[15]

Ethnicity is not only class-contingent but is laden with gendered values
as well. For women, as Glenn suggests, "modernity meant breaking down
traditional negative female stereotypes and expanding the feminine presence and voice beyond the customary spheres of home and marketplace."[16] From the 1917 publication of Elizabeth Stern's *My Mother and
I* through the 1958 printing of Rose Pesotta's *Days of Our Lives*, the autobiographies of Jewish women clearly challenge Old World constructions

of femininity: in a wide range of reminiscences, the promised land looks particularly promising for the girl who wishes to become a scholar. Despite their formal differences, women's narratives describe Jewish ethnicity in Russia in surprisingly uniform terms, depicting Judaism as an experience not only of external racial oppression (the devastation of the pogroms, for instance, is a literary constant) but of gender discrimination within the family as well.[17]

Although texts by immigrant women that are incompatible ideologically and rhetorically nevertheless share a tendency to describe the move to America as a feminist defiance of masculine privilege, their descriptions of the relations between gender and culture in the immigrant once she is established as "American" are far from uniform. Masculine representations of cultural practice in the New World tend to look for ways to reclaim a patriarchy made servile through unceasing economic pressure; even goyim like Riis celebrate the reinstatement of the "priest and patriarch" in their descriptions of household rituals, descriptions which use gendered values to invoke class oppression. In "Lost Children" a feminized street seller invokes "the Sabbath blessing upon his house and all it harbored," dissipating through prayer "every trace of the timid, shrinking peddler" and restoring himself to his rightful place as familial "head."[18] A similarly gendered iconography operates in "The Slipper-Maker's Fast," where a shoemaker's struggle to maintain tradition has as its aim the need to obliterate not so much a religious "bondage" as a sexual one: "To-morrow was the feast . . . the first Yom Kippur since they had come together again . . . the feast when, priest and patriarch of his own house, he might forget his bondage and be free" (28–29).

If men's recollections maintain the integrity of religious/cultural authority in order to invest it with a value gendered masculine, women's texts are more likely to decouple Judaism as religious practice from Judaism as cultural articulation in order to open a space for feminine authority. This divorce between a religious authority that speaks in the name of the Father's law and a feminized cultural practice conflates femininity and maternity, however, so that writing, cooking, and storytelling become specifically motherly arts.

The often vexed relation between feminine culture and masculine law in the texts of Jewish American women is evoked succinctly in Pauline Leader's *And No Birds Sing*.[19] Like assimilationist texts more generally,

Leader's autobiography wields the image of the New America in a polemic against the masculine feudalism of Russia. The Old World "was a world for men," but, Leader suggests, the New one will be different: "Are all men like my father? I wonder. Not American men, I am sure. American men are different. It is only Jews who let their wives work in ice-cold markets, who let their wives lift sides of beef until they rupture themselves" (62). In this very troubled account of upward rise, the Old World division of labor in which wives work while husbands read the Torah is symptomatic of the pathology of Jewishness itself, a working-class culture which must be cast off in order for women, in particular, to get ahead. Where Riis's "The Slipper-Maker's Fast" sympathizes, if condescendingly, with a head of household who is devoid of authority in the world outside the home, Leader's representation of Jewish American domestic life casts the father as a tyrant whose only reason for existing is to obliterate her independent spirit, a strength of will she has inherited from her mother. Envious of her clumsy attempts at poetry writing, an art he had himself attempted before the demands of a growing family foreclosed the possibility, he now tried "to break my will as his had been broken. But he could not. For I had [my mother] in me as well as him. I had her endurance that would persist, that would not admit failure" (137).

Acknowledging that the literary tendencies she inherits are a paternal legacy does not prevent Leader from condemning masculine tyranny. Her autobiography is perhaps most excoriating in its fraught depiction of the relation between mother and daughter, however. In the United States, it is ultimately the maternal figure who must be denied because as a worker she is most steeped in the associations of Jewish culture. While Leader as autobiographer demands readerly sympathy for this progenitor whose poverty and unceasing toil are the measure of a constricted life, her own response as a character mimes the condescension of the Americans who despise this woman, "so much more clever" than they, for her lack of "fine clothes" (173) and her inability to play the lady: " 'I hate you,' I cried. 'I hate you. I wish you were dead. I never have anything like other girls. They laugh at me. The way my coat stinks of the market. They hold their noses when I come near them. . . . Damned dirty Jews.' I turned on my mother with *their* cry. 'Damned Jews!' I said" (18).

Mary Antin provides another working out of the relation between cultural loss, class rise, and the gendered metaphors often used to express these changes. In *The Promised Land,* whose title clearly identifies the book as a narrative of assimilation, Antin explicitly documents the sexism of Russian Jewish practice, quoting a common prayer that begins, "I thank Thee, Lord, for not having created me a female" (33) and scorning matrimony as a process that objectifies women with a terrifying economy: as a bride, her mother has "submitted to being weighed, measured, and appraised before her face" (56).

But references to the difficulties women endure at the hands of patriarchal institutions drop out of the autobiography when it begins to describe Antin's life in America; substituted in their place is an affirmation of upward mobility. Just as narratives by blacks written during the latter part of the nineteenth century and Mexicano literature post-1848 often signal the assumption of bourgeois status via feminine characters whose physical and social marks of "refinement"—blue eyes, light skin, golden hair, and, of course, an immobilizing chastity—approximate whiteness,[20] so turn-of-the-century Jewish texts like Antin's chart their subjects' class rise and their distance from ethnic culture by celebrating the American "lady" as icon of Anglo-American middle-class culture. Like more recent academic success stories (Richard Rodriguez's 1982 *Hunger of Memory,* for instance),[21] the tale of the education of Mary Antin teaches readers as much about cultural endeavors and class maneuvering as it does about scholarly activity. If the author of *The Promised Land* indicts the charity of her Beacon Hill friends as bloodless in comparison with the heartfelt aid of her Dover Street neighbors, she nevertheless devotes her time, if not her sympathies, to the Brahmins.

I would suggest that the ambivalence Antin demonstrates concerning the values of labor and leisure is the outcome of the text's very conflicted sense of ethnic identity. As she dramatically announces in her preface, her narrative will provide an example of the melting-pot plot: "I was born, I have lived, and I have been made over" (xix). Critics of the autobiography often position Antin as "sure she achieves" her goal of becoming "wholly assimilated,"[22] but the phrases that follow this apparently confident assertion of (Anglo) American identity suggest otherwise. In fact, her clean break with tradition is made possible only through a concerted—and ultimately unsuccessful—effort to deny a past she describes as a dead weight, a "heavy garment" that "clings to your limbs when you would run" (xix). Read against even more orthodox assimilationist narratives (consider the formulation of Jewish American identity in Riis's celebrated *The Battle with the Slum:* "If ever there was material for citizenship, this Jew is such material. Alone of all our immigrants he comes to us without a past. He has no country to renounce, no ties to forget" [192]), Antin's ambivalent rendering of Jewish cultural memory appears hesitantly subversive. Because she calls attention to the instability of this self-imposed schism, Antin's insistence on pushing Jewish life beyond the pale of her personal narrative indicates her continuing sense of cultural identity. She attempts to resolve this cultural schism through the conventions of fictional representation and the binary logic of gender: "I can analyze my subject, I can reveal everything; for *she,* and not *I* is my real heroine" (xix). Yet such distancing only calls attention to the difficulty of self-making. Similarly, hyperbolic announcements such as "I am just as much out of the way as if I were dead, for I am absolutely other than the person whose story I have to tell" (xix) succeed merely in emphasizing the impossibility of self-denial. The transition from the observance of Yom Kippur to the celebration of Thanksgiving is not without complications.

By the concluding paragraphs of her preface Antin has come full circle, leaving readers with a distinctly clichéd trope of Jewish identity. Acknowledging her autobiographical double bind—"I can never forget, for I bear the scars. But I want to forget" (xxii)—she likens her condition to that of the estranged Russian-Jewish army conscript, "wandering among Jewish settlements, searching for his family; hiding the scars of his torture under his rags" (xxii).[23] This highly colored testament to the oppressiveness of the past and the impossibility of escaping it suggests that we should rethink recent critical formulations about the book, arguments like Richard Tuerk's or Raymund Paredes's, which mistakenly equate Antin's eagerness to remake herself with a sense of ease concerning such cultural metamorphosis. Paredes asserts: "In a familiar pattern of heedless assimilation, Antin never connects her readiness to cast off her ethnic heritage to her childhood experiences of bigotry and barely questions the socializing aspects of her American education; she merely celebrates its accessibility."[24] Yet Antin's preface employs precisely this type of the cast-off Jew to describe her own ethnicity. "It is painful to be consciously of two worlds," she acknowledges. "The wandering Jew in me seeks forgetfulness. I am not afraid to live on and on, if only I do not have to remember too much" (xxii). With this curiously inappropriate autobiographic gesture Antin introduces her reminiscences, dramatically undercutting the ostensible purpose of her narrative by calling up a quintessentially Jewish figure, one whose masculinity allows her to flout a securely gendered identity and thus to further question the apparent impregnability of her American (dis)guise. Protestations of successful Americanization to the contrary, what we are left with in *The Promised Land* is a warning about the dangers of ethnic disaffiliation. As mirror image to her own cultural and sexual confusion, the figure of the estranged soldier reminds readers that the practice of forced assimilation, with its consequent disorientation, is not exclusive to Russia.

The kind of ideological confusion that marks Antin's autobiography is equally characteristic of Elizabeth Stern's *My Mother and I*. As with other personal narratives by Jewish American women which chart movement up from poverty, the language of class mobility speaks for cultural accommodation here. Distinguished by an introduction from Theodore Roosevelt which scraps one thousand years of Jewish history as insignificant compared with the Americanizing of its author, Stern's book was clearly marketed for a readership eager for immigrant success stories.[25] The writer presents herself with becoming humility as one of "America's foster-children" (11), an image recalling scores of photographs of Ellis Island hopefuls.

Like Antin, Stern insists early on in her narrative that "I could make myself an American," and her rehearsal of Franklinian self-authoring is equally fettered by old affiliations. As with American ethnic autobiography more generally, Stern's narrative casts the (English) word as providing the way out of the ghetto; yet language, although it acts as the medium for acculturation, is equally the means by which the writer reconnects, if only in memory, to her origins. "The mere writing of this account is a chain, slight but never to be broken," Stern asserts (11), identifying the autobiographical act as one that reconstructs ethnicity as well as disavows it. Throughout this assimilationist bildungsroman, the act of writing resonates with Jewish cultural practice as Stern's mastery of language reaffiliates her with a specifically feminine and maternal community. Its author may work to distinguish this text from her previous literary attempts: "Now I was writing only to my own mother, and only for myself." But she reminds us that she has written for others as well: having learned to write in American schools, she recalls the practice of her childhood, when, with the help of her mother, she penned letters home on behalf of those who could not write.

Explicitly, however, *My Mother and I,* like *The Promised Land,* is an immigrant success story. As I noted earlier, in narratives of the first half of this century Jewish culture is inevitably associated with poverty: to become an "American lady" (75), as Elizabeth Stern describes her own transformation, is to figure class rise as well. Yet the success of this enterprise is itself predicated upon a gendering of culture, a sexualized mapping of ethnic identity that uses the bipolarity of gender to literalize the bicultural self. Like other assimilationist narratives by women, Stern's book mirrors Antin's image of the wandering Jewish conscript torn from home and hearth in seeing cultural change as a function of increasing distance from the maternal. Ethnicity, that is, is embodied in her mother and signified through images of writing and cooking. Given the gendered division of labor that narratives like Leader's, Stern's, and Antin's critique, however, it is not surprising that becoming "American-feminine"[26] means learning not to work at all, means becoming a lady rather than living the life of a professional woman. This model of gender identity, like Antin's metaphor of the past as a garment that "clings to your limbs when you would run," is backward-glancing, nostalgic for nineteenth-century formulations of separate spheres rather than anticipating twentieth-century celebrations of (feminist) desire to partake in the political world.[27]

Like Pauline Leader, Stern uses the changing power relations between mother and daughter to describe her own accommodations in the New World. If it is her mother who guides the pen of the nine-year-old letter-writer, for instance, it is this same woman who is represented as farthest from the academic and social successes of her high-school-age daughter. Marooned at home, stumbling over the English words her daughter has long since mastered, she lives vicariously through a child who provides her only grudgingly with small gifts of information. Wrenching the authority of language from this woman now depicted as powerless, Stern paints a bitter portrait of maternal isolation, a revenge fantasy sharpened by guilt and loss.[28] Transforming one of her mother's old copper cooking pots from functional object into artifact—it now stands in the daughter's living room as art—allows the author to claim American territory for herself. As an assimilationist narrative, then, Stern's book makes cultural loss into a kind of repatriation, a choice between her mother and the adopted "mother country" (197) of America.

The Spirit of Socialism:
Class Struggle and Cultural Practice
in the Garment Industry

To say that work was difficult in the garment industry is like suggesting that funding is useful in obtaining election to political office. Stitching shirtwaists during the first half of the twentieth century, like sewing designer labels onto sweaters today, was misery. Trying to make a living in factory or sweatshop occupied virtually every waking hour, exhausting the body and beating down the spirit:

Work was seasonal, which meant weeks of unemployment each year. Employees paid for their needles and a fee for electricity, and often were charged for the boxes they sat on and for coat lockers (when there were any). They paid for any damaged work and were fined if they were late. Clocks were set back so workers would not be able to calculate how much overtime they worked. Frequently their paychecks were "short," but the process of correcting "mistakes" was so complex that it discouraged them from complaining.[29]

Those who did complain were subjected to various kinds of abuse; for the largely Jewish union organizers of New York City, hostility was often framed in the language of anti-Semitism. In his classic history of the International Ladies' Garment Workers' Union, Louis Levine notes that in order to explain the conditions in sweatshops, investigators "took the view that the sweat-shop was the result of the inferior standards introduced by the immigrants. Some even declared it a special Jewish institution explicable by the 'racial' and 'national' characteristics of its Jewish workers. An official of the State of Pennsylvania wrote that the Russian Jews 'evidently prefer filth to cleanliness.' "[30]

Similarly, union propaganda writer Joseph Schlossberg's complaint on behalf of the Amalgamated Clothing Workers of America reflects the anxiety many Russian Jewish workers must have felt about the necessity of "becoming American" and the apparent impossibility of doing so, given the racist language employed in anti-union resistance. "We have shown how seriously we have taken the American institutions. We began to American-

ize. We learned eagerly all we could about this country," Schlossberg insists. But organizing efforts only resulted in the rhetorical equivalent of a
quarantine on immigrant workers: "Then the cry of un-American 'cheap
labor' and 'reducing the American standard of living' was changed to the
cry of un-American 'wage profiteering' and 'ruining the industry.'"[31]

When it identifies the sweatshop as a Jewish "institution" and claims
that Jewish workers prefer its "going and coming," early twentieth-century
anti-Semitic language recapitulates nineteenth-century racist depictions of
the happy darky content to labor in the cotton fields from before dawn to
after dark and the happy-go-lucky railroad worker working "all the live
long day," as the song goes, "just to pass the time away." The writings
of Jewish workers themselves, however, resonate with the conviction that
immigrants are struggling to change the nature of work itself: in their
narratives, labor organizing becomes a peculiarly Jewish métier. Schlossberg goes so far as to affirm categorically that "the early class struggles in
the modern clothing industry in New York were Jewish class struggles"
(6), a dramatically ethnocentric rhetorical gesture which insists on the contributions of Jewish unionists at the expense of everyone else. Clearly,
however, in the eyes of many Jewish organizers—including the women
who were to record their activities in the pages of their personal narratives—the union was, as California historian Douglas Monroy describes it,
"a Jewish cultural institution as well as an economic organization."[32]

Labor historians also document socialism as a secular form of Jewish
practice, identifying such activism as a constant across continents. Susan
Glenn describes the Bund, which "spread its message among artisans and
laborers, adopting a program of revolutionary agitation and building a secret, underground Jewish workers' movement that culminated in massive
strikes in the industrial centers of the Pale" as an organization, like Zion-
ism, at once political and ethnic.[33] Henry Tobias cites Litvak, who argues
that the Central Committee of the Bund became for Jewish workers in
Russia "a kind of holy of holies," the words "the organization has decided"
a sort of "commandment."[34] Rischin uses similar language to describe the
(generic) sweatshop worker of the United States, who "embraced the socialist message with the piety with which he performed his devotional ex-
ercises." Calls to socialist action not only advocated class struggle but
pleaded for "the protection and preservation of Jewish life."[35] For garment
workers the International Ladies Garment Workers Union (ILGWU),

"with its affinity for socialism and moral reform," Ann Schofield argues, "came to represent a secular alternative both to religious orthodoxy and radical socialist politics for working class Jewish men."[36] And not just men: by 1910, Russian Jewish women represented 55 percent of garment workers; within the ILGWU they formed an even larger majority, making up somewhere between 66 and 70 percent of the strikers.[37]

"House-keeper" of the Union: Metaphors of Gender and Culture in Women's Labor Autobiographies

While their modes of self presentation vary, the personal narratives of such women radicals as Emma Goldman, Elizabeth Hasanovitz, and Rose Cohen all contain references to socialist literature like Nikolay Chernyshevsky's novel *What Is to Be Done?* (1863), as well as allusions to the political legacy of the Bund. Their prose, fervent with exclamations of faith in the working masses, draws upon the Yiddish *zargon* (polyglot tongue) of Russian socialist propaganda and the Yiddishized English of the American popular socialist press, a language and literature gilded with "scriptural invocations and preambles and the prophecies of Isaiah and Jeremiah . . . almost Talmudic in their tortuousness."[38] The commercial language of capitalism in advertising even took on the impassioned vocabulary of the labor organizers, banking upon the close connection between the culture of Brownsville and the fight for better working conditions. This notice, for instance, in the November 1897 Jewish newspaper the *Jewish Daily Forward* called for consumers to attend "A Protest meeting—All are invited to gather at 81 Delancey Street. Express your protest against the present cold by purchasing good warm gloves."[39]

Reading the writings of immigrant women like Goldman, Hasanovitz, and Cohen in relation to the language of protest—Bundist political tracts, Russian novels, and American labor propaganda, newspapers, and advertising copy—which colors Jewish life across two continents is suggestive not merely because this configuration reiterates on the level of personal narrative the historical relation between Russian socialism, Jewish resistance to czarist oppression, and American labor organizing.[40] Linking Jewish agitation in the United States with Jewish protest in Russia offered immigrant women an opportunity not without its own literary restraints, but one that allowed writers to present, albeit at a "slant," a model of Jewish cultural practice less exoticized and hence less self-estranging than assimilationist prototypes like those the American Immigration Library provided. The kind of Jewish American "tradition" established by such texts may be spoken through the language of class struggle rather than of cultural nationalism; nevertheless, it provided Jewish women autobiographers with what may have seemed a more palatable alternative to texts like *The Promised Land,* which in facing the question of ethnic identity squarely, seem compelled to represent their subjects as Jews *manqués,* as women who, if nostalgic for the challah and gefilte fish of their childhood, are apparently successfully assimilated "Americans."

I have suggested that the stories of class rise by immigrant women, despite their vehemence in indicting paternal tyranny, tend to close by disavowing a maternal legacy. Since Jewish cultural practice is figured through the mother, such a rift between generations becomes a denial of ethnicity as well. Autobiographies by labor leaders, by contrast, are more likely to suspend criticism of familial relations as gendered systems of power in favor of rendering home as a sustaining ground, a sanctified space in which continuing forms of cultural practice become the mechanism for bridging the continents and provide the immigrant speaker with a sense of Jewish identity in the New World.

Not surprisingly, whereas in assimilationist autobiography the mother's hard work keeping kosher is vilified as demonstrating a slave mentality that prevents daughters from becoming American-feminine, autobiographers affirming a working-class consciousness take her labor as a gendered precedent for their struggles on behalf of the union.[41] For Rose Schneiderman, for instance, as for Elizabeth Stern, culinary artifacts associated with the mother are redolent with cultural value, while acculturation is distinguished as a paternal edict.[42] Yet where Stern transforms the Russian cooking pot into an objet d'art, Schneiderman refuses to make her maternal legacy obsolete. Like Fabiola Cabeza de Baca in her celebration of *The Good Life* and Cleofas Jaramillo in her insistence on *The Genuine New Mexico Tasty Recipes,* Schneiderman uses cooking as a trope for cultural practice. And as in the culinary narratives of African American women, ethnic identity in *All for One* is, paradoxically, made richer through geographical dislocation. "I shall never forget our first Passover in the U.S.," Schneiderman recalls, invoking the conventional Jewish paradigm of Old

World racial oppression. "Everything was scrubbed shining clean and the room was filled with light from candles as well as the lamp. The table had a new white cloth and we all had new clothes which mother made. There was an abundance of food but, more important, there was a sense of safety and hope that we had never felt in Poland" (25). Just as, in Gamio's report, Elisa Silva maintains cultural stability across borderlines through the figure of her mother, who "cooks at home as if we were in Mexico" (161), Schneiderman insists on ethnic continuity; in this reminiscence, however, transposition to the United States sustains rather than deters ritual.

But not all of Schneiderman's culinary metaphors describe the process of cultural translation so smoothly. The relation between Old World traditions and life in the New World requires compromise, adjustment, and negotiation. The family's samovar, for instance, is sacrificed to the cultural confusion of the passage from Russia to the United States. Yet one like it provides a later substitute, suggesting that ethnic continuity can be maintained despite resettlement:

In all the confusion of landing, Mother forgot some of our baggage, and our linens and bedding and the precious samovar disappeared forever. We were so happy at being together that we weren't as depressed over our loss as we probably should have been. But somehow tea never tasted as good to me again until, many years later, we used to make it in a samovar at the Women's Trade Union League. (24)

Schneiderman's anti-assimilationist parable cautions against a too easy dismissal of cultural value ("we weren't as depressed over our loss as we probably should have been") at the same time as it emphasizes the damage such loss inflicts upon the self ("tea never tasted as good to me again"). It refuses as well the seductions of elegy; cultural continuity may be difficult to maintain across borders, but, given a little flexibility, it is not impossible.

Rose Pesotta's recollection of her organizing work for the ILGWU uses a similarly gendered vocabulary of cooking terms to represent cultural practice. In *Bread upon the Waters* she frames union labor as a series of domestic tasks. Styling herself as the "house-keeper" (345) of the ILGWU allows the only female member of the union's executive board to take on an authority gendered masculine. This apparently idiosyncratic appellation is less dissonant with the language of labor activism than late twentieth-century readers might think, since women's organizing work, as a number

of feminist labor historians have noted, has consistently taken place in areas where a feminine presence appears "natural." At the turn of the century male unionists often discouraged women from entering the work
force; fearing competition for jobs, the men censured women's wage labor
as a betrayal of the principle of separate spheres. Their "contributions to
the home and their duties as mothers were so valuable that women ought
not to be in the labor force at all," many argued.[43] Such judgments shaped
both the fields of action for women workers and the ways they talked
about their work. Historian Françoise Basch notes that beginning in 1901
and for the first six or seven years of the American Socialist party's existence, native-born women "worked in auxiliaries and ladies' branches of
the party and left the leadership to the men. Reaching out from their
female spheres, the Pillars of the Home, for example, organized charity
sales, bazaars, choirs, and other fund-raising membership events."[44]

Middle-class gendering of the division between public and private life
drove a wedge between "women" and "work" that made it impossible to
include Anglo-American working-class women in conventional discussions
about labor. At first glance, Jewish immigrants, whose "cultural tradition
and the exigencies of poverty . . . in no way forbade, and even encouraged,
economic activity on the part of [Jewish] women,"[45] enjoyed a less fraught
relation to work and, at least in the Jewish press, greater visibility as workers. As Schofield suggests, women's public activity in the labor movement
"met with cultural and community approval rather than censure. . . . The
working woman was a 'central figure' in Jewish community and popular
literature. For inexperienced teenagers, the reference points of the Bund
and the consumer riots guided their actions, while politicized women in
their neighborhoods provided role models and leaders."[46]

But did standing behind the counter of the family grocery store carry
the same political weight as standing in front of the union podium? With
the advantage of hindsight, Schofield reads the contributions of ILGWU
women back into the labor movement, but the rhetorical patterns of the
leaders themselves suggest that their public activities on behalf of the
union were not without conflict. In fact, gendered arguments in the narratives of women like Rose Schneiderman and Rose Pesotta seem curiously
muted. As with the hesitance to name anti-Semitism, such silence can be
read to reveal self-censorship rather than the absence of patriarchal disapproval. In none of the recollections I have read have I seen more than

quick swipes at masculine arrogance. But neither have I seen more than passing glances at the activities, let alone the accomplishments, of male labor organizers. If, in deference to the cause of workers, the women active in the ILGWU restricted their criticism of masculine coworkers to the pages of their letters and diaries, they also limited their praise of these men in their more public accounts of labor struggles.

Like the "articulate silences" King-kok Cheung's study of Asian-American writing appraises,[47] the refusal of Jewish women organizers to discuss their male coworkers is, then, a conscious strategy of omission which speaks to the almost exclusively masculine focus of contemporary accounts of union organizing.[48] Despite the fact that the ILGWU rank and file were two-thirds female, for instance, not a single woman's name is mentioned in the minutes of congresses before 1909.[49] Small wonder that in their autobiographical recountings female organizers redress such slights and omissions by not bothering to address them at all. Elizabeth Hasanovitz describes her growing friendship with union coworker Clara in loving detail, yet masculine organizers are absent from *One of Them,* and even her fiancé is relegated to the margins of the autobiography.[50] Rose Schneiderman records her debts and difficulties with the women of the Women's Trade Union League (WTUL) and eulogizes dozens of other women who worked alongside her in the ILGWU. Yet so rare is her mention of masculine organizers that, were you to read this autobiography as the definitive history of the ILGWU, you would assume that the rank and file and the union's directors were all women. On the exceptional occasions where men are acknowledged, their contributions are ironized: "His name was Samuel Shore, and he was bright, young, and had done some volunteer trade-union work in Philadelphia. He and I worked together. I must say he wasn't too energetic but he was a very handsome young man and a good speaker. Although he was a bit pompous and inclined to promise everything in the world, the girls liked him and believed in him" (105). In addition, Schneiderman scathingly indicts champions of the sexual double standard:

When the senator said that he was against suffrage for women because he was afraid that if women had the vote they would lose their feminine qualities, I pointed out to him, not too gently I hope, that women were working in the foundries, stripped to the waist because of the heat, but he said nothing about their losing their charm. Nor had he mentioned the women in laundries who stood for 13 and 14 hours a day in terrible heat and steam with their hands in hot starch. I asked him if he thought they would lose more of their beauty and charm by putting a ballot in the ballot box than standing around all day in foundries or laundries. (120–21)

Like other narratives of labor by women organizers, Pesotta's *Bread upon the Waters* critiques the masculine fraternity of executive board members and elected officials by celebrating the achievements of the feminine rank and file. In Puerto Rico, "as in our union in the States," she recalls of a 1933 organizing trip, "I found women taking the lead" (107). In the context of a long history of sexed union labor, however, the decision to represent her own participation in the ILGWU as a "house-keeper" is a conciliatory rather than inflammatory rhetorical strategy, one designed, not to redress masculine authority by ironizing "modesty," but instead to include her in the tradition of the union's feminine rank and file by a form of self-address that negotiates the blurred boundaries between family, home, and workplace so as to conform with the gendered divisions between them.

But staging her union work as maternal labor does reauthorize culture. As in Schneiderman's recollection of the WTUL, in Pesotta's narrative organizing activity speaks to ethnic practice as well as to class action. The meals she prepares for striking workers encourage collective bargaining by focusing on community traditions, because they are depicted using a series of culture-specific catalogues of edibles that signal Pesotta's attentiveness not only to gender but to racial difference. Ann Schofield documents Pesotta's careful attention to cooking:

Through all these campaigns a central motif was food. In Montreal she served cookies and hot chocolate to picketers and, as she writes, "went out of my way to get delicacies for lunch, starting with shrimp cocktail and ending with chocolate layer cake and ice cream" (260). In Seattle the choices were Scandinavian "edibles," and in Cleveland, where Rose herself gained ten pounds, soups, goulash, and homemade sausage were served to strikers in the Hungarian Social Hall.[51]

Pesotta's descriptions of ethnicity and labor neither conflate the two nor make them mutually exclusive, but, rather, represent them as interdependent; it is by recognizing cultural difference that the organizer is able to unite the ILGWU membership in a common struggle for better working conditions.

Dignifying labor by respecting and reproducing race-consciousness is not only an outsider's strategy for obtaining the esteem and cooperation of a non-Jewish rank and file, however. As a narrative device, attention to the culture of work provides Pesotta with a means of ethnic self-identification that will sustain the entire autobiographical project. The analogy with which she begins *Bread upon the Waters* makes her account of organizing work structurally contingent upon her childhood experience of racial oppression as a Jew; as with other immigrant texts, ethnicity is expressed in terms of the speaker's relationship with her mother. Pesotta begins by narrating her flight to Los Angeles, where her task is to revitalize the strike energies of divided garment workers. But after an introductory paragraph about her departure from Newark, the autobiography changes form. The following paragraph begins with an italicized heading reading "September 17, 1933," leading readers to anticipate receiving ILGWU history in diary form. Yet what follows on the next few pages is actually not the memories of a particular day in 1933, but a rehearsal of her previous work on behalf of the garment union.

Pesotta directs our attention to the immediacy of the diary in order to introduce a chronologically more distant but emotionally more resonant set of memories. En route to California, as it were, the text suddenly changes direction. From the recollection of her mother's "sad face at the airport gate," Pesotta flashes back "across time and space" to remember this scene as the repetition of another: "Derazhnia, my home-town in the Ukraine, in the dismal railway station there, on the day I left for America" (4). Although they span twenty years, the memories that follow this dramatic jump-cut to childhood are all framed in the present tense: "Now I am a child again in Derazhnia," the writer begins (4); similarly, introducing a late-night discussion of pogroms and repression: "Our family is seated at the Sabbath dinner table" (6); finally, on her passage to the United States: "I see myself leaving Antwerp, a friendly city, in the rain" (10). By contrast, the return to the relatively more immediate past of the plane flight to Los Angeles, with which Pesotta closes the chapter, is framed in the past tense. Titling this first chapter "Flight to the West," Pesotta provides readers with an even more explicit parallel between her individual struggles as a union organizer in the United States and her people's struggles against czarist policy in Russia. The second, literal plane flight to Los Angeles recalls her first flight to the West, through the Ukraine and Poland, around the German border, past the port city of Antwerp, over the ocean to New York. These rhetorical and syntactical inflections privilege the earlier memories of Jewish life in Russia; later chapters do not refer explicitly to Jewish identity, yet their structural dependency on the Russian section suggests a thematic connection as well.

Even Emma Goldman's willfully iconoclastic *Living My Life* gestures toward cultural community, if we read the narrative with attention to its discursive as well as historical contexts. Alice Wexler documents Goldman's resistance to speaking in her native tongue, that "jargon without syntax, conjugation, or declension," according to Commons (94): "Although Jewish immigrants were beginning to swell the urban working class, and Yiddish-speaking anarchists now outnumbered the old German émigré revolutionists, Goldman as late as 1906 addressed Jewish audiences in German, insisting that she did not speak 'jargon.' Not until 1908 did she begin lecturing in Yiddish."[52] Given the scorn of some native speakers for any "dialect" that diverges from the English of the Cabots and the Lodges, we need not read such hesitation as a pure function of ethnic self-denial or class-consciousness, however. At other instances, indeed, Goldman calls attention to herself as a Jew. She responds to Johann Most's jealous description of Alexander Berkman as " 'that arrogant Russian Jew'. . . . I, too, was a Russian Jew. Was he, Most, the anarchist, an anti-Semite?" (72–73). Or consider the relation between Goldman's awareness of the pressures tending on the one hand to affirm identity and on the other to revise it, as this tension is played out in the following description of a colleague. Once again an immigrant text provides us with a gendered reading of culture:

Zhitlovsky had come to America with Babushka. A Socialist Revolutionist, he was also an ardent Judaist. He never tired urging upon me that as a Jewish daughter I should devote myself to the cause of the Jews. I would say to him that I had been told the same thing before. A young scientist I had met in Chicago . . . had pleaded with me to take up the Jewish cause. I repeated to Zhitlovsky what I had related to the other: that at the age of eight I used to dream of becoming a Judith and visioned myself in the act of cutting off Holofernes' head to avenge the wrongs of my people. But since I had become aware that social injustice is not confined to my own race, I had decided that there were too many heads for one Judith to cut off. (370)

"My own race": for Goldman, as for Antin and Stern, Schneiderman and Pesotta, cultural fidelity is epitomized by the faithfulness of the good daughter. If the passage reflects the carefully cultivated amusement of someone on the defensive, Goldman's praise of her own nonpartisan political efforts reinforces the reader's sense that this response is also an escape from a gendered form of cultural work.

Toward the close of the autobiography, Goldman reaffirms her ethnic affiliation with studied offhandedness. A Zionist doctor and poet asks her to celebrate Rosh Hashanah and she replies: "We confessed that we had not been aware of the approach of the Jewish New Year, but we were Jews enough to want to spend the holiday with him" (841). The irreverence Goldman displays toward the high holy days is put to even better use in a comic anecdote about the over(ac)culturated:

I met a young anarchist, Stefan Grossmann, who was remarkably well informed about the life of the city. He had many traits I disliked: his efforts to hide his origin in chameleon-like acceptance of every silly Gentile habit irritated me. The very first time I met Grossmann he told me that his fencing-master had admired his *germanische Beine* (Germanic legs). "I don't think that's much of a compliment," I replied; "now, if he had admired your Yiddish nose, that would be something to boast about." (172)

Nor are Goldman's less acerbic assessments of what she types as Jewish foibles a simple matter of internalized anti-Semitism. The anarchist's critiques of Chasidic evangelicalism, for instance, do not necessarily prove her desire to assimilate. Such willingness to critique religious practice may on the contrary signal to readers an assurance of ethnic identity, just as Sholom Aleichem's own parodies of the shtetl reaffiliate him with community life there.

Responses to American Anti-Semitism

Talk about nerve, I really think them Jew girls have it all.
  Theresa Malkiel, *The Diary of
  a Shirtwaist Striker*

Affectionate criticism can slide into a less sympathetic mockery. Because twentieth-century Jewish autobiographers were writing in the wake of a decade of heavy immigration from Eastern Europe, they are often defensive in their affirmation of Jewish manners and Jewish life. Not infrequently this defensive posture turns to self-contempt, a deflecting strategy in which the language of anti-Semitism is appropriated in anticipation of its use by a less sympathetic Other.

The ideological ambivalence such mimicry produces is evident in Elizabeth Hasanovitz's autobiography *One of Them,* whose choice of title pronouns demonstrates the shifting ground on which the author stands as stranger and estranged, at once in solidarity with a community oppressed in Russia and repressed in the United States, yet wishing to keep herself at a measured distance from "them." Reminiscent of more uncompromisingly assimilationist narratives, Hasanovitz represents Jewish ethnicity in the Old Country straightforwardly. There, to be a Jew was quite clearly to live as an outcast: "Members of the human family, people with brains and ambition, we were not citizens; we were children of the cursed Pale, with our rights limited, the districts in which we could live and the trades and professions we could follow, all prescribed for us" (8). The status of those children of the Pale who migrated to the Promised Land, however, is far less defined. Hasanovitz is quick to criticize those overeager to assimilate: "The children are not taught that the traditional customs and old-fashioned ways of their parents may be just as valuable as their modern American ones. In their ignorance everything not American is repellent to them" (82). But she is more hesitant in defining just which "American" ideas might be worth adopting. The working-class subject she defends in the following lines, for instance, envies the advantages the more acculturated flaunt: "They deemed that she lacked culture and refinement because in the public schools they had received false ideas of externals. Their understanding of Americanism was limited to speaking English, wearing high pompadours and powdering their noses" (42–43).

She does not develop such resentment into a critique of the ideological pressures the public schools exert upon apt students, however, but instead redirects it at the cultural ingenue, the greenhorn, and the sweatshop boss. In one passage, she exploits the same anti-Semitism she indicted in the too-hastily-converted to express working-class solidarity. Recalling a time when she was looking for a job, she describes a potential employer with merciless caricature: "We waited for a long time, until, at last, His Majesty the Employer came out, a very unsympathetic-looking fellow with a long curved nose and still more unattractive voice. 'Vot you vant, girls?' he asked in dry broken English" (62).

Other writers avoid this self-reflexive antipathy only to displace it elsewhere. Theresa Malkiel uses an Anglo-American narrator to sing the praises of Jewish workers in her fictionalized *Diary of a Shirtwaist Striker*. If, as Françoise Basch notes in her Introduction to the novel, this strategy acts as a form of "antiracist pedagogy" (65) by speaking obliquely against anti-Semitism, it is also celebratory at the expense of others:

The Italian girls are like a lot of wild ducks let loose. I ain't a bit surprised that our bosses are so anxious to replace us girls by Italians—they're good workers and bad thinkers—just what suits the bosses, but it is pretty hard on us. To tell the truth, I don't know as these simple souls can be blamed much—their thinking machines were never set in working order. (141)

More common than this explicit racism is an equation of labor agitation with Jewish struggle so complete that it writes out the contributions and conflicts of other workers. The Russian Jewish immigrant women who organized for the ILGWU frequently complained about the insensitivity the wealthy WASP women of the WTUL demonstrated toward Jewish workers. "They don't understand the differences between Jewish girls and gentiles," Pauline Newman wrote to Rose Schneiderman. As Basch notes, "The 'allies' could not speak Yiddish and would schedule events on Jewish holidays, even on Yom Kippur" (27). Overcorrecting for such cultural indifference, the narratives of Jewish women frequently represent both the rank and file and the organizers of the ILGWU as a united front, working in perfect harmony and accord.

In this rewriting of union history as working-class romance, much is ignored: complaints that holding meetings in Yiddish prevented non-Jewish workers from participating, disenchantment on the West Coast with an organization singularly uninterested in Mexicano community outreach, anger in New York over the refusal of ILGWU locals to permit the few black women in the garment industry from becoming members. The autobiographies of union organizers write cultural difference as a phenomenon that involves only Jew and gentile; discussion of any other racial conflict is quickly suppressed. Thus in *All for One*—published in 1967, at the height of the civil rights struggles—Rose Schneiderman raises the issue of black-white race relations only twice, dispatching what she calls "the colored question" with a readiness that raises more questions than her quick closure addresses:

The first year the outgoing students recommended that Negro women be admitted to the school. When the question came up before the Board of Directors there was much discussion about it but we voted to admit two Negro women each year. Sometimes, the women recommended from the south did not meet our educational requirements but we took them anyway. The first two were Southerners. They made good records and were much liked by all the students, even the white Southerners. And that settled the colored question at the Bryn Mawr Summer School. (144)

Schneiderman's other mention of integration is even briefer, reducing the complicated tangle of segregation politics to a few concise sentences:

The highlight of the course was always a weekend trip to Washington. There were usually several Negro girls in the class and it was impossible to get a hotel to take both groups in. Nor could they eat in the same restaurants. Finally, after several years, the whole group went to an interracial hotel which had just been established by Negroes. (159)

Published some two decades earlier, Rose Pesotta's autobiography *Bread upon the Waters* offers a more complex account of the relation between class-consciousness and cultural difference. Organizing workers is made contingent upon an awareness of and respect for community traditions. Pesotta's attention to the ways strikers maintain unity through cultural practice suggests that her organizing technique was to affirm cultural ties as an analogy for class affiliations. Nevertheless, the autobiography hardly offers a sustained cultural critique. As Joan Jensen affirms, the published account, which "carefully defends the ILGWU leadership," represents Pesotta's organizing work in a fashion distinctly at odds with the frustration she voiced in her correspondence and unpublished diary over the lack of consideration accorded her by an overwhelmingly male union leadership and the sometimes muted, sometimes explicit anti-Semitism of a non-Jewish rank and file.[53]

While anti-Semitism in the Promised Land is as rarely chronicled in personal narrative affirming labor as in autobiography that works to efface it, antipathy toward the "real Americans" (those robust farmer-pioneers who metaphorically pledge allegiance to the flag every time they put hoe to ground) and criticism of their hostility toward immigrant workers surfaces in the private correspondence not only of ILGWU organizers but also of those who, like Elizabeth Stern, are trying to pass as middle-class. If resentment toward the native-born is hard to find in Pesotta's *Bread upon the Waters,* disgust with shiksa workers sounds loud and clear in her private communications. Labor historian Alice Kessler-Harris documents such complaints by quoting portions of a letter Pesotta wrote to David Dubinsky, in which she speaks of Anglo-American workers in Seattle as those "100% American white daughters of the sturdy pioneers. They are all members of bridge clubs, card clubs, lodges, etc. Class consciousness is as remote from their thoughts as any idea that smacks with radicalism."[54] Whether it is justified or not, the open contempt of this account and the frankness with which it identifies racial difference as a serious impediment to sustained class-based alliance provide us with a different gloss on the organizing efforts of immigrants like Schneiderman and Pesotta, and a way of reading ethnic identity back into autobiographical accounts that appear to efface it. Perhaps most important, it demonstrates how the "quick fix" provided by the suturing over of long-standing cultural differences in assimilationist narrative and labor autobiography conflates ethnicity and immigration in American life and letters.

Finally, and in contrast to such explicit acknowledgment of conflict, cultural contact remains in *Bread upon the Waters* a sanitized arrangement. Framed as a historical phenomenon rather than a political reality, exploitation based on race is distanced from the literary present of the narrative, because it is contained in a series of vignettes that offer accounts of labor conflicts in relation to national policy—but never in relation to the activities of the ILGWU. I have suggested that this kind of refusal to acknowledge the nuances of intercultural conflict stems from pressures exerted upon the labor leaders of the ILGWU as Jews. If it was designed to maintain working-class solidarity and thus implicitly affirm Jewish culture, such erasure of the interracial differences between women in the garment industry unions ends, however, by reducing the picture of class struggle, leaving us with a largely monochrome daguerreotype of feminine working-class relationships.

Chapter Six

"I was there in the front lines, though I may not always have been visible"

Self-Determination in the Autobiographies of Jewish Women Labor Organizers

"One who represents the type": Critical Characterizations of Immigrant Autobiography

All the scenes and experiences of the past year chased through my brain: my home, Russia with its persecutions, my departure, my journey, my arrival in America, the factory in Canada where I worked first, my arrival in New York, five weeks of work in a factory in New York,—and then the nine weeks of searching for work. The memories crowded my brain and numbed me with their hopelessness.

> Elizabeth Hasanovitz, *One of Them: Chapters from a Passionate Autobiography*

One of the difficulties in writing about the autobiographies of Russian Jewish immigrants is their susceptibility to overgeneralization: the blood and bitterness of life in the Pale, the struggle for bread in the New York tenements—such was the stuff publishers' dreams were made of in the first years of the twentieth century. For a reading public schooled in Dickensian melodrama and the sentimental fiction of Louisa May Alcott, the recollections of workers in Brownsville's garment district provided satisfying "real-life" prototypes of heroines like Little Nell and Beth March. Rose Schneiderman's description of the sweatshops where child seamstresses hunched thin-shouldered over sewing machines reads as luridly as any Dickensian rendering of London's boot-blacking factories. Similarly, the "little woman" of Rose Cohen's autobiography *Out of the Shadow* (1918) recalls the consumptive New England heroine of Alcott's novel:

Sister was happy in a friendship she had formed. The little girl was the old-est in a family of boys . . . and this little woman of eleven went to school, where we heard she was remarkably bright. And between times she took care of the mother and the boys and the house. She went patiently, with her back a little bent, from task to task and was always sweet and bright.[1]

The catalogue of work and worries I have cited as an epigraph and with which Elizabeth Hasanovitz opens her recollection of life in America draws far less heavily on the sentimental novel in its efforts to enlist the reader's sympathy.[2] But insofar as discursive pressures pushed her to style herself as the model assimilated citizen—heroine of America's romance with the melting-pot plot—her narrative, like Cohen's and Schnei-derman's, rehearses the autobiographies of Russian Jewish immigrants more generally. All of these writers adapted their histories to the publish-ing avenues open to them: Joseph Ozier's American Immigrant Library series, such journals as the *Atlantic Monthly*, and the periodicals of the trade unions.

Both the pointed intertextuality of Cohen's autobiography (which ex-plicitly acknowledges a debt to *Little Women* and *David Copperfield*) and the focus on cultural accommodation in immigrant narratives more gener-ally make an aesthetic virtue out of historical necessity. In the eyes of many anxious natives, literary resemblance to blue-blooded American nov-elists like Alcott helped to domesticate the "exotic" people squeezing their way through the gates of Ellis Island by fictionalizing their narratives out of existence—or, at the very least, by recasting their peculiar customs as anachronisms in the world of modern America, a coda to their inevitable assimilation in the melting pot of immigrant workers. The demands of a readership preoccupied with "the Great Jewish Invasion" of the first de-cades of the century—what Henry James called "swarming Israel"—en-couraged Jewish autobiographers to characterize themselves as exemplary "new Americans" rather than as exceptional immigrants struggling to succeed in the "Golden Land."[3]

Curiously, many labor historians and literary critics recapitulate this typecasting, so that even as their texts are being considered as historical documents or their narrators as speaking on behalf of an unspecified working-class collective, the actual subjects of Jewish autobiography remain "not always visible." In this chapter I wish to locate those autobiographical impulses in writing by women that work *against* such conglomerating discursive pressures. Before analyzing more closely the strategies three labor leaders use to articulate selfhood, however, I would like to consider the ways that current critical exigencies reproduce the rhetorical pressures of the past. Just as publishing configuration urged immigrant writers to frame their histories in terms of successful assimilation, so the tendency to see people en masse for their own scholarly purposes causes critics to develop a vision of a representative working-class self which overwrites particular autobiographers' attempts at self-depiction. Consider Mexicana personal narratives such as Fabiola Cabeza de Baca's *We Fed Them Cactus* (1954), for instance, which is marketed on its back cover as a literary souvenir, a "piece of genuine Southwest Americana." Like *We Fed Them Cactus* or editorial shaping in collaborative narratives such as *La Partera* and *Motherwit*, which bend discrete memories to fit a generic frame, academic attention to Jewish narrative is often ethnographic, listening to particular lives only insofar as they serve as cultural artifact.

Regenia Gagnier suggests that her analysis of the narratives of nineteenth-century British working-class writers will develop "an alternative rhetorical strategy . . . not, as historians have, as data of varying degrees of reliability reflecting external conditions, but as texts revealing subjective identities embedded in diverse social and material circumstances."[4] Gagnier's distinction holds for critics of American working-class texts as well; for the most part, these readers of the autobiographies of Jewish American women workers have followed the rhetorical lead of the authors, justifying such books as valuable by mining them for data on the relation between women and labor in the United States. From Moses Rischin's classic *The Promised City* and Melvyn Dubofsky's *When Workers Organize* to Philip Foner's three-volume *Women and the American Labor Movement* and more recent feminist revisions of the history of women workers including

Susan Estabrook Kennedy's *If All We Did Was to Weep at Home* and Susan Glenn's *Daughters of the Shtetl*,[5] the complicated textual patterning Jewish women writers develop to represent their lives has been glossed mimetically, cited as documentation of organizing efforts, strike protests, and working conditions but rarely considered in light of the complex relations it traces between subjectivity and rhetorical figuring.[6]

A critic of my argument here might suggest that I am conflating two forms that should remain separate: the historical project and the literary agenda. Granting the sanctity of a traditional scholarly geography, however, does not make the problem of typecasting disappear, for critics of autobiography are as quick as students of labor history to resort to the kind of generalization that obscures rather than explains the forms immigrant autobiography takes.

Certainly the rhetoric of much personal narrative by female labor unionists directs readers to see life in political context, often justifying the story of the "One" as significant because it speaks on behalf of the "All." Theresa Malkiel's 1910 novel *The Diary of a Shirtwaist Striker* was advertised in the *Progressive Woman* as providing women workers with an inspirational model of feminine political activism: "Don't fail to read this book," the insert announced. "Give it a big circulation. It shows what women can and are doing, in the industrial world."[7] The didacticism of this literary announcement, which justifies novel reading as a form of political education, characterizes the publishing context of the *Diary,* first circulated in its entirety by the socialist Cooperative Press. Such an advertisement does not necessarily offer an interpretive index for situating the particular voice of its heroine in relation to its author, nor does it unconditionally define the writer's project in relation to the historical events the novel retraces, however. Moreover, as I have argued throughout this book, autobiographers are often impelled by conditions of publication to justify their self-scripting with reference to a certain representative status. In the case of Jewish labor organizers, the writer may bow to discursive pressures encouraging her to present herself as immigrant, as Jew, or as working woman in a way that creates tension with (and often masks) rhetorical gestures that develop a distinct identity. Conflating— or, rather, equating—a given discursive formation with the narratives formed by its rhetorical conditions, then, will prevent us from hearing what is distinctive about a specific voice.[8]

Nuancing the Collaborative Model
of the Female Subject:
Rose Cohen's *Out of the Shadow*

*Yet worse than poverty and as painful "as the gout or stone"
is neglect. The poor man suffers most because "he is only not
seen."*

John Adams, *Discourses on Davila*

*I may not have been seen but I saw it all: first as a cash girl in
department stores . . . then as a machine-operator in cap factories, and finally as organizer and later president of the New York
Women's Trade Union League—with time out from the latter
job to organize for the International Ladies' Garment Workers'
Union, to work for women's suffrage, and to serve my state as
secretary of the Department of Labor and my country as the
only woman on the Labor Advisory Board of the National Re-
covery Act.*

Rose Schneiderman, *All for One*

*Do the masses become masses by themselves? Or are they the
result of a theoretical and practical operation of "massifica-
tion"? From where onward can one say of a "free" work of art
that it is written for the infinite numbers which constitute the
masses and not merely for a definite public stratum of society?*

Trinh H. Minh-ha, "Commitment
from the Mirror-Writing Box"

In the preceding chapter I read a number of Jewish American women's
personal narratives against their discursive contexts in order to consider
how each negotiates the relation between immigrant consciousness and a
distinctly Jewish American culture. In this chapter I would like to consider
how such texts become a forum for self-distinction. As an overcorrection
for masculinist readings that define identity within the narrow limits of
traditional autobiography theory, readers of women's narratives have often
advanced a collaborative model of identity that indiscriminately polarizes
every feminine voice as speaking on behalf of the collective, each masculine one as insistently autonomous. Bella Brodzki and Celeste Schenck, for
instance, juxtapose "representative masculine autobiographies" (Benjamin
Franklin's *Autobiography,* Henry Adams's *Education,* Walt Whitman's
Song of Myself, and Norman Mailer's *Advertisements for Myself*) which

"rest upon the Western ideal of an essential and inviolable self," against women's autobiography as "relational." From Margaret Cavendish's *The True Relation of My Birth and Breeding* (1656) to Gertrude Stein's *The Autobiography of Alice B. Toklas* (1933), the feminine personal voice is displaced, they argue, becoming a textual space of "blurred boundaries" with virtually no relation to "traditional selfhood." This affirmation of what Susan Friedman characterizes as "the feminine capacity for empathy and identification" operates as a largely uninflected critical constant in feminist autobiography theory: as Sherna Gluck and Daphne Patai put it, from Anaïs Nin's autobiographical "abnegation" to oral history, "concern with connection and collaboration emerges as a clear theme."[9]

Given the historical neglect of working-class texts by literary scholars, it is not surprising that readers as attentive to class as to gender are occasionally overzealous in formulating models of the subject that will justify further research. Yet as critic and filmmaker Trinh Minh-ha points out, a class-inflected reading of narrative that is overly dependent on a rigid distinction between the "upper classes" and the "lower orders" does little to develop our sense of the variety and richness of working-class literature: "To oppose the masses to the elite is already to imply that those forming the masses are regarded as an aggregate of average persons condemned by their lack of personality or by their dim individualities to stay with the herd, to be docile and anonymous."[10]

Although in countering this tendency to describe working-class autobiography en masse one must be careful to avoid overgeneralizing in the other direction, I would argue that too fixed an idea of collaboration in the texts of women autobiographers may itself be class-based; regardless of ethnicity, working-class women may be inclined to represent themselves more on the basis of what makes them distinctive *from* rather than similar *to* others. Insisting on the value of the "I," after all, compensates in some measure for an exchange economy that standardizes individual achievement as so many units of labor/time. Given that labor in the service of another more often undermines than generates self-assertion, that is, workers may turn to autobiography precisely in order to escape the anonymity of "the masses."[11]

Consider the personal narratives of working-class Jewish women active in the labor movement. Here is a kind of autobiography that describes what appears to be a most adamantly collective history: the documentation of joint effort on behalf of the garment unions. Ostensibly it is the union, not the self who works on its behalf, that is granted pride of place in the recollections of women like Rose Schneiderman, Elizabeth Hasanovitz, and Rose Pesotta, as a glance at the titles of Schneiderman's autobiography, *All for One*, and Hasanovitz's story, *One of Them: Chapters in a Passionate Autobiography*, makes clear. Their shared commitment to recording the achievements of the ILGWU means that such autobiographers are obligated to narrate their particular accomplishments as metonyms for the "larger struggle" of organized labor, a textual vantage point which subordinates the activities of the "I" to the history of this movement. In the labor press, sustained reference to personal impressions runs the risk of being read as intolerable self-absorption, a betrayal of the collective. Given their firsthand experience in the sweatshops (a dehumanizing " 'process of grinding the faces of the poor' ")[12] and their own class-consciousness, it is not surprising to find these writers cognizant that they are "to many potential readers ... but 'social atoms' making up the undifferentiated 'masses.' "[13] Consider how Rose Cohen recollects the humiliations of poverty in *Out of the Shadow* (1918): "We were all ashamed of showing our ignorance. A girl who could not read and write would do anything to hide it. We were as much ashamed of it as we were of our poverty. Indeed, to show one was to show the other. They seemed inseparable" (251). Defensiveness about this distinction (whether real or imagined) between a self-assured reading public and the writer's own painstakingly cultivated literary authority, then, defines an autobiographical subject hesitant to distinguish herself further from others.

Yet a close look at these books finds in every case a series of narrative interventions of the autobiographical self which cannot be justified as furthering the story of union organizing that stands as their apparent subject. Reminiscences of relations with parents and siblings, remarks on the pleasures and difficulties of travel, and reflections on philosophical and metaphysical problems demonstrate a tension between, on the one hand, the status of the autobiographer as privileged because of her part in the life of the union, and, on the other hand, the need to identify the singular achievements of the self as noteworthy in their own right. The ambiguity of this kind of self-representation, a tension which, I would argue, is not successfully resolved in the reminiscences of Emma Goldman, Rose Schneiderman, Elizabeth Hasanovitz, and others, suggests that both the collaborative model of feminine self-representation privileged by much feminist autobiography theory and the class-contingent generalizations of labor historians are in need of further scrutiny. In fact, while their memoirs frequently invoke a collective subject, this "we" is both more various—signifying different communities in different textual instances—and more accommodating than the plural subject as defined by such critics.

In autobiographies like Rose Cohen's *Out of the Shadow*, for example, what looks like an indiscriminate collective "we" carries distinct inflections that vary with context. Consider her recollection of a hospital stay:

What with the long periods of idleness after each job, the months of inactivity in the hospital, the natural apathy due to the illness, the miserable conditions in the shops, I lost all taste for work, I lost my pride of independence, I lost my spirit. . . . And when I put on my wrapper I felt that I became a part of the rest of the dependents, a part of the house, a part of all that I saw about me. (259)

More enervating than the back-breaking labor of the garment industry is the enforced inactivity of the hospital, an idleness which drains her independent spirit, substituting a faceless, characterless "I." Although she is discouraged by the brutalizing conditions of the sweatshop, the writer's sense of herself rests in her work: it is pride in her labor that provides her with the authority necessary to insist upon self-distinction.

The relationship among collective subjectivity, the singular subject, and labor becomes clearer in the comparison Cohen draws between her experience as a domestic worker and her recollections of labor in the sweatshops: " 'I should not like to be a servant all the time,' I thought. I looked out of the window and gradually I began to reason it out. I realized that though in the shop too I had been driven, at least there I had not been alone. I had been a worker among other workers who looked upon me as an equal and a companion" (180). Working-class community is based precisely on that recognition of the independent "I" that a class-inflected feminist scholarship denies in its celebration of the collective. Here, solidarity is produced, not by obliterating the "I" and replacing it with a communal consciousness, but by developing a respect for the individual that builds bonds among equals.

Nor does the whole turn out to be greater than the sum of its parts in Rose Schneiderman's *All for One*. As in Cohen's recollection of union work, Schneiderman asserts herself through the collective struggle for union recognition. Yet even a quick glance at the epigraph that begins this section demonstrates that affiliation is not the same thing as amalgamation. To feel a part of the community of workers is not, after all, to relinquish one's belief in one's uniqueness. The value Schneiderman accords to union organizing is inextricably linked to her sense of self-worth; her statement that she worked "to serve my state" and "my country" expresses both patriotism and pride. Not surprisingly, this long cumulative sentence articulating service on behalf of others builds to a final phrase which spotlights the autobiographer's "I": she is "the only woman" to serve on the Labor Advisory Board.

"I am a modest woman usually": Rose Schneiderman's *All for One*

Despite her insistence on individual achievement, locating this singular woman in the pages of a narrative which acts simultaneously as historical chronicle, personal record, and collective tribute to ILGWU and WTUL labor calls for an interpretive model best approximated by Schneiderman's own formulation: "I was there in the front lines, though I may not always have been visible." To read the "auto" back into an autobiography that inscribes not only the author's own reflections but the memories of many women unable to write themselves into the history of the American labor movement demands that we train our attention on what is often partially obscured.[14] Frequently, Schneiderman is crowded out of her own narrative. The insistence that she is struggling for a goal shared by working women generally, for instance, demands an equally collective subject. When she wishes to emphasize the oppression of women, she writes the agent of change in the plural: "The fight for legislation to protect the rights of working women was only part of our job. We used the soapbox, we used the picket line, we used every means we could think to advance the labor movement among women" (7). Similarly, the tragedy of the Triangle Shirtwaist Company fire calls for collective mourning: "From 10 in the morning until 4 in the afternoon we of the Women's Trade Union League marched in the procession. . . . In our grief and anger we, who were dedicated to the task of awakening the community to the plight of working women, would not remain silent" (98–99). In general, explicit censure in

All for One (be it a condemnation of the National Association of Manufacturers or an indictment of the upper-middle-class reformers of the Women's Trade Union League, women as interested in socializing immigrant woman as in making socialists of them)[15] is leveled not by the personal "I" but in the name of a more diffuse spirit of feminine community.

Schneiderman's autobiographical "I" hardly occupies a Rousseauian center stage even when the author is not engaged in direct political commentary, however. You can find observations acknowledging the personal—brief confessions of anger at the boorish behavior of masculine colleagues (117), moments of self-doubt when exhaustion and frustration overpower the effort of positive thinking (113, 115), thumbnail descriptions of excitement at the beginning of a new job (50)—but these are quickly checked, slight gestures tossed off as if in the middle of a conversation about something more important.[16] More sustained attention to autobiographical accomplishment is developed circuitously, framed at an angle which requires the reader to exercise peripheral vision so as not to miss it. At one point, for example, Schneiderman allows herself a (muted) expression of pride over the fact that she has saved the lives of four relatives, her own hard-earned money having been used for their passage to the United States before the onset of the Second World War. She credits this accomplishment only at a remove, however: "It will always be a mystery to me how Mother could save so much out of the allowance I gave her for our household, but she did and she brought over three nieces and a nephew, which is why they were here in America when Hitler massacred all the Jews in Khelom" (17).

Where self-references are less oblique and the "I" bolder on the page, the author prefaces them with disclaimers that use the language of feminine humility in order to advance herself without fear of censure. The collaborative nature of Schneiderman's book prevents us from identifying this hesitancy as hers alone. Yet such modesty places her autobiography squarely within a tradition of public women's personal narrative that frames feminine moral goodness as altruism and in so doing discourages its textual affirmation as inappropriately self-aggrandizing. In an essay on the autobiographies of public women, Patricia Spacks identifies this paradox particularly succinctly: "The impossibility of laying public claim to essential virtue generates a curious tension in these records. . . . Goodness *is* selflessness, these autobiographies suggest; and vice versa—a notion by its nature unlikely to make for effective autobiography, since autobiographies are about selves."[17] For Schneiderman, as for Rose Pesotta, such discursive constraints require that pride in personal accomplishments be muted and public recognition styled as accidental rather than intentional: "I had a call one day from Elmer Andrews, State Commissioner of Labor, asking me to come to see him. I had no idea what was up and no one could have been more surprised than I when he asked me if I would like to be secretary of the State Department of Labor. At first I thought he was joking" (221).

Humility aside, Schneiderman's "not so eminent me" (99) frequently finds herself among very select company. Visits to the White House and the Roosevelts' vacation home are common: "Maud and I were invited to both places many times for, according to Frances Perkins in her book *The Roosevelts I Knew,* Maud and I were among the people who could bring F.D.R. new and stimulating ideas after his illness" (176). More notable than the fact that this self-praise requires introduction is its implication: where cabinet members and the rich and famous have failed, the garment worker has triumphed.[18] Perhaps the most interesting allusion to the presidential circle, however, is Schneiderman's acknowledgment of Eleanor Roosevelt: "Eleanor Roosevelt urged me to write the story of my years in the labor movement. She would have written the introduction for it, but now that she is no longer here, I do not want anyone else to substitute for her; that is why there is no introduction to my book. It will have to stand on its own merits" (preface). By invoking and then withdrawing the First Lady as her literary sponsor, Schneiderman defines a moment of unapologetic self-advancement. Clearly this memorializing statement is a tribute to Roosevelt, but by indicating that no one other than the wife of the president of the United States can effectively introduce her recollections, Schneiderman implies that her own stature is far from humble. By refusing to entertain another word on the question of the book's introduction, the terse closure of the final sentence reinforces this sense of personal command.

Like Rose Pesotta's uncompromising self-representation as an "Admiral Dewey" (96) for the ILGWU in *Bread upon the Waters,* Schneiderman's narrative of organizing work and union struggle suggests that the most brazenly self-assertive statements are acceptable so long as they are articulated using the language of (feminine) service. "I am a modest woman

usually but in her book Frances [Perkins] paid Maud and me a great compliment which I am going to quote, for it is about what we did for the
trade-union, not for ourselves," Schneiderman assures us at one point
(177); or, at the outset, "This is quite a statement coming from me because, though I find it hard to ask for things for myself, I could ask for the
moon if I needed it for the [WTUL] League" (10).

By invoking a collective, Schneiderman also opens the space for herself.
Styling her reminiscences as spoken on behalf of a community allows her
to assert an independent "I" without being indicted as immodest. At moments, this relationship of the worker's "we" to the speaker's "I" is even
structured so that the history of labor is subordinated to the struggles of
the subject working on its own behalf. In the following prefatory remarks,
for example, collective organizing provides the justification for self-
assertion:

For more than 50 years I was part of the most exciting movement in the
United States, the fight of workers for the right to organize. I was there
in the front lines, though I many not always have been visible, for by no
amount of stretching have I ever achieved a height of more than four and
a half feet. And in the early days of the fight I never weighed more than
ninety pounds. (vii)

Similarly, despite the ostensible aim of the phrase, the autobiographical
moment rather than the historical record attracts attention in the following
passage: "And so, with the blessings of labor and laymen the National
Women's Trade Union League was born, an organization which was to be
the most important influence in my life" (76).

That Schneiderman privileges the autobiographical "I" in a narrative
whose ostensible aim is to record a history of union organizing suggests
that we reappraise those texts that at first appear to favor historical documentation and cultural accounting over self-reflection. Granted, in their
discouragement of extended references to personal experience, the forms
such personal narratives take seem compromised at best; yet in a discursive context that allows immigrant women so few opportunities for self-
expression, this intermittent focus on singularity is hardly surprising. Pesotta gestures to the pressures representative status—as Jewish, as female—
exert upon self-representation when she compares her difficulties as the
only woman on the executive board of the ILGWU with David Dubinsky's

position on the executive council of the American Federation of Labor: "There you were considered the Jew and here I am considered the Woman and at times I feel just as comfortable as you did."[19]

One of Them: Elizabeth Hasanovitz's Autobiographical Hard Labor

Like Schneiderman, who scripts a personal history under the rubric of memorializing the "larger cause of labor," the title of Elizabeth Hasanovitz's memoir plays on the conflict between received categories of representation and the need for self-voicing. "One of Them" signifies group identity, but with a difference. Maintaining both class allegiance and cultural identification, it suggests estrangement as well. If the title pronoun "them" invokes a working-class consciousness and indicates the author's cultural status as a Jew, the text as a whole focuses most explicitly on class. Large portions of the narrative read like a textbook chronicling the history of the garment industry: they explain the collective bargaining process, summarize union protocols, and describe the efforts of the manufacturing lobby to resist workers' organizing efforts, with little or no commentary to distinguish them as the product of an idiosyncratic "I." "The Manufacturers' Association in the dress and waist industry controlled nearly two thirds of the trade," a bodiless voice announces early in the narrative (53), continuing: "On January 18, 1913, a protocol agreement was consummated between the Manufacturers' Association and the union. It aimed to enlist both parties in an effort to improve conditions and to obtain the equalization of standards throughout the industry by peaceful and honorable means" (54).

What saves *One of Them* from the anonymity of the government document is the determined presence of the autobiographer herself. Moving in and out of the narrative in a fashion more clunky than graceful, Hasanovitz punctuates the historical record with meditations on the nature of her singular existence. These existential musings mime on the rhetorical level the work of the sweatshop; lapses in (textual) concentration, they interrupt the narrative like the mind wandering away from the drone of the assembly line. Note, for instance, how this solitary "I" demystifies the book's more celebratory recollections of collective struggle: "A heavy melancholy swept over me. I looked around me. What was I doing here on this roof among all these people? I felt the roof, the people, the thick air, as a million-pound weight on me" (88). Poverty; a desire, largely unrealized, for a more expansive cultural life; the constant, mind-numbing anxiety of the struggle for bread—all her worries close in upon her in merciless imitation of the fetid, constricting air of the tenement where, late at night, she finds herself despairing of success, "too weak, too helpless against life" (33).

Such explicitly confessional moments remain the exception rather than the rule in Hasanovitz's narrative, but the pull toward autobiographical self-determination is strong in passages intended, not to dramatize the self, but, rather, to eulogize the work of the laboring masses. Over and over again, the need to assert the self distracts the writer from her focus on the representative "we" of union labor; it will suffice to consider one such moment in full. Here, a parable designed to describe the condition of working women as a group becomes an opportunity for self-expression. "She" is transmuted into "I," and the administrative anonymity of the passage is exchanged for the direct appeal of active verbal effort:

Conditions must be created so that the girl shall not be driven from the shop. The long hours, the unsanitary conditions, the small wages, the frequent slack seasons, drive the self-supporting, unprotected girl sometimes to a life of shame. . . . Eh! What an ugly, contemptible world this is! I am trying so hard to bring my family over here to save them from the Russian autocratic teeth, but I would rather see my sisters dead than see them enduring humiliations from such a debauchee as that jobber. Brr! It throws me into a fever when I think of it. (102)

Even when the collective subject is most wholeheartedly championed, narrative energy is inevitably trained on the singular experience of the "I" who is singing its praises. In the following passage Hasanovitz invokes the discourse of union leaflets and periodicals in order to argue the merits of the closed shop:

Our higher bosses raged at *me*, thinking that it was only *I* who was responsible for those demands. But *I* was the shop representative, and spoke not only for *myself*. *I* expressed the wish of all the workers in *my* shop. Still they treated *me* worse than the others. They tried to rid themselves of *me*, thinking that with *me* out of the way, they would accomplish their task, and at the first opportunity *I* was fired. But *I* was taken back the same day, for as soon as *I* took my hat ready to leave the shop, the rush, the noise of the machines, suddenly stopped. Everything came to a standstill. Over 200 workers folded their hands, quietly protesting against the firm's action. They refused to resume work until their shop delegate returned—and *I* was taken back the same day. (260; emphasis added)

Ostensibly, this anecdote bears out the thesis articulated at its outset: collective struggle, not individual will, characterizes union organizing efforts. But even as Hasanovitz disparages her own singularity (my voice is important only insofar as it expresses the wishes of the community; I am merely the mouthpiece for the group), her constant invocation of the "I" ends by subverting her claims of personal insignificance. Sound and syntax counterpoint rather than compound sense here, the very words with which the author expresses individual insignificance affirming self-distinction instead. The stress on her singularity may be framed in negative terms (I am *not* responsible, I do *not* speak for myself), but the resonance of "only I" with "only for myself" plays up what is uncommon about the speaker.

This almost imperceptible slide away from the self-in-relation, a shift which begins with the quiet transformation of "the shop" into "my shop," ends by calling attention to itself in the dramatic description of work stoppage that closes the passage. Here, the concerted effort of the garment workers is directed toward the autobiographical subject. The actions of two hundred, that is, are framed as a struggle to reinstate the self, ending not so much in collective victory as in a supremely personal triumph: "and I was taken back the same day." Anticipating the punch line, the repetition of this phrase indicates self-promotion rather than self-denial, encouraging readers to gloss the struggle between shop owners and workers as a more personal contest of wills.

Despite an insistence on the collective self, then, narrative energy and focus in *One of Them* seem disproportionately directed toward the "One," toward affirming what Hasanovitz calls at the close of her book "my hard labor" (289). As in Rose Schneiderman's recollection of union work, Hasanovitz's history of the collective enables rather than discourages self-assertion, the text's attention to community allowing for the articulation of a personal voice as well. Because it exploits the language of feminine service on behalf of others ("I spoke not only for myself") the book can focus on the predicament of the "I" without fear of censure. The description of collective "struggle and hardship" (253) sets the scene for individual success: "I was determined to have order in the shop, to get everything that was coming to the workers according to the agreement, to encourage, to show the workers the value of organization and the strength of unity" (253). In this narrative about "getting employment" and fighting to maintain it, insisting on pride in labor opens space for the working-class autobiographer to be "something else" (303) as well.

Contextualizing Emma Goldman's
Living My Life

I was not hewn of one piece, like Sasha or other heroic figures. I had long realized that I was woven of many skeins, conflicting in shade and texture. To the end of my days I should be torn between the yearning for a personal life and the need of giving all to my ideal.

Emma Goldman, *Living My Life*

As if bound to take their cues from the force of her own personality, critics of Goldman's two-volume, 993-page memoir tend to reiterate the mixed message of the quote above: the book is narcissistic but impersonal, a self-glorifying tract that nevertheless manages to leave the reader with an indistinct impression of autobiographical identity.[20] Critical appraisal of the autobiography as the product of a "conflicting" and complicated discursive structure accords it a privileged position not out of line with Goldman's own shrewdly romantic assessment of her life and character.[21] Following her lead, scholarly readers have tended to position Goldman as "something of an anomaly,"[22] her memoir as the exception to literary rules, whether of the autobiographical genre in general or, more specifically, of the personal narratives of public women.

Such a sense of distinctiveness, however, is in no small degree the product of the critical methods used to obtain it. Reading this text without sufficient regard for its historical and discursive contexts virtually guarantees that it will jump out of the literary background. If we resituate Goldman's recollection of her life as a Russian Jewish anarchist in the context of her political and cultural milieu, however, what appeared exceptional about the narrative begins to look typical.[23] While her pointed reference to the conflict between personal life and political ideal marks her life story as a glamorously turbulent one, comparison with the personal narratives of labor organizers Rose Schneiderman, Rose Cohen, and Elizabeth Hasanovitz indicates that what is unusual about the work's uneasy mixture of self-promotion and self-denial is simply the writer's glorification of this tension.

As in the recollections of Schneiderman and Hasanovitz, in Goldman's, too, the relationship between the histories of labor and the self is a complex one, foregrounding the story of the movement and the struggles of diverse activists at the same time as it calls attention to the particular achievements of the "I" who is recording the drama. Like Schneiderman, Goldman follows descriptions of her own speeches and their reception with biographical vignettes of others working to promote the socialist cause in the United States. Albeit framed as contingent upon the recognition of the "I," the following recollection provides a tribute to the work of a community: "Miss Lillian D. Wald, Lavinia Dock, and Miss MacDowell were among the first American women I met who felt an interest in the economic condition of the masses. They were genuinely concerned with the people of the East Side" (16). Frequent, too, are more extensive portraits of friends and coworkers: a memorial to Robert Reitzel after his death from tuberculosis ("A thinker and poet, he was not content merely to fashion beautiful words; he wanted them to be living realities, to help in awakening the masses to the possibilities of an earth freed from the shackles the privileged few had forged," [222]) and a lengthy paragraph commending the "inexhaustible energy" and "keen intellect" of William Shatoff, who "devoted his life to the enlightenment of the Russian refugees" (595).

If the combination of historical exposition and biographical cameo in *Living My Life* recalls the personal narratives of immigrant Jewish women labor organizers, so, too, Goldman's more self-referential rhetorical patterns mirror the oblique strategies of writers like Cohen, Schneiderman, Pesotta, and Hasanovitz. Granted, the book carries an assertively self-reflexive title, and its length does not suggest an author tentative about self-promotion. Yet even Goldman's "narcissism" is often rendered apologetically, while those memories approaching the bildungsroman are described more allusively than explicitly. Goldman most often invokes childhood scenes and emotional confessions as corollaries to political ideas, framing the personal as contingent upon the "ideal." In a particularly telling example, she conflates a Russian landscape of her youth with a description of her feelings for Alexander Berkman ("Fedya awakened in me the mysterious yearning I used to feel in my childhood at sight of the sunset turning the Popelan meadows golden in its dying glow," [33]). Both auto-biographical admissions are subordinated to an ostensible thesis that hon-ors a political aesthetic as ultimately more compelling than the artist's ap-prehension of beauty: Berkman discredits the "importance of beauty in one's life" but still "stirs" Goldman more "when speaking of revolutionary ethics" than when others discourse on "bad taste" (33).

But it is the carefully offhanded acknowledgment of the book's genesis that provides the closest link to Rose Schneiderman's own characteristi-cally humble self-advancement. Toward the close of the autobiography, Goldman devotes two full pages to a description of the autobiographical impulse that motivated it. Where Rose Schneiderman invokes the author-ity of Eleanor Roosevelt as literary sponsor, Goldman suggests that her own memoir is written at the behest of Theodore Dreiser. In its self-deprecatory lightheartedness, her allusion to this literary benefactor's prompting recalls Schneiderman's "surprise" when she is asked to become secretary of the State Department of Labor. To the novelist's suggestion that she write the story of her life, Goldman responds:

I told him that Howard Young had put the question first. I had not taken it very seriously and I was not surprised that I had received no word from him, though he had been back in America several months. Dreiser protested that he was greatly interested in seeing my story given to the world. He would se-cure a five-thousand-dollar advance from some publisher and I would hear from him very soon. (986)

The cultivated tone of amusement, the offhand dismissal of Young's pro-posal, and the questioning of Dreiser's own intention through the un-dermining verb "protested" are certainly characteristic of Goldman's irrev-erent, sardonic speechifying; at the same time, however, the need to authorize her own literary labor by invoking a more prominent sponsor echoes the rhetorical gestures characteristic of the personal narratives of immigrant Jewish labor leaders more generally.[24] Despite the proprietary insistence on marking out a space for the self, the autobiographical voice of *Living My Life* proves far more contingent upon the demands of history and significantly more accommodating to the voices of others than the bravura of its title promises.

A historicizing anecdote may serve to illustrate. Quitting her first job is a romantic if dangerous gesture for the young anarchist, according to *Living My Life*. Taking the unusual step of throwing away her meager living ("I had come to ask for a rise. . . . Mr. Garson replied that for a factory girl I had rather extravagant tastes, that all his 'hands' were well satisfied . . . that I, too, would have to manage or find work elsewhere," [17]), Goldman leaves Garson's "employ" (17), finds another job at a rival factory days later, maintains her own dignity as a worker and, years later, enjoys the opportunity to teach the sweatshop boss a lesson about working people's justice in a passage that simultaneously underscores her own distinctive achievements: "Who would have thought that the little girl in my shop would become such a grand speaker?" (352) a more humble Mr. Garson asks rhetorically. The autobiographer characterizes this action as idiosyncratic, yet historians suggest that electing to leave one job for another was in fact "a favorite tactic for self-promotion, a 'trick of the trade' as one observer noted. . . . Job-changing by women seeking higher wages was commonplace in an industry noted for a high rate of labor turnover. . . . Low wages and an interest in finding better work were given as reasons for quitting a job by 29% of the clothing workers surveyed."[25]

Likewise, reading Goldman's narrative with attention to its discursive contexts reveals a text that speaks of community as frequently as it does of iconoclasm. Blanche Gelfant distinguishes Goldman's strategy of "rhetorical excess" as a form of "rhetorical overdetermination" comparable only to that in Theodore Dreiser's *Sister Carrie:* "Instead of selecting a single predominant discourse, Dreiser and Goldman conflated the various modes available to them, as though hoping that rhetorical excess would make their unacceptably radical social criticism seem cogent, logical and, as expressed in familiar literary conventions and clichés, acceptable."[26]

Such a characterization is possible, however, only if we ignore Goldman's literary milieu—Yiddish newspapers, strike bulletins, union calls to action, Russian novels, the personal narratives of her Jewish contemporaries, and the journalistic pieces of her political coworkers. In fact, the Jewish anarchist's blurring of "history, journalism, philosophy, myth, melodrama, romance, apologias and confessions, and propaganda"[27] is not so much the distinguishing characteristic of her prose as its generically defining one. Creating a literary prototype inadequately rooted in history prevents us from reading her rhetorical practices as culturally contingent, yet her vocabulary of faith as well as her impassioned tone identify her narrative as a structural exemplar of the writing of Jewish immigrant activists. Readers today may wince at the purple prose of this elegy to a coworker: "Now Robert was dead, his ashes strewn over the lake. His great heart beat no more; his turbulent spirit was at rest. Life continued on its course, made more desolate without my knight, robbed of the force and beauty of his pen, the poetic splendour of his song" (222). But this paean is no more "excessive" than is Theresa Malkiel's tribute to the persuasive power of Mother Jones: "One glance into her glittering eyes, a glimpse at the noble face and outstretched arms that are anxious to embrace the whole human race, is enough to make you understand how she does it, not to say anything of the words of wisdom that flow from her lips" (115).

I have suggested that the multiplicity of rhetorical forms in the personal narratives of immigrant Jewish women—what Blanche Gelfant has singled out in Goldman's autobiography as a literary "pastiche"—can look like discursive confusion if we do not adequately historicize them. Comparing Goldman with "other radical women of her time—Mother Jones, Elizabeth Gurley Flynn, C. P. Gilman, and Margaret Sanger, all of whom wrote autobiographies," Gelfant finds that the Jewish exception to this Anglo-American rule is exceptional ("Goldman shattered the stereotype of woman as private, selfless, and submissively conforming to social expectations she sought secretly to subvert"),[28] hardly a surprising deduction if you define *woman* as excluding working-class and Jewish immigrants.

It must, however, be said that putting a writer's memoirs in context may involve working against the grain of the autobiographer's own interpretive directives. In the case of *Living My Life,* such a reading clearly puts pressure on Goldman's self-representation as glorious iconoclast, but it also provides us with a more nuanced picture of a subject negotiating her relationship to her community by exploiting the rhetorical forms provided by that community. Ultimately, what such representational conflicts demonstrate is that the relationship between historical exposition and autobiographical voicing in personal narratives like Goldman's is neither self-evident nor straightforward. By reevaluating what initially appears as so much discursive "noise" drowning out the autobiographical register, we may refine the entire literary score as well.

Coda

*A letter from my father in August 1914 said that count-
less Russian regiments were again passing through Derazhnya, en route to the Western front in the Carpathian
Mountains. Then all mail stopped. In that first year I had
become an American.*

Rose Pesotta, *Days of Our Lives*

By the standards of assimilationist autobiography, the closing paragraphs
of Rose Pesotta's description of her Old World beginnings are nothing if
not conventional: the brutality of the Russian regime, dispatching its
troops "ill-fed, ill-equipped and ill-clad. . . . as always" to the firing lines of
the First World War; the estrangement of Jewish residents implied in the
father's third-person witnessing of "Russian regiments" traveling through
a town claimed by Sholom Aleichem for Yiddish culture; the epistolary
synecdoche for family, simultaneously intimate and distanced from the immigrant narrator; the amputation of the past necessary for Americanization—these images of acclimatization are so familiar they are almost styl-
ized.[1]

What makes this avowal of legal permanent residency more complicated
is that it was published thirteen years after Pesotta's first personal narrative, *Bread upon the Waters*. As introduced by "native-born" American
Norman Thomas, *Days of Our Lives* supplements rather than upstages the
union organizer's first autobiographical performance, describing her "earlier years in Old Russia" (Introduction, unpaginated). But as an autobiographical bildungsroman it disappoints. Like *A Vanished World*, photogra-

pher Roman Vishniac's tribute to the Warsaw Ghetto,[2] *Days of Our Lives*
is true to type—less "an absorbingly interesting picture . . . of the author's
own childhood" than a postwar memorial to "an era that is gone forever"
(Introduction).

As "a record of that time and place" rather than a recollection of that
"dynamic, well-educated, charming woman . . . who has given her life and
energy to the American labor movement" (Introduction), Pesotta's 1958
narrative resonates with a discursive context that predates it by some half
a century. I have suggested that turn-of-the-century autobiography by Jewish immigrants most often tells the story of class rise and the denial of
culture, whereas the labor narratives of midcentury more commonly affirm
both their subjects' working-class origins and their ethnic identity. *Days of
Our Lives* disrupts this chronological sequence, allowing me the luxury of
self-criticism prior to publication and the satisfaction of textual closure.
If the narrative complicates some of my generalizations about immigrant
autobiography, it also provides a postscript to the discussion of literary
history with which this book opened. The curious textual chronology of
Days of Our Lives, that is, clarifies how text and context—the substance
and style of a book and the conditions of its publication—inform one another.

On the one hand, *Days of Our Lives* speaks to its contemporary political environment—what else would one expect during the height of the
Cold War but a story about Soviet barbarism, after all? On the other hand,
its iconography looks back to *The Promised Land. Days of Our Lives* does
not so much echo the celebratory rhetoric with which earlier Jewish autobiographers gilded the Statue of Liberty as reinvigorate this language.
Thomas's Introduction invites comparison with Theodore Roosevelt's essay
for Elizabeth Levin Stern's 1917 *My Mother and I.* Like Roosevelt's paean
to "Americanizing," Thomas describes Pesotta—the labor organizer who
enlists workers in Cleveland by feeding them the soups, goulash, and sausage she recalled from her early years in the Ukraine—as the assimilationist poster "girl . . . [who] emphatically made good in America as an American." Pesotta herself calls the United States "the Golden Land" (237),
which recalls even earlier immigrant terms such as "Gold Mountain,"
which many first-generation Chinese Americans used to describe gold-rush
California. Like Antin, like Stern, like scores of other emigrants from Russia and Poland, the narrator of *Days of Our Lives* escapes "to" America as

much as "from" the Old World (237), and, like their narratives, hers too pauses a moment to genuflect in front of "the Great Lady of Promise . . . holding high the torch of freedom" (244).

Other standards of early immigrant autobiography resurface here. Pesotta stages the parting from family as a choice requiring emotional and cultural denial rather than as a necessity forced by historical circumstance (and thus to some extent open to spiritual if not geographical backsliding): "I had made my choice. There could be no turning back. The gate closed behind me, shutting out my past" (233). And while anti-Semitism in America gets short shrift, she describes Old World pogroms and other systemic abuses against Jews in grim detail. The "Black Hundreds, the so-called official citizens' army of anti-Semites," are depicted as "beating, torturing, and killing Jews"—and here we see a glimpse of the militant narrator of the earlier autobiography—as well as "students, workers, and strikers, in the name of law and order" (71). What look like isolated instances of "anti-Semitic literature" she exposes as part of "a great stream . . . of anti-Jewish propaganda . . . from an official printing plant in St. Petersburg, operated by agents of the Okhranam, the imperial secret police. The flames of anti-Semitism had to be kept burning in Tsarist Russia, as in recent years in the Soviet Union" (140–41).

This kind of historicizing supplies the book with a cultural context by working against the explicit exhortation of the text to invoke the past only to push it beyond reach of the "American" self who recollects it in tranquillity. It does not, however, clear a space for sustained autobiographical expression. Despite the contrast Thomas implies between Pesotta's apparently objective account of her "work as an organizer here in America" in *Bread upon the Waters* and the more "personal story" of her Russian years promised in *Days of Our Lives,* this second narrative delivers (sociological) instruction rather than (autobiographical) intimacy.

Agency in *Days of Our Lives* is collective and ethnographic, as the objectified first-person plural of Pesotta's title makes clear. Even the ritualized description of the making of an American the final paragraphs deliver recalls a mass pledging of allegiance rather than a Franklinian self-making, as Pesotta's explanatory passage reveals: "We were on our way to a new world, a new life; we were escaping to the Golden Land. I didn't know then how great was the surge of people like us to the U.S. at that time. In the fiscal year ending in mid-1914, a total of 255,660 left the Russian Empire and Finland, mostly Jews fleeing pogroms" (237). Simultaneously rehearsing and dismantling the trope of the model citizen by revealing it to be a process more akin to the generic multiplication of cloning than the idiosyncrasies of a (re)naissance, this almost postmodern moment (almost, because the Althusserian self-subjection of the "I" is unconscious rather than self-conscious), is merely the last of a series of autobiographical sabotages.

The ostensibly collective subject of *Bread upon the Waters* is flexible enough to permit self-voicing, but *Days of Our Lives* inverts the dynamic this first book established between "I" and "we." Whereas the 1945 text uses the plural agency of the ILGWU in order to foreground the activities of its single and singular "housekeeper," the 1958 publication invokes the "I" as cultural authority for ethnic storytelling. In the face of the mass erasure of the Holocaust, Pesotta implies, *Days of Our Lives* cannot afford the luxuries of memoir. It is a requiem rather than a recollection, permitting autobiographical memory only rarely, and then as ground for the kinds of cultural recording books like Fabiola Cabeza de Baca's *The Good Life* and Gregorita Rodríguez's *Singing for My Echo* begin with only to move away from.[3]

The first sentence of the book announces this equation. "As we grow older," Pesotta begins, "we frequently try to dig up from a tiny cell in the brain the memory of some ritual which grew out of family ways from time immemorial and became a tradition or folklore" (1). Where folklorists like Cabeza de Baca and Cleofas Jaramillo inflect their depictions of familial and community ritual with autobiographical intentionality, invoking tradition in order to ground memory, Pesotta honors memory in order to reestablish a community that continues to exist only within the pages of her narrative. On the relatively rare occasions when she distinguishes herself from "the Jews of Derazhnya" (1), the "I" serves as cultural ambassador, introducing readers to Shabbat rituals (in "Family and Friends"), translating terms like "Pesach" and "matzoth" (in "Memories"), explaining the significance of the "mitzvah" and how to recite "Kaddish" (in "Our Town"). Even when Pesotta glances at those periods of personal crisis where autobiographical disclosure would be most appropriate, she introduces herself only as an illustration of sociocultural phenomena. Her near-death from croup as a child, for instance, is used to make a point about community health care:

With anxious heart Dad went to Zhmerinka, and was back by daybreak. Meanwhile, the old doctor watched by my bedside through the night. The new medicine eased the tightened throat, the choking stopped, and in another day I was out of danger. I think that both Pan Kazimir and father, in their first-aid activities, were actuated as much by self-preservation as by altruism. In a region without medical facilities, an uncontrolled disease might quickly mushroom into an epidemic, and they knew well that epidemics made no distinction among Jews, peasants, and land-owners. (96)

As ethnographic documentation, however, *Days of Our Lives* succeeds brilliantly. The social history of Derazhnya—a town which exists because of anti-Semitic laws creating the Pale, and which flourishes despite them—is richly recorded, a place of busy, energetic life, testimony to cultural survival under bitter poverty. Jewish achievement is celebrated through vignettes of writers like Sholom Aleichem and Mocher-Seforim, authors whose championing of Yiddish is all the more respected for its vernacular status ("Sholom Aleichem . . . has often been compared to Mark Twain for his humor. But Mark Twain had a relatively easy time gaining recognition as an author. He was writing in the spoken language of his own land and for people eager to read, while Sholom Aleichem was groping in the dark, endeavoring to create enduring literature in a jargon that was widely scoffed at," [143]), and lesser-known schoolteachers and religious scholars are honored as heroes, guiding studies "taught surreptitiously" (105) lest they be punished by Russian civil authorities. Time and time again, Pesotta compares the working-class aesthetic of Jewish life in the Pale to the achievements of American high culture, always to the advantage of the former. She attests to the prowess of "visiting cantors . . . invited to officiate on the Sabbath. . . . Those singers, tenors, baritones, basses, who had excellent voices, performed before an appreciative audience of Jews who occupied every available seat in the synagogue and their response was comparable to that of a modern audience listening to an accomplished artist at the opera or at a concert" (203–4); and she cites Mocher-Seforim's evocative names as instance of his literary prowess: "*Kaptzansk,* Povertyville; *Glupsk,* Fooltown; *Tuneyadevki,* Parasiteville," bearing "names quite as revealing as the American designations of the depression period, Tobacco Road, or Sinclair Lewis's Babbitt-town" (142).

To some extent, Pesotta's class-conscious reading of Jewish cultural life works against the book's memorializing pull, recalling the sense of agency that informs her first autobiography. When the organizer makes connections between the laboring artists of prewar Russia and the working writers of contemporary television, for instance, she discourages that fetishization of the past that the narrative structure of *Days of Our Lives* confirms more generally. Passages like the following politicize art and, unlike the majority of scholarly studies, celebrate popular culture without deracinating it from the aesthetic expressions of previous generations: "Nowadays, humor, quips, tall tales, anecdotes, and even ad libs, voiced with apparent spontaneity by leading comedians, are the result of grinding labor by anonymous factory toilers called gag-writers, who often dip into the treasure-house of immigrant grandparents' memories for the mirthful wisdom of Hershel and his contemporaries" (171).

Once again, however, "memory" is pushed to the margins. Ironically, a text that announces itself as a sustained personal narrative provides us with comparatively fewer glimpses of the "I" than do the culinary narratives of Fabiola Cabeza de Baca and Cleofas Jaramillo, narratives, I have argued, that are both cultural expression and entrée into autobiography. Pesotta's rare personal admissions—of a youthful attraction to a boy of "meager schooling" (225) that is cut short by parental edict, of the teasing she receives from peasant boys and her revenge upon them, of her high-spirited sister's humiliation by a severe father—demonstrate that she had access to a more confessional language. Why, then, did she use it so sparingly?

Throughout this book I have suggested that ethnic autobiographers are often compelled to make use of languages damaging to autobiographical expression. But, as I have also tried to demonstrate, this kind of publishing configuration does not prohibit writers from creating more self-possessed personal narrative; it merely means they have to work harder to get around the textual obstacles placed in their way. *Days of Our Lives* should be no exception to this rule—and when it comes to eulogizing others rather than focusing on herself, Pesotta suggests a way out. In a discussion of Russian censorship, she explains, "I came to know that certain writers had adopted an ingenious code, characterized by the intelligentsia as *The Conscience of Russia.* By means of humor and satire, which served the writers as a shield, the rottenness of those in power was frequently exposed" (121–22).

Whether this observation gestures toward the autobiographical indirection of Pesotta's own text is unclear, although the brief but telling example of familial censorship I alluded to above provides a stunning metaphor for her self-silencing. Her sister has lately returned from a visit to the big city of Odessa, where she has learned of the revolutionary movement (as, presumably, Pesotta herself will do later). "As soon as Esther entered the house, she began to spread her lately acquired knowledge," the organizer recalls:

Before she had time to finish the sentence, father walked in. "Stop that kind of talk at once!" he commanded. "If there's any such talking to be done in this house, I'll do it. Comb out that silly looking pompadour and take off those stilts before you break an ankle. Give the children their supper and put them to bed" (70–71).

A clearer illustration of the punishing of feminine high spirits would be hard to find. The father's "commandment," designed to crush this self-possessed young woman at the threshold of adult sexuality ("Esther was fifteen that year, and became a glamour girl wearing her hair high in a pompadour style of that period," [70]), is a gendered bruising as humiliating as it is sexualized. Given this warning about the dangers of speaking as a political woman, what is surprising is not the head-averted autobiographical stance of Pesotta's second memoir but the flagrant defiance of the first, which, post-1958, reads as a sustained transgression against not only political conservatism but paternal rule.

It is unfortunate for readers interested in the life of Rose Pesotta that the autobiographer does not take the same kind of rhetorical risks with *Days of Our Lives* that she did with her initial personal narrative. "My performance was too good," she says of her work in a Russian tea-house—but also, metatextually, of her autobiographical performance as well. ". . . That was what had led me into this pitfall. I would escape from it by being not so good. . . . At that age the word sabotage had never come to my ears. . . . But that was the process, nameless in my mind, that would liberate me from the drudgery into which I had been maneuvered" (116). In *Days of Our Lives,* such tricksterism turns to self-sabotage. Yet in providing us with an example of the myriad difficulties women autobiographers face as they labor toward self-possession in prose, Pesotta's second autobiography is very useful. What this autobiography-that-is-not-one confirms is that conventional genre distinctions are inadequate for assessing the work of ethnic American women. Like the literary forms working-class women make use of to script the stories of their lives, what constitutes autobiographical utterance is more elastic—and ultimately more compelling—than the parameters we often use to describe it.

Notes

Preface

1. William Boelhower, "The Making of Ethnic Autobiography in the United States," in Paul John Eakin, ed., *American Autobiography: Retrospect and Prospect* (Madison: University of Wisconsin Press, 1991), 126.

Introduction

1. Fabiola Cabeza de Baca, *The Good Life: New Mexico Traditions and Food* (1949; Santa Fe: Museum of New Mexico Press, 1982); Rose Schneiderman with Lucy Goldthwaite, *All for One* (New York: Paul S. Erikson, 1967); [Jesusita Aragón as told to] Fran Leeper Buss, *La Partera: Story of a Midwife* (Ann Arbor: University of Michigan Press, 1982). Further citations will appear in the text.

2. By using the phrase "making the self," of course, I mean to distinguish between the textual self and the actual "I"; between the subject represented in narrative, that is, and the authorial "I" that constructs this self on the page.

3. Californios writing as early as 1885 insist that it is the "Spanish" who are "native" to the state. See María Amparo Ruiz de Burton, *The Squatter and the Don*, ed. Rosaura Sánchez and Beatrice Pita (1885; Houston: Arte Público, 1992), 66.

4. Jacob A. Riis, *The Battle with the Slum* (New York: Macmillan, 1902), 364.

5. As late as 1993, Margo Culley's introduction to her edited collection, *American Women's Autobiography: Fea(s)ts of Memory* (Madison: University of Wisconsin Press, 1992)—a text which includes a range of autobiographical voices—tends in rehearsing a conservative model of American autobiography to shut out many writers whose autobiographical practices have roots in other long-standing American traditions: "The dominant tradition of American women's autobiography has roots in Puritan beliefs about the self and the Puritan practice of conversion narra-

tives. . . . Even in periods when autobiography has become a thoroughly secular enterprise its forms and purposes can be traced to these earlier traditions" (10).

6. Sonia Saldívar-Hull, "Feminism on the Border: From Gender Politics to Geopolitics," in Hector Calderón and José David Saldívar, eds., *Criticism in the Borderlands: Studies in Chicano Literature, Culture, and Ideology* (Durham: Duke University Press, 1991), 206.

7. Sidonie Smith, *Subjectivity, Identity, and the Body: Women's Autobiographical Practices in the Twentieth Century* (Bloomington: Indiana University Press, 1993), 23.

8. Julia Watson and Sidonie Smith, "Introduction: De/Colonization and the Politics of Discourse in Women's Autobiographical Practices," in Sidonie Smith and Julia Watson, eds., *De/Colonizing the Subject: The Politics of Gender in Women's Autobiography* (Minneapolis: University of Minnesota Press, 1992), xvii.

9. Sau-ling Cynthia Wong, *Reading Asian American Literature: From Necessity to Extravagance* (Princeton: Princeton University Press, 1993), 14.

10. Fabiola Cabeza de Baca, *We Fed Them Cactus* (1954; Albuquerque: University of New Mexico Press, 1989) (further references will appear in the text); Cleofas M. Jaramillo, *Romance of a Little Village Girl* (San Antonio: Naylor, 1955).

11. Genaro M. Padilla, "Imprisoned Narrative? Or, Lies, Secrets, and Silence in New Mexico Women's Autobiography," in Calderón and Saldívar, eds., *Criticism in the Borderlands*, 47. See also Padilla's *My History, Not Yours: The Formation of Mexican American Autobiography* (Madison: University of Wisconsin Press, 1993) for a more extended discussion of the discursive context within which Cabeza de Baca and Jaramillo wrote and published. My own readings of both writers owe much to the brilliant historiographic and textual analysis Padilla has brought to bear on their writing, and to whose work here as elsewhere I am indebted.

12. Many feminists have been quick to claim autobiography as the genre most hospitable to women writers. Certainly, as Patricia Spacks asserts, "Women, for obvious social reasons, have traditionally had more difficulty than men about making public claims of their own importance. . . . The housewife seldom offers her life to public view" (cited by Estelle Jelinek, "Women's Autobiography and the Male Tradition," in Estelle C. Jelinek, ed., *Women's Autobiography: Essays in Criticism* [Bloomington: Indiana University Press, 1980], 112). But to suggest, as Jane Marcus does in "Invincible Mediocrity: The Private Selves of Public Women," that because "the memoir made no grand claims to high artistic achievement . . . women could write in this genre without threatening male hegemony" (in Shari Benstock, ed., *The Private Self: Theory and Practice of Women's Autobiographical Writings* [Chapel Hill: University of North Carolina Press, 1988], 120) ignores the fact that for most women—women granted less privilege than that of the white middle class—even this apparently less intimidating avenue does not offer any easy literary entrée. See also Frances Smith Foster's attention to the politics of publishing for nineteenth-century black women in "Autobiography After Emancipation:

The Example of Elizabeth Keckley": "Racism and sexism made literacy difficult and often illegal for the white women and the people of color who together constituted then, as now, the majority of Americans. Those who were able to write or to dictate their stories generally found few publishing opportunities. And those who both wrote and published their versions of self found that the readers' expectations and prejudices required particular modifications of style and content and even then often distorted what was written" (in James Robert Payne, ed., *Multicultural Autobiography: American Lives* [Knoxville: University of Tennessee Press, 1992], 35).

13. Ramón Saldívar, *Chicano Narrative: The Dialectics of Difference* (Madison: University of Wisconsin Press, 1990), 42.

14. Personal Narratives Group, eds., *Interpreting Women's Lives: Feminist Theory and Personal Narratives* (Bloomington: Indiana University Press, 1989), 7.

15. Raymond A. Paredes, "The Evolution of Chicano Literature," in Houston A. Baker Jr., ed., *Three American Literatures* (New York: Modern Language Association, 1982), 37.

16. William Boelhower, "The Making of Ethnic Autobiography in the United States," in Paul John Eakin, ed., *American Autobiography: Retrospect and Prospect* (Madison: University of Wisconsin Press, 1991), 125.

17. Onnie Lee Logan, *Motherwit: An Alabama Midwife's Story*, as told to Katherine Clark (New York: E. P. Dutton, 1989). Further citations will appear in the text.

18. Narratives of women of color are not only exploited for their ethnographic value, however. bell hooks suggests another (mis)use of personal narrative: "Often novels or confessional autobiographical writings are used to mediate the tension between academic writing, theory, and the experiential. This seems to be especially the case when the issue is inclusion of works by women of color in feminist theory courses" (*Talking Back: thinking feminist, thinking black* [Boston: South End Press, 1989], 37–38).

19. [Aragón as told to] Buss, *La Partera*, vii.

20. Sau-ling Cynthia Wong, "Autobiography as Guided Chinatown Tour? Maxine Hong Kingston's *The Woman Warrior* and the Chinese American Autobiographical Controversy," in Payne, ed., *Multicultural Autobiography*, 262.

21. Wong, "Autobiography as Guided Chinatown Tour?" 264.

22. Wong, "Autobiography as Guided Chinatown Tour?" 262.

23. James Clifford's characterization of the nineteenth-century ethnographer as attaining ethnographic authority by "undergoing a personal learning experience comparable to an initiation" is suggestive here (*The Predicament of Culture: Twentieth-Century Ethnography, Literature, and Art* [Cambridge: Harvard University Press, 1988], 28). The "initiation" accords the ethnographer cultural mastery, identifying him as bicultural: fluent in the cultural codes of his own world *and* the one he is studying. The presumed subject (object) of study, meanwhile, represented as ever more firmly rooted in his own world—or, rather, in the world the ethnogra-

pher makes for him in print—becomes by comparison far less of an authority. Thus ethnographic narrative in this sense works to (re)produce the ethnographer, rather than his apparent object, as subject. For a concise history of American anthropology in relation to its objects of inquiry, see Arnold Krupat, *Ethnocriticism: Ethnography, History, Literature* (Berkeley: University of California Press, 1992), especially chapter 1, "Ethnography and Literature: A History of Their Convergence."

24. Some readers may see the absence of theorists of the subject like Lacan, Derrida, Kristeva, Butler, and Fuss in this study as a conspicuous lack, but this gap is studied. Certainly, these writers challenge universalist, humanist assumptions about subjectivity, as the attention they have received by autobiography scholars makes evident. I have chosen not to treat their work in any sustained way here, however, because a great number of studies of autobiography have already provided us with useful and extensive treatments of their theories in relation to the study of women's personal narratives. (The reader might wish to consult Françoise Lionnet's *Autobiographical Voices: Race, Gender, Self-Portraiture* [Ithaca: Cornell University Press, 1989] and Sidonie Smith's more recent *Subjectivity, Identity, and the Body,* two fine contemporary studies that do engage these theorists.) More important, notwithstanding crucial differences among them, the models of the subject such theorists produce appear essentially ahistorical and thus ill suited to illuminating the texts this study considers. The sweeping assertions they make about subjectivity are largely inhospitable, that is, to this project, which works to formulate and to privilege a theory of the concrete and which interests itself in arguing for the usefulness of a methodology of the local.

25. Zora Neale Hurston, *Dust Tracks on a Road: An Autobiography,* ed. Robert Hemenway (1942; Urbana: University of Illinois Press, 1984), 237.

26. Jade Snow Wong, *Fifth Chinese Daughter* (New York: Harper and Brothers, 1945), 90.

27. From Georg Misch's compendium, *A History of Autobiography in Antiquity,* trans. E. W. Dickes (Cambridge: Harvard University Press, 1951), to James Olney's collection, *Autobiography: Essays Theoretical and Critical* (Princeton: Princeton University Press, 1980), autobiographical identity is markedly isolationist. Hertha D. Wong provides a particularly useful discussion of this standard subject in chapter 1 of *Sending My Heart Back Across the Years: Tradition and Innovation in Native American Autobiography* (New York: Oxford University Press, 1992). See also her identification of "the Eurocentric insistence on such literary conventions as chronology, unity, and closure" (87) as the defining markers of traditional autobiography. See, in addition, Sidonie Smith's cogent description of the "universal subject" in *Subjectivity, Identity, and the Body:* "Imperial interpreter, provocateur of totalization, the essential self is likewise a 'free' agent, exercising self-determination over meaning, personal destiny, and desire. Neither powerless nor passive, it assumes and celebrates agency. Its movement through time/history is purposeful, consistent, coherent, hence teleological" (8). For other useful critiques of autobiography theory's privileging of a model of the self that celebrates autonomy to the

exclusion of community, see Regenia Gagnier's "The Literary Standard, Working-Class Autobiography, and Gender," in Susan Groag Bell and Marilyn Yalom, eds., *Revealing Lives: Autobiography, Biography and Gender* (New York: State University of New York Press, 1990); Jane Marcus's "Invisible Mediocrity: The Private Selves of Public Women." In Shari Benstock, ed., *The Private Self: Theory and Practice of Women's Autobiographical Writings* (Chapel Hill: University of North Carolina Press, 1988); Arnold Krupat's discussion of "The Concept of the Canon" in his *The Voice in the Margin: Native American Literature and the Canon* (Berkeley: University of California Press, 1989); Sidonie Smith's *A Poetics of Women's Autobiography: Marginality and the Fictions of Self-Representation* (Bloomington: Indiana University Press, 1987); Bella Brodski and Celeste Schenck's Introduction to their *Life/Lines: Theorizing Women's Autobiography* (Ithaca: Cornell University Press, 1988); Smith and Watson, eds., *De/Colonizing the Subject;* and Lionnet's *Autobiographical Voices,* among others.

28. In his 1970 Introduction to the autobiography, for instance, Robert Hemenway describes Hurston as "nonconfrontational" and her book one that "sacrifices truth to the politics of racial harmony" (xiii). His 1984 edition of a less bowdlerized version of the text acts as a corrective to this earlier assessment, however, as does Claudine Raynaud's analysis of omitted sections of the narrative. In " 'Rubbing a Paragraph with a Soft Cloth'? Muted Voices and Editorial Constraints in *Dust Tracks on a Road*" (in Smith and Watson, eds., *De/Colonizing the Subject*), Raynaud suggests that the censored portions emphasize "the complexity of [Hurston's] resistance to the white publishing world, and the ways in which she eventually complied. . . . It restores from the original text a more accurate, if still extremely puzzling, portrait of Hurston" (35). See Françoise Lionnet's discerning reading of *Dust Tracks* for another important exception to this critical history. In the following passage, for instance, Lionnet critiques those scholars who have held Hurston to account for careless record-keeping and suggests that we discard the notion that autobiography enjoys a closer relation to referentiality than do other genres: "If over-enthusiasm can be seen as another word for hyperbole, then Hurston the writer is hereby cautioning her own reader to defer judgment about the explicit referentiality of her text. Why come to it with preconceived notions of autobiographical truth when the tendency to make hyperbolic and over-enthusiastic statements about her subject matter is part of her 'style' as a writer? Couldn't we see in this passage Hurston's own implicit theory of reading and thus use it to derive our interpretive practice from the text itself, instead of judging the work according to Procrustean notions of autobiographical form?" (*Autobiographical Voices,* 101–2).

29. Frank Chin, "Come All Ye Asian American Writers of the Real and the Fake," in Jeffery Paul Chan, Frank Chin, Lawson Fusao Inada, and Shawn Wong, eds., *The Big Aiiieeeee! An Anthology of Chinese American and Japanese American Literature* (New York: Meridian, 1991). In her analysis of Christian Indian autobiography, A. LaVonne Brown Ruoff suggests that apparently assimilationist texts

may use tropes of acculturation subversively: "The spiritual confessions linked Indian autobiographers to Protestant literary traditions and identified these authors as civilized Christians whose experiences were as legitimate subjects of written analysis as the experiences of other Christians. Apes, Copway, and later American-Indian autobiographers, like the slave narrators, used personal and family experiences to illustrate the suffering their people endured at the hands of white Christians" ("John Joseph Mathews's Talking to the Moon: Literary and Osage Contexts," in Payne, ed., *Multicultural Autobiography*, 3). Granting the different historical and cultural trajectories of two distinct American literary traditions, Ruoff's argument about Native American personal narrative nevertheless provides a useful methodological corrective to Chin's "either/or" reading of Chinese American autobiography.

    30. Lionnet, *Autobiographical Voices*, 128.

    31. Thus, for instance, Chin's reading of Wong's narrative as acculturated because it espouses a "Western" idea of individualism ignores this writer's frequent invocation of a specifically Chinese American collective. Consider the following description of mutual aid associations: "Family associations took care of personal and business matters for Chinese in America. Controversies without legal status in American courts could be taken up in association meetings; destitute Chinese families or widows who were not American citizens could get immediate assistance; men without relatives could have their funeral arrangements assured" (Come All Ye Asian American Writers," 118). It is just as easy to find passages celebrating a distinctly Chinese American culture as it is to locate what Chin might characterize as more ideologically compromised portions of the narrative.

    32. This formulation means neither to suggest that all white autobiographers refuse to assign cultural coordinates to their self-representations nor to assume that all writers of color are focused primarily on enunciating their cultural and ethnic origins, but merely to assert that until very recently, autobiography critics have either ignored the cultural inflections of Anglo-American canonical texts or have described them all as variations on a single Puritan theme in such a way as to preclude comparative cultural study.

    33. For an example of this tendency to overcorrect for the "existential" model of the subject by celebrating a wholly collaborative idea of identity, see hooks in *Talking Back:* "I evoked the way of knowing I had learned from unschooled southern black folks. We learned that the self existed in relation, was dependent for its very being on the lives and experiences of everyone, the self not as signifier of one 'I' but the coming together of many 'I's, the self as embodying collective reality past and present, family and community" (30–31). This formulation seems to me to oversimplify the range of representational strategies African American autobiography provides readers, but hooks's assertion that we read the self historically ("Social construction of the self in relation would mean . . . that we would be in touch with what Paule Marshall calls 'our ancient properties'—our history") is crucial.

See chapter 6 for a more sustained discussion of critical constructions of the relational self.

34. In "Women's Autobiographical Selves: Theory and Practice," in Benstock, ed., *The Private Self,* 43.

35. Krupat, *The Voice in the Margin,* 133–34.

36. With our sometimes foreshortened scholarly memories we may take such correctives for granted, yet these revisions are both relatively recent and hard won, and the ground they question remains a contested site. Thus as late as 1980, Roger Rosenblatt supported what Krupat identifies as "egocentric individualism" (*Ethnocriticism,* 29) when he described autobiography as "one person in relation to one world of that person's manufacture, which is that person in macrocosm, explained and made beautiful by that same person in the distance, playing god to the whole unholy trinity" ("Black Autobiography: Life as the Death Weapon," in Olney, ed., *Autobiography,* 169), and in the same collection James Olney rehearses the standard definition of autobiography as deriving from a tradition inaugurated by St. Augustine, celebrating the "dawning self-consciousness of Western man that found literary expression in the early moments of modern autobiography" ("Autobiography and the Cultural Moment: A Thematic, Historical, and Bibliographical Introduction," 13). It is pronouncements like these, by no means exceptional, that make the argument for the kind of more expansive definition advanced implicitly by Blackburn, and more explicitly by Krupat, so necessary.

37. See William L. Andrews, *To Tell a Free Story: The First Century of Afro-American Autobiography, 1760–1865* (Urbana: University of Illinois Press, 1986), and *Sisters of the Spirit: Three Black Women's Autobiographies of the Nineteenth Century* (Bloomington, Indiana University Press, 1986); Joanne M. Braxton, *Black Women Writing Autobiography: A Tradition Within a Tradition* (Philadelphia: Temple University Press, 1989).

38. Carolyn Porter, "Are We Being Historical Yet?" *South Atlantic Quarterly* 87 (Fall 1988): 782.

39. Mourning Dove, *Cogewea, the Half-Blood: A Depiction of the Great Montana Cattle Range,* ed. Lucullus Virgil McWhorter, introduction by Dexter Fisher (Lincoln: University of Nebraska Press, 1981), 149.

40. Michael M. J. Fischer, "Ethnicity and the Post-Modern Arts of Memory," in James Clifford and George E. Marcus, eds., *Writing Culture: The Poetics and Politics of Ethnography* (Berkeley: University of California Press, 1988), 125. Fischer does not deny that cultural practice may be undertaken consciously, but his use of a psychoanalytic model of transference and of what he calls "dream-work" to explain ethnicity tends in practice to privilege unconscious mechanisms of transmittal as more "sophisticated"—and thus more worthy of study—than more direct means of cultural reproduction. See, for instance, the following weighted comparison: "Ethnicity is something reinvented and reinterpreted in each generation by each individual and . . . it is often something over which he or she lacks control.

Ethnicity is not something that is *simply passed on* from generation to generation, taught and learned; it is something *dynamic*, often unsuccessfully repressed or avoided" (195; emphasis added).

41. Elizabeth Fox-Genovese, "My Statue, My Self: Autobiographical Writings of Afro-American Women," in Benstock, ed., *The Private Self*, 83.

42. Cf. Françoise Lionnet's discussion of ethnic and autobiographical authority in Hurston's *Dust Tracks:* "Despite its rich cultural content, the work does not authorize unproblematic recourse to culturally grounded interpretations. It is an orphan text that attempts to create its own genealogy by simultaneously appealing to and debunking the cultural traditions it helps to redefine" (*Autobiographical Voices*, 101). Orphan and affiliate, Hurston is at once a presence distinct from others and a cultural arbiter wholeheartedly engaged with a racial collective. According herself the power to revise the cultural standard also grants her more weight as an autobiographical subject.

43. Michael Omi, *Racial Formation in the United States from the 1960s to the 1980s* (New York: Routledge, 1986), 72–73.

44. Evelyn Nakano Glenn, *Issei, Nisei, War Bride: Three Generations of Japanese American Women in Domestic Service* (Philadelphia: Temple University Press, 1988), 38.

45. Fredric Jameson, *Postmodernism; Or, The Cultural Logic of Late Capitalism* (Durham: Duke University Press, 1990), 49.

46. This formulation is Genaro Padilla's in *My History, Not Yours*. Padilla suggests that "ideologically subordinate speech . . . actually constitutes multi-addressed utterance in which pragmatic appeasement reads at one surface of language while anger and opposition read at other, and often within the same, surfaces. Such strategic utterance constitutes a form of rhetorical camouflage which first appropriates a public 'voice' for an individual from an otherwise 'silenced' group and then turns that voice to duplicitous purpose. Such discursive duplicity functions to communicate different stories to different audiences, with an implicit understanding that one's own people will . . . someday read them 'de una manera digna de ellos' " (draft version of chapter 1, msp. 42). Given the all too common practice of figuring the speaker as "always already" silenced, the focus on speech is crucial here. Although her essay works in general to deconstruct reductive notions of oppressor/oppressed power relations, Chandra Talpade Mohanty's description of resistance as inhering "in the very gaps, fissures, and silences of hegemonic narratives" is illustrative of this tendency to deny voice to those who lack political authority (Introduction to her *Third World Women and the Politics of Feminism* [Bloomington: Indiana University Press, 1991], 38). This focus on silence may be an eloquent metaphor for oppression, but I would argue that it is inaccurate at the level of the literal and disabling as a trope.

47. VertaMae Smart-Grosvenor, *Vibration Cooking; Or, The Travel Notes of a Geechee Girl* (1970; New York: Ballantine, 1986), xv.

48. Omi, *Racial Formation,* 67–68.

49. John Brenkman, *Culture and Domination* (Ithaca: Cornell University Press, 1988), 24. Mohanty makes a similar point in *Third World Women* when she suggests that "it is possible to retain the idea of multiple, fluid structures of domination which intersect to locate women differently at particular historical conjunctures, while at the same time insisting on the dynamic oppositional agency of individuals and collectives and their engagement in 'daily life' " (13).

50. Ronald Takaki, *Strangers from a Different Shore: A History of Asian Americans* (New York: Penguin, 1989), 168.

51. José Antonio Villareal, *Pocho* (New York: Doubleday, 1959), 108.

52. Evelyn Brooks Higginbotham, "African-American Women's History and the Metalanguage of Race," *Signs* 17 (Winter 1992): 258.

53. Maxine Baca Zinn, Lynn Weber Cannon, Elizabeth Higginbotham, and Bonnie Thornton Dill, "The Costs of Exclusionary Practices in Women's Studies," in Gloria Anzaldúa, ed., *Making Face, Making Soul/Haciendo Caras: Creative and Critical Perspectives by Women of Color* (San Francisco: Aunt Lute Foundation Books, 1990), 34. For another useful critique of Anglo-American feminism see Norma Alarcón, "The Theoretical Subject(s) of *This Bridge Called My Back* and Anglo-American Feminism," in Calderón and Saldívar, eds., *Criticism in the Borderlands.* Alarcón argues that privileging gender effaces the ways in which " 'one becomes a woman' in opposition to other women" as well as in "simple opposition to men" (33).

54. Julia Watson, "Toward an Anti-Metaphysics of Autobiography," in Robert Folkenflik, ed., *The Culture of Autobiography: Constructions of Self-Representation* (Stanford: Stanford University Press, 1993), 71.

55. Sau-ling Cynthia Wong, "Immigrant Autobiography: Some Questions of Definition and Approach," in Eakin, ed., *American Autobiography,* 161.

56. Fox-Genovese, "My Statue, My Self," 71.

57. Charlotte L. Forten [Grimké], *The Journal of Charlotte L. Forten: A Free Negro in the Slave Era,* ed. Ray Allen Billington (1953; New York: W. W. Norton, 1981; Alice James, *The Diary of Alice James,* ed. Leon Edel (New York: Penguin, 1964); Marita Golden, *Migrations of the Heart: An Autobiography* (New York: Ballantine, 1983); Maya Angelou, *All God's Children Wear Traveling Shoes* (New York: Random House, 1986).

58. Mary G. Mason, "The Other Voice: Autobiographies of Women Writers" in Olney, ed., *Autobiography,* 210.

59. Margo Culley, "What a Piece of Work Is 'Woman'!" in her collection, *American Women's Autobiography,* 15–16.

60. Elizabeth Hasanovitz, *One of Them: Chapters from a Passionate Autobiography* (Boston: Houghton Mifflin, 1918).

61. Schneiderman with Lucy Goldthwaite, *All for One,* 76.

62. Rose Cohen, *Out of the Shadow* (New York: George H. Doran, 1918), 259.

63. Mathews's recognition of the specificity of women's lives is worth quoting in full: " 'Moreover, beyond acknowledgment of diversity among the groups of women, there is the need to acknowledge the diversity of each individual woman. . . . Each woman in any society is not simply a member of one definite social category, but is a unique and female focus of a multitude of coexisting and competing social groups and relationships' " (as cited by Mary Jo Maynes, "Gender and Narrative Form in French and German Working-Class Autobiography," in Personal Narratives Group, eds., *Interpreting Women's Lives,* 40–41). Acknowledging the specificity of such narratives allows us a measure of defense against the critical complacency which can follow upon any sustained inquiry. It allows us, for instance, to read a critique of paternal authority encoded in a text that presents itself as all filial duty, without discrediting a more affirmative representational moment of the relation between father and daughter. Consider the irony with which Jade Snow Wong mocks this moment of fatherly self-importance: "One day when the family was at dinner, father broke the habitual silence by announcing a new edict: 'I have just learned that the American people commonly address their fathers informally as "Daddy"! The affectionate tone of this word pleases me. Hereafter, you children shall address me as "Daddy." ' No comment was required; the children mentally recorded this command" (12). Or this remembrance by Marita Golden: "My father was the first man I ever loved. He was as assured as a panther. His ebony skin was soft as the surface of coal. . . . In school he went as far as the sixth grade, then learned the rest on his own. . . . By his own definition he was 'a black man and proud of it.' Arming me with a measure of this conviction, he unfolded a richly colored tapestry, savored its silken texture and warned me never to forget its worth. Africa: 'It wasn't dark until the white man got there.' Cleopatra: 'I don't care WHAT they tell you in school, she was a black woman' " (3).

64. hooks, *Talking Back,* 4.

65. Sarah Rice, *He Included Me: The Autobiography of Sarah Rice,* transcribed and ed. Louise Westling (Athens: University of Georgia Press, 1989), 77.

66. Takaki, *Strangers from a Different Shore,* 9.

Chapter One

1. Ernesto Galarza, *Barrio Boy* (Notre Dame: University of Notre Dame Press, 1971). The section epigraph is taken from p. 33. M. F. K. Fisher, *The Gastronomical Me* (1943; San Francisco: North Point Press, 1989). The section epigraph is taken from p. 18.

2. Cleofas Jaramillo, *The Genuine New Mexico Tasty Recipes* (1939; Santa Fe: Seton Village Press, 1942) (further citations will appear in the text); Fabiola Cabeza de Baca, *Historic Cookery* (1949; Las Vegas, N.M.: La Galería de los Artesanos, 1970).

3. Joan Aleshire, "Exhibition of Women Artists (1790–1900)," in Elaine Hedges

and Ingrid Wendt, eds., *In Her Own Image: Women Working in the Arts* (Old Westbury, N.Y.: Feminist Press, 1980), 57.

4. C. Kurt Dewhurst, Betty MacDowell, and Marsha MacDowell, eds., *Artists in Aprons: Folk Art by American Women* (New York: E. P. Dutton in association with the Museum of American Folk Art, 1979), xviii.

5. Alan Grubb, "House and Home in the Victorian South: The Cookbook as Guide," in Carol Bleser, ed., *In Joy and in Sorrow: Women, Family, and Marriage in the Victorian South, 1830–1900* (New York: Oxford University Press, 1991), 157.

6. Ibid., 160; Fabiola Cabeza de Baca, *The Good Life: New Mexico Traditions and Food* (1949; Santa Fe: Museum of New Mexico Press, 1982); Cabeza de Baca, *Historic Cookery*.

7. Tey Diana Rebolledo, "Narrative Strategies of Resistance in Hispana Writing," *Journal of Narrative Technique* 20, no. 2 (Spring 1990): 136.

8. Susan Leonardi, "Recipes for Reading: Summer Pasta, Lobster à la Riseholme, and Key Lime Pie," *PMLA* 3 (May 1989): 343. Further references to this essay will appear in the text.

9. Cleofas M. Jaramillo, *Romance of a Little Village Girl* (San Antonio: Naylor, 1955), 173. Further citations will be given in the text.

10. Back cover to Diana Kennedy, *The Cuisines of Mexico* (1972; New York: Harper and Row, 1986).

11. In full, Craig Claiborne's accolade to Diana Kennedy, reprinted on the back cover of *The Art of Mexican Cooking*, reads as follows: "Diana Kennedy is the ultimate authority, the high priestess, of Mexican cooking in America. Her previous works have set the standard for any subsequent south-of-the-border cookbooks that might appeal to the English-speaking public. In this present work she has exceeded herself. If you want to cook with the most authentic Mexican taste, this volume should be your guide. I thought I knew Mexican food. This book has been an education!" (*The Art of Mexican Cooking: Traditional Mexican Cooking for Aficionados* [New York: Bantam, 1989]).

In a recent essay, food writer Jim Wood identifies Kennedy herself as the most vigorous marketing agent on her own behalf: "The recognized expert on Mexican food, she once told me, 'Don't let some wretched editor put in "one of the recognized; I am *the* recognized.'" Like Craig Claiborne's accolade, Wood's own assessment of Kennedy as a "worthy interpreter" of Mexican cuisine demonstrates how recipe exchange figures as a trope for intercultural relations more generally. ("In the Mexican Kitchen," *Image* [*San Francisco Examiner*], 10 March 1991, 30).

12. In the case of *The Cuisines of Mexico*, as Kennedy acknowledges, the book's recipes are based on the meals the author's Mexican maids cooked for her during her various sojourns in Mexico. Kennedy herself obliquely acknowledges her own anxiety about cultural appropriation in her acknowledgments to her most recent book, *The Art of Mexican Cooking*, which introduce the text as follows: "I should like to include . . . a quotation from Poppy Cannon (in her introduction to *Aromas*

and Flavours by Alice B. Toklas): 'Little by little I began to understand that there can be value in giving a fine performance of another's compositions . . . that an exquisite interpretation can be in its own way just as creative, just as imaginative as an invention' " (x).

Such anxiety is reproduced by Wood in his essay honoring Kennedy. Praising her powers not only as "a literary and culinary stylist" but as an "environmentalist" as well, he describes her ranch eighty miles outside of Mexico City as taking "sustainable agriculture to a new level. She made the place self-sufficient in the sense that a ship must be self-sufficient while at sea" ("In the Mexican Kitchen," 30). A different kind of "barco que nunca atraca/ship that will never dock" (Lorna Dee Cervantes, "Barco de Refugiados/Refugee Ship," *Emplumada* [Pittsburgh: University of Pittsburgh Press, 1981], 40–41), Wood's metaphor describes Kennedy's intercultural foray not so much as affiliating but isolating, the besieged stranger in a strange land.

13. Tey Diana Rebolledo, "Tradition and Mythology: Signatures of Landscape in Chicana Literature," in Vera Norwood and Janice Monk, eds., *The Desert Is No Lady: Southwestern Landscapes in Women's Writing and Art* (New Haven: Yale University Press, 1987), 102.

14. Marialisa Calta quotes Shange in "Take a Novel, Add a Recipe, and Season to Taste," *New York Times*, 17 February 1993, B1.

15. Calta, "Take a Novel," B1.

16. Clearly, power relations do not cease to operate at the front door of the family home. Nevertheless, I would argue that despite its being politically fraught, the intimacy of this space often makes it appear a less intimidating locus within which to work toward self-assertion. bell hooks frames this complex relation with particular eloquence: "Usually, it is within the family that we witness coercive domination and learn to accept it whether it be domination of parent over child, or male over female. Even though family relations may be, and most often are, informed by acceptance of a politic of domination, they are simultaneously relations of care and connection. It is this convergence of two contradictory impulses—the urge to promote growth and the urge to inhibit growth—that provides a practical setting for feminist critique, resistance, and transformation" (*Talking Back: thinking feminist, thinking black* [Boston: South End Press, 1989], 21).

Contemporary women writers continue to use the image of home to evoke the relation between autobiographical identity, familial history, and cultural practice. Consider, for instance, Rosemary Cho Leyson's articulation of this triad via the edible metaphor in her story "The Visit Home": "The white, short-grained rice her mother scoops into her bowl never looked so precious sitting full along the top edge of the bowl ready to be eaten. She reaches for the pyrex bowl on the table and scoops a little bit of the content onto her bowl with her chopsticks. It is chut: salted baby shrimps, fermented Korean style with ferocious Korean chili powder, garlic and all sorts of other potent ingredients. Spread across a little bit of rice, it really hits the spot. She almost feels like crying as the sensation of the food sinks into her taste buds. It is an old familiar feeling, one too precious to ever take for granted. It is the only link she has to who she is and where she is from" (in Gloria Anzaldúa, ed., *Making Face, Making Soul/Haciendo Caras: Creative and Critical Perspectives by Women of Color* [San Francisco: Aunt Lute Foundation Books, 1990], 100.

17. [Jesusita Aragón as edited by] Fran Leeper Buss, *La Partera: Story of a Midwife* (Ann Arbor: University of Michigan Press, 1980). The question of mediation in Aragón's narrative, and in collaborative autobiography more generally, deserves sustained attention. See the discussion of relations between editor and speaker in *La Partera* in chapters 3 and 4.

18. Norma Jean and Carole Darden effect a similar association of material and moral nourishment in *Spoonbread and Strawberry Wine: Recipes and Reminiscences of a Family*: "Our mother used to tell us that good food inspires good thoughts, good talk, and an atmosphere of happiness" ([New York: Fawcett Cress, 1978], 11). I am indebted to P. Gabrielle Foreman for calling my attention to this book.

19. Jessica B. Harris, *Iron Pots and Wooden Spoons: Africa's Gifts to New World Cooking* (New York: Atheneum, 1989), xxii.

20. Maya Angelou, *All God's Children Wear Traveling Shoes* (New York: Random House, 1986), 26.

21. I wish to distinguish here between those particular languages circulated in the 1960s and 1970s that make ethnic politics synonymous with the specific historical needs of cultural nationalism, and a more expansive and open-ended idea of ethnic identity itself; ethnic identity, that is, as a form of self-identification that may exploit any number of languages in order to further itself.

22. Sau-ling Cynthia Wong considers *Fifth Chinese Daughter* and Wong's exploitation of the culinary metaphor as a form of "food pornography," (after Frank Chin), in a provocative exploration of edible tropes in Asian American literature published as my own book goes to press (See 61ff. in "Big Eaters, Treat Lovers, 'Food Prostitutes,' 'Food Pornographers,' and Doughnut Makers," in *Reading Asian American Literature: From Necessity to Extravagance* [Princeton: Princeton University Press, 1993]). Her critique of Jade Snow Wong's tendency to act as "culture-broker" for a voyeuristic Anglo-American reading public is compelling, but I would argue that her characterization of Wong's "eagerness for acceptance" (64) as the "ingratiating posture" (67) of the "food pornographer" is, finally, too severe. My own reading, as framed in this chapter, stresses not so much the humility with which Wong describes her activities in the kitchen as their self-congratulatory effects. Nor can we really expect—given the exigencies of publication for American women of color during wartime (recall Hurston's *Dust Tracks*)—to hear the confident feminine speaking voice the critic describes in her call for "a robust culture created and maintained by free-acting, self-possessed men and women" (61). I

would argue that resistive utterance within such discursive and historical contexts is more likely to consist of sidelong remarks and oblique parries than straightforward, sustained criticism.

23. Thanks to Genaro Padilla for his contributions to this discussion of *Fifth Chinese Daughter.*

24. Although this chapter focuses on their culinary texts, both writers are better known for their more sustained personal narratives. If they are less clearly hybrid texts than the earlier cookbooks, both Cleofas Jaramillo's *Romance of a Little Village Girl* and Fabiola Cabeza de Baca's *We Fed Them Cactus* combine folklore and cultural history with personal reminiscence. See below, this chapter, for a discussion of the relation between ethnography and autobiography in the work of these two writers.

25. As virtually every scholar of Chicano literature notes, native Mexican people of the United States use a variety of self-identifiers to signify their ethnic identity: *Mexicano, Latino,* and *Hispano* constitute only a partial list. Each of these terms, as Ramón Saldívar indicates, "has a different psychological, historical, and political connotation that sets it apart from the others" (*Chicano Narrative: The Dialectics of Difference* [Madison: University of Wisconsin Press, 1990], 12). I use *Hispano* to refer to native Mexicans of the state of New Mexico, *nuevomexicano* as the adjectival form designating what is native Mexican New Mexican, and *Mexicano* to refer to Mexicans who are native to the United States.

26. Joan M. Jensen, "Canning Comes to New Mexico: Women and the Agricultural Extension Service 1914–1919," in Joan M. Jensen, ed., *New Mexico Women: Intercultural Perspectives* (Albuquerque: University of New Mexico Press, 1986), 207. (Further references will be included in the text). Jensen points out that Cabeza de Baca was in fact the "first demonstration agent to be assigned to the Pueblos in the 1930s" (205). While I do not concur with Jensen's conclusions, I am indebted to her essay for its historical analysis of the work of the New Mexico home demonstration agents.

27. Fabiola Cabeza de Baca, "Los Alimentos y Su Preparación," Extension Circular 129 (New Mexico: New Mexico College of Agriculture and Mechanic Arts, Agricultural Extension Service, 1934), 4. Further references will be cited in the text.

28. And see Genaro M. Padilla, "Imprisoned Narrative? Or, Lies, Secrets and Silence in New Mexico Women's Autobiography," in Hector Calderón and José David Saldívar, eds., *Criticism in the Borderlands: Studies in Chicano Literature, Culture, and Ideology* (Durham: Duke University Press, 1991): "The dominating culture . . . must make the subject forget the details of its domination and make it believe that it has not surrendered so much as availed itself of a more progressive sociocultural national experience. . . . The dispossessed elite, in addition to the modicum of political power they are granted, are also fitted with a socioideological discourse that not only accedes to their dispossession, but actually becomes the

official cultural discourse through which the subject group makes sufferable its subordination" (43–44). Further references to this essay will appear in the text.

29. Scholars of western American history have acknowledged the significant role Spanish colonization plays in understanding the region as a whole ever since historian Herbert Eugene Bolton published *The Spanish Borderlands: A Chronicle of Florida and the Southwest* (New Haven: Yale University Press, 1921). For other readings of the Southwest Conquest and its contemporary political legacies for Chicanos see, among others, Carey McWilliams, *North from Mexico: The Spanish-Speaking People of the United States* (1949; Westport: Greenwood Press, 1990); David J. Weber, *The Mexican Frontier, 1821–1846: The American Southwest Under Mexico* (Albuquerque: University of New Mexico Press, 1982); David J. Weber, ed., *Foreigners in Their Native Land: Historical Roots of the Mexican Americans* (Albuquerque: University of New Mexico Press, 1973); Rodolfo Acuña, *Occupied America: A History of Chicanos* (3d ed. New York: Harper and Row, 1988); Patricia Limerick, *The Legacy of Conquest: The Unbroken Past of the American West* (New York: W. W. Norton, 1987); and Richard White, *"It's Your Misfortune and None of My Own": A New History of the American West* (Norman: University of Oklahoma Press, 1991). For studies of the colonization of New Mexico and its aftermath, see George I. Sánchez, *Forgotten People: A Study of New Mexicans* (Albuquerque: University of New Mexico Press, 1940); Roxanne Dunbar Ortíz, *Roots of Resistance: Land Tenure in New Mexico, 1680–1980* (Los Angeles: Chicano Studies Research Center Publications, U.C.L.A., 1980); and Benjamín R. Read, *Illustrated History of New Mexico* (New York: Arno Press, 1976).

30. Rebolledo, "Tradition and Mythology," 102. See also her "Foremothers," in Tey Diana Rebolledo and Eliana S. Rivero, eds., *Infinite Divisions: An Anthology of Chicana Literature* (Tucson: University of Arizona Press, 1993).

31. Fabiola Cabeza de Baca, "New Mexican Diets," *Journal of Home Economics* (34 November 1942) 669.

32. I am writing here in dialogue with Genaro Padilla, Raymund Paredes, and Tey Diana Rebolledo, all of whom develop arguments about cultural representation in the work of Fabiola Cabeza de Baca and Cleofas Jaramillo. See Padilla and Rebolledo for other readings of cultural resistance in what appear to be purely "accommodationist" texts. For a critique of such New Mexican writers as retreating "from the contemporary world into nostalgia," their work as a "literature created out of fear and intimidation" in which "we find . . . a rather ingenuous hopefulness, a submissiveness, and a contrived and derivative romanticism," see Paredes, "The Evolution of Chicano Literature," in Houston A. Baker Jr., ed., *Three American Literatures* (New York: Modern Languages Association, 1982), 52–53.

What such productive disagreements suggest is that the terms *oppositional* and *accommodationist* are not sufficient parameters to describe the works of texts like Cabeza de Baca's and Jaramillo's, where we see *both* what Ramón Saldívar characterizes as gestures of subordination *and* those of opposition. (See, for instance, the following from Saldívar's *Chicano Narrative:* "It has been debilitating when as the contrastive other of the dominant culture, Chicano culture has become for Anglos subordinate in all respects. It has been potentially liberating when as the contrastive other Chicano culture has produced for Chicanos a consistent and highly articulated set of oppositions to the dominant cultural system surrounding it" [4]). Literary culture is rarely merely one or the other, however, nor do oppositions here necessarily have to be "highly articulated" in order to be understood.

33. Clearly such nostalgia for a "Spanish" order, in that it attempts to define Hispanos as "pura Español" (of "pure" Spanish blood) invokes a colonial frame of reference. I will argue that Jaramillo and Cabeza de Baca both tend to signify Hispano/Native American cultural difference obliquely; class inflection, to an extent, simultaneously masks and speaks for this ethnic difference. (See the discussion below of "Señora Martina" in Cabeza de Baca's *The Good Life.*) Nevertheless, I would suggest that current power relations make it impossible to discuss Spanish imperialism over indigenous populations separately from Anglo imperialism over both Mexicano and Native American people. Just as gender relations for African Americans are to a degree informed by white-black race relations in the United States (not to mention race relations in this country more generally), so Anglo-Americans, Hispanos, and Native Americans exist in an unequal, sometimes triangulated, relation to one another. In the texts of both Jaramillo and Cabeza de Baca, colonial representations are to a degree contingent upon, and work as unattractive but nevertheless understandable responses to, racism exerted over Mexicanos by the Anglo-American order. Critiquing the dominant discourse that lumps all Mexican people together as other, Cabeza de Baca insists on a less monolithic picture of Hispano life, but she does so by invoking—obliquely—Hispano colonialism over Native Americans: "Many historians and writers have contended that there was no wealth in colonial New Mexico, but there was. It was strictly a feudal system and the wealth was in the hands of the few. The *ricos* of colonial days lived in splendor with many servants and slaves. Their haciendas were similar to the Southern plantations. To those coming from what was then the United States of America, the life of the New Mexican *ricos* was not understood because they kept their private lives secure from outsiders" (*We Fed Them Cactus* [1954; Albuquerque: University of New Mexico Press, 1989], x).

34. Cleofas M. Jaramillo, *Sombras del Pasado/Shadows of the Past* (Santa Fe: Ancient City Press, 1941).

35. Lest we be too quick to criticize Jaramillo as "old-fashioned" or naive for representing culture as "pure," consider that such assurances of authenticity remain a contemporary marketing staple. See Jim Wood on Diana Kennedy's books, for instance: "Kennedy's success inspired at least half a dozen others to publish excellent cookbooks of authentic Mexican recipes. But none has sold as well" ("In the Mexican Kitchen," 30).

36. Erna Fergusson, *Mexican Cookbook* (Albuquerque: University of New Mexico Press, 1934), foreword. Page numbers are provided in the text for further quotes from this book. Citations without page numbers are from the book's unpaginated foreword.

37. This apparently unbridgeable rift in chronological, cultural, and ideological perspective becomes easier to negotiate if we consider the different subject positions the author occupies in the two texts. I have previously suggested that "Los Alimentos" locates the author as a kind of cultural intermediary, a state "agent," if you will. Writing in Spanish, speaking to an Hispano readership, the author of the "Boletín" need not articulate her identity as nuevomexicano. Cultural difference is not at issue here; what is problematized instead is her position as worker for the state. *The Good Life*, by contrast, assumes an extra-cultural audience and constructs its subject accordingly. Here it is the author's affiliation with an ethnic community that authorizes her to speak about "New Mexico Traditions and Food." The Introduction to *The Good Life* concisely traces this shift in self-representation: "As a home economist I am happy to see modern kitchens and improved diets, but my artistic soul deplores the passing of beautiful customs which in spite of New Mexico's isolation in the past, gave us happiness and abundant living" (*The Good Life*, 4).

38. For other representations of this cultural plenitude, see the narrative of Leonardo Martínez, as transcribed by Patricia Preciado Martin in *Images and Conversations: Mexican Americans Recall a Southwestern Past* (Tucson: University of Arizona Press, 1983); see also that of Jesusita Aragón in *La Partera*. Interestingly, the same kinds of food catalogues appear in black culinary narrative too. Operating out of a different historical problematic, however, their cultural and political resonances are distinct as well. See chapter 2 for a reading of some of these lists.

39. As cited by Calta, "Take a Novel," B1. See also Margaret Abreu's "In the New Mexico Kitchen," *New Mexico* (March 1940), 36. In a recipe for menudo, Abreu practices a similar kind of cultural proprietorship. Although she offers her recipes to an intercultural audience, her narrative drives a wedge between native and nonnative readers: "It is too bad that American slang has given some words a ridiculous slant and made such classics as 'balmy,' 'nuts' and 'tripe' derisive in meaning. *Menudo* is tripe, a delicious dish when properly prepared. . . . *Menudo*, as prepared in a New Mexican kitchen is indeed a great delicacy. Its preparation from the source to the cooking pot is not a very enjoyable task unless one is used to it. I am and I like it. There is a feeling there, in taking the article in the raw, emptying its contents and through a series of operations preparing for the table and my guests a white, spotless and fascinating dish" (36). As in Cabeza de Baca, language here is culturally contingent—both the dish itself and the undefined "feeling" accompanying it cannot be properly enjoyed by the "uninitiated cook," who instead "may order one, already prepared, from the butcher."

40. The same kind of attention to the limits of cultural translation are operative

in the writer's *Historic Cookery*. See, for instance, her discussion of "guisar": "Your experiments in New Mexican cookery can be fascinating. Remember, though, that when you try any of these recipes, you should be prepared to spend plenty of time. *Guisar*, which has no exact English equivalent, is the most popular word in the native homemaker's vocabulary. Roughly translated, it means to dress up food, perhaps only by adding a little onion or a pinch of oregano; good food always deserves a finishing touch. Food must never taste flat, but it will—if it's not guisado" (1).

For a more contemporary revoicing of the limits of extra-cultural access, see Susana Archuleta's recollections in Nan Elsasser, Kyle MacKenzie, and Yvonne Tixier y Vigil, eds., *Las Mujeres: Conversations from a Hispanic Community* (Old Westbury, N.Y.: Feminist Press, 1980), 36–41: "Think about making tortillas. You can read about making tortillas from a recipe and you most likely will be able to make the dough. But to roll them? And to cook them? You can't learn that from a recipe" (40).

41. Like the *partera* (midwife), curanderas have historically worked in opposition to the (Anglo) medical establishment. The American Medical Association has consistently attempted to undermine their practices in order, at least in part, to secure a monopoly over medical service. See chapters 3 and 4 for a discussion of midwifery in collaborative personal narrative.

42. In one sense, then, the author herself takes on the work of curandera by providing her readership with this description of alternative medical practices.

43. Rebolledo, "Tradition and Mythology," 105.

44. Abreu, "In the New Mexico Kitchen," 36. Note how cultural affirmation also gives voice to an uncompromising "I": "Menudo, as prepared in a New Mexican kitchen is indeed a great delicacy. Its preparation from the source to the cooking pot is not a very enjoyable task unless one is used to it. *I am and I like it*" (emphasis added).

Chapter Two

1. LeRoi Jones, "Soul Food," in Gladys J. Curry, ed., *Viewpoints from Black America* (1962; Englewood Cliffs, N.J.: Prentice Hall, 1970), 85–86.

2. VertaMae Smart-Grosvenor, *Vibration Cooking; Or, The Travel Notes of a Geechee Girl* (1970; New York: Ballantine, 1986). Further references will appear in the text.

3. María Amparo Ruiz de Burton, *The Squatter and the Don*, ed. Rosaura Sánchez and Beatrice Pita (1885; Houston: Arte Público, 1992); "Poema para los Californios Muertos" in Lorna Dee Cervantes, *Emplumada* (Pittsburgh: University of Pittsburgh Press, 1981), 42–43.

4. This is not to say that an interest in defining what constitutes a national literature (more precisely, a nationalist literature *de la raza*) does not operate in

Chicano narrative contemporaneous with the Black Arts Movement of the late 1960s and early 1970s, merely that what is defined as Chicano/Mexicano at this particular historical moment often involves redrawing or ignoring international boundaries in such a way that distinctions between Mexicanos of Mexico and of the United States become less important, for Chicanos, than their shared mythopoetic heritage, a heritage most concisely represented by the invocation to Aztlán. Nevertheless, writers of both sides define themselves in contradistinction to one another as well.

5. Joanne M. Braxton, *Black Women Writing Autobiography: A Tradition Within a Tradition* (Philadelphia: Temple University Press, 1989), 2.

6. Houston A. Baker Jr., *Blues, Ideology, and Afro-American Literature: A Vernacular Theory* (Chicago: University of Chicago Press, 1984), 202.

7. Alan Grubb, "House and Home in the Victorian South: The Cookbook as Guide," in Carol Bleser, ed., *In Joy and in Sorrow: Women, Family, and Marriage in the Victorian South, 1830–1900* (New York: Oxford University Press, 1991), 173.

8. Judith Rollins, *Between Women: Domestics and Their Employers* (Philadelphia: Temple University Press, 1985), 230.

9. Sarah Rice, *He Included Me: The Autobiography of Sarah Rice,* transcribed and ed. Louise Westling (Athens: University of Georgia Press, 1989), 52. In full, the passage reads: "She could take a cookbook and then use her own ingenuity and imagination and invent wonderful things. Whatever she did, she did with a love for doing it well and put her imagination in it. She wanted her work to look good, taste good, and last long. She believed in quality."

10. That recipes have an exchange value, quite literally, is noted by Michelle Cliff in her reading of Fanny Hurst's *Imitation of Life*, which resonates with Nell Kane's story: "Delilah carries with her various recipes, and these prove to be the 'salvation' of Miss B. and family. In a relatively short time, Miss B. is the proprietor of a chain of restaurants in which Delilah's food is the main attraction, and which are recognized by a likeness of Delilah on the sign" ("Object into Subject: Some Thoughts on the Work of Black Women Artists," in Gloria Anzaldúa, ed., *Making Face, Making Soul/Haciendo Caras: Creative and Critical Perspectives by Women of Color* (San Francisco: Aunt Lute Foundation Books, 1990), 277.

11. Genaro M. Padilla, *My History, Not Yours: The Formation of Mexican American Autobiography* (Madison: University of Wisconsin Press, 1993), 223.

12. Stokely Carmichael, "Toward Black Liberation," in Larry Neal and LeRoi Jones, eds., *Black Fire* (New York: William Morrow, 1968), 129.

13. Don E. Lee, *Think Black* (New York: Broadside Press, 1969); Don E. Lee, *Black Pride* (New York: Broadside Press, 1968); Larry Neal, *Black Boogaloo: Notes on Black Liberation* (San Francisco: Journal of Black Poetry Press, 1969).

14. Houston A. Baker, Jr., ed., *Black Literature in America* (New York: McGraw-Hill, 1971), 17.

15. Ralph Ellison, *Invisible Man* (1947; New York: Vintage, 1972); James Bald-

win, *Shadow and Act* (New York: Random House, 1955); James Baldwin, *The Fire Next Time* (1962; New York: Vintage, 1993) (further citations to this book will appear in the text); LeRoi Jones, *Blues People: Negro Music in White America* (New York: William Morrow, 1963); James T. Stewart, "The Development of the Black Revolutionary Artist," James Boggs, "Black Power—A Scientific Concept Whose Time Has Come," and Larry Neal, "An Afterword," all in Neal and Jones, eds., *Black Fire.*

16. Larry Neal, "An Afterword: And Shine Swam On," in Neal and Jones, eds., *Black Fire,* 654–55. Further references will appear in the text.

17. William J. Harris calls attention to Baraka's change of heart in LeRoi Jones, *The LeRoi Jones/Amiri Baraka Reader,* ed. William J. Harris (New York: Thunder's Mouth Press, 1991); LeRoi Jones, "The Myth of a 'Negro' Literature," in Curry, ed., *Viewpoints from Black America,* 110.

18. Hertha D. Wong, "Pictographs as Autobiography: Plains Indian Sketchbooks of the Late Nineteenth and Early Twentieth Centuries," *American Literary History* (Summer 1989): 297.

19. Arnold Krupat, *Ethnocriticism: Ethnography, History, Literature* (Berkeley: University of California Press, 1992), 20.

20. Cited in Kristal Brent Zook, "Light Skinned-ded Naps," in Anzaldúa, ed., *Making Face, Making Soul/Haciendo Caras,* 89.

21. N. Scott Momaday, *The Way to Rainy Mountain* (Albuquerque: University of New Mexico Press, 1969).

22. Karen Fields, Introduction to Mamie Garvin Fields with Karen Fields, *Lemon Swamp and Other Places: A Carolina Memoir* (New York: Free Press, 1983), xiii–xiv. Further references will appear in the text.

23. Here, of course, I am referring to Booker T. Washington, whose famous 1895 address at the Atlanta Exposition, and its recapitulation in the pages of his autobiography, *Up from Slavery* (New York, 1902), advocated a program of vocational education for blacks that was decried by W. E. B. DuBois and others as excessively conciliatory.

24. It would be interesting to compare the cultural politics of Ntozake Shange's 1982 novel *Sassafras, Cypress and Indigo* (New York: St. Martin's Press) with the Dardens' representation of the familial and cultural collective (*Spoonbread and Strawberry Wine: Recipes and Reminiscences of a Family* [New York: Fawcett Cress, 1978]). Like the Dardens' culinary autobiography, Shange's novel represents the exchange and reproduction of recipes as intrafamilial (and, as in *Spoonbread and Strawberry Wine,* recipes are interwoven into a story narrated by sisters). A recipe for Christmas duck accompanying a letter from a mother to a daughter, for instance, is described as "a dish full of love and history" (133).

25. Carmichael, "Toward Black Liberation," 128.

26. James T. Stewart, "The Development of the Black Revolutionary Artist," in Neal and Jones, eds., *Black Fire.* Further references will be cited in the text.

27. I am borrowing Joanne Braxton's assessment in *Black Women Writing Autobiography*, 30.

28. Marialisa Calta,"Take a Novel, Add a Recipe, and Season to Taste," *New York Times,* 17 February 1993, B1, B4.

29. Republished in Amiri Baraka, *Home: Social Essays* (New York: William Morrow, 1966).

30. Stokely Carmichael, "Power and Racism," in Curry, ed., *Viewpoints from Black America,* 226.

31. Addison Gayle, "Cultural Strangulation: Black Literature and the White Aesthetic," in Baker, ed., *Black Literature in America,* 374.

32. This trope for cultural poverty is not limited to the African American literary tradition. Consider, for instance, Teatro Nuestro's play *La Boda* (1989), where the contrast between the Mexican hero's spiritually and culturally full family life and his Anglo boss's emotionally impoverished existence is demonstrated through a comparison between the former's enjoyment of a carefully prepared supper, complete with homemade tortillas, and the latter's birthday dinner—a lavish affair of Kentucky Fried Chicken and Safeway birthday cake. Compare this passage from Alfredo Véa Jr.'s novel *La Maravilla* (New York: Dutton, 1993): "He's gonna need a balanced diet, Vernetta. You got to learn to cook *adobo* and *lechon* and *pancit* to go along with the red beans and chitlins. Otherwise, his soul will be starving and you won't even know it. You feed him that white food and you take the red out of his marrow, kill his spirit. That other food will stick in his gullet. . . . Then he'll probably be lost like all them disconnected white folk eatin' all that processed food" (136).

33. And see James Baldwin's exhortation in *The Fire Next Time,* where white bread represents a similar lack of cultural sustenance: "To be sensual, I think, is to respect and rejoice in the force of life, of life itself, and to be *present* in all that one does, from the effort of loving to the breaking of bread. It will be a great day for America, incidentally, when we begin to eat bread again, instead of the blasphemous and tasteless foam rubber that we have substituted for it. And I am not being frivolous now, either" (43).

34. Amiri Baraka, *Black Magic: Collected Poetry, 1961–1967* (Indianapolis: Bobbs-Merrill, 1969).

35. Michael M. J. Fischer, "Ethnicity and the Post-Modern Arts of Memory," in James Clifford and George E. Marcus, eds., *Writing Culture: The Poetics and Politics of Ethnography* (Berkeley: University of California Press, 1988).

36. S. Frank Miyamoto's introduction to Monica Sone's *Nisei Daughter* (1953; Seattle: University of Washington Press, 1987) provides an interesting example of how complex the reproduction of culture can be. Describing the kind of cultural work the Japanese Language School provided for Seattle Nisei before the Second World War, he comments: "The School . . . was minimally successful in teaching the language but highly effective in establishing lasting associations" (xi).

37. John Brenkman, *Culture and Domination* (Ithaca: Cornell University Press, 1988), 24.

Chapter Three

1. [Jesusita Aragón as edited by] Fran Leeper Buss, *La Partera: Story of a Midwife* (Ann Arbor: University of Michigan Press, 1980). Further citations will be given in the text. For Buss's assessment of AMA medicine see, in particular, 6–7 of her Introduction and Appendix 1, "Network," 113–18, 121.

2. As with autobiographical texts more generally, many attempts have been made to define what constitutes a life history/first-person oral account. Bob Blauner's "Problems of Editing 'First-Person' Sociology," *Qualitative Sociology* (Spring 1987), provides a particularly cogent definition: "I define the first-person study as any book or article in which the findings are presented predominantly directly through the narratives or accounts of interview subjects, rather than distilled through the summaries or analysis of the writer, and in which the presentation of such 'personal document' material rather than the author's point of view is considered the primary goal" (47). Further references to this article will appear in the text.

3. Onnie Lee Logan, *Motherwit: An Alabama Midwife's Story*, as told to Katherine Clark (New York: E. P. Dutton, 1989). Succeeding references will appear in the text.

4. See the publisher's comments on the back cover of *La Partera*.

5. J. Whitridge Williams, "Medical Education and the Midwife Problem in the United States," *Journal of the American Medical Association* 58 (January 1912), in Judy Barrett Litoff, *The American Midwife Debate: A Sourcebook on Its Modern Origins* (Westport: Greenwood Press, 1986), 95, 97.

6. Judy Barrett Litoff, *American Midwives: 1860 to the Present* (Westport: Greenwood Press, 1978), 73.

7. Litoff, *American Midwives*, 99.

8. Statistics are from Litoff, *American Midwives*, 99, 55–58.

9. Jessica Mitford, "Teach Midwifery, Go to Jail," *This World* (San Francisco *Chronicle*), 21 October 1990, 8.

10. Pat Ellis Taylor, Introduction to Jewel Babb, *Border Healing Woman: The Story of Jewel Babb as Told to Pat Ellis Taylor* (Austin: University of Texas Press, 1981), 109. Further citations will be given in the text.

11. Litoff, *American Midwives*, 103.

12. E. R. Hardin, "The Midwife Problem," *Southern Medical Journal* 18 (May 1925), in Litoff, *The American Midwife Debate*, 148.

13. As quoted in Litoff, *American Midwives*, 78.

14. United States Department of Labor, *Proceedings of Conference on Better Care for Mothers and Babies: Held in Washington, D.C., January 17–18, 1938,*

Bureau Pub. No. 246 (Washington, D.C.: U.S. Government Printing Office, 1938), 95.

15. Quoted in Litoff, *American Midwives,* 72.

16. Texas State Board of Health, Bureau of Child Hygiene, "Report on the Midwife Survey in Texas, January 2, 1925," (1924), in Litoff, *The American Midwife Debate,* 69, 70, 69.

17. In her discussion of Plains Indian pictographic autobiography in *Sending My Heart Back Across the Years* (New York: Oxford University Press, 1992), Hertha Wong points out that the titles of such sketchbooks as "The Life of the Red-Man, Illustrated by a Kiowa Brave" and "Scenes for Indian Life, Drawn by Howling Wolf," both edited by Anglo-Americans, make clear that the editorial interest lay in "depicting a generalized presentation of Indians, rather than the personal artistic interpretations of individuals" (66). In the chapter "Pictographs as Autobiography," among others, Wong's readings of Native American collaborative autobiography focus in suggestive ways on many of the issues discussed in this chapter.

18. Hamilton Holt, ed., *The Life Stories of (Undistinguished) Americans as Told by Themselves* (1906; New York: Routledge, 1990), unpaginated "Note." Further citations will appear in the text.

19. Mary Paik Lee, *Quiet Odyssey: A Pioneer Korean Woman in America,* ed. Sucheng Chan (Seattle: University of Washington Press, 1990); Rigoberta Menchú, *I . . . Rigoberta Menchú: An Indian Woman in Guatemala,* ed. Elisabeth Burgos-Debray (New York: Verso, 1984).

20. Or, as Theresa Tensuan pointed out to me, it involves writers in disputes about inauthenticity and narrative discontinuity, charges which demonstrate "people clinging to the idea that the writer of color presents a transparent narrative which critics and editors can then reconstruct and interpret." Personal communication, 7 December 1990.

21. Philippe Lejeune, "The Autobiography of Those Who Do Not Write," in his *On Autobiography* (Minneapolis: University of Minnesota Press, 1989), 185–215 (further citations will appear in the text). In addition, a number of scholars have been critical of the speaker-editor relation in collaborative texts. See, for instance, Cletus E. Daniel's Introduction to Victoria Byerly's *Hard Times Cotton Mill Girls: Personal Histories of Womanhood and Poverty in the South* (Ithaca: ILR Press, 1986); Arnold Krupat's *The Voice in the Margin: Native American Literature and the Canon* (Berkeley: University of California Press, 1989); Genaro M. Padilla's "Leaving a 'Clean and Honorable Name': Rafael Chacón's 'Memorias,' " in his *My History, Not Yours: The Formation of Mexican American Autobiography* (Madison: University of Wisconsin Press, 1993); Greg Sarris's *Keeping Slug Woman Alive: A Holistic Approach to American Indian Texts* (Berkeley: University of California Press, 1993); and Hertha Wong's *Sending My Heart Back Across the Years: Tradition and Innovation in Native American Autobiography* (New York: Oxford University Press, 1992). For considerations of specific feminine collaborations, see

Katherine Borland, " 'That's Not What I Said': Interpretive Conflict in Oral Narrative Research," Daphne Patai, "U.S. Academics and Third World Women: Is Ethical Research Possible?" and Claudia Salazar, "A Third World Woman's Text: Between the Politics of Criticism and Cultural Politics," all in Sherna Berger Gluck and Daphne Patai, eds., *Women's Words: The Feminist Practice of Oral History* (New York: Routledge, 1991); as well as Carole Boyce Davies's essay, "Collaboration and the Ordering Imperative in Life Story Production" in Sidonie Smith and Julia Watson, eds., *De/Colonizing the Subject: The Politics of Gender in Women's Autobiography* (Minneapolis: University of Minnesota Press, 1992). All these essays acknowledge the editor as helping to construct, not simply relaying, the speaker's narrative. Borland cautions editors not to assume that their gloss matches the speaker's: "Presumably, the patterns upon which we base our interpretations can be shown to inhere in the 'original' narrative, but our aims in pointing out certain features, or in making connections between the narrative and larger cultural formations, may at times differ from the original narrator's intentions" (64). Salazar considers Rigoberta Menchú's collaboratively produced *I . . . Rigoberta Menchú*, suggesting that what is most "revealing" about editor Elisabeth Burgos-Debray's contributions is "how deeply transformed Rigoberta's way of talking becomes, despite the editor's naive beliefs to the contrary. . . . Burgos-Debray's editorial orchestration in the highly problematic role of Rigoberta's transparent 'double' produces a text that is more informative of her and her readers' own interpretive agendas . . . that reflects our own assumptions about what a narrative by someone like Rigoberta should look like" (99). Carole Boyce Davies develops a similar critique of editorial repression, commenting on the erasure of the speaker in a number of jointly produced texts that attribute authority only to the editor. Like me, Patai sets the "average U.S. female academic—white and middle-class" in opposition "to her average 'Third World' object of research—nonwhite and/or poor" (137).

22. Joan M. Jensen, "Oral History of Working Class Women in the Southwest," in Nancy E. Loe, ed., *A Sense of Community: A Framework for Women's Oral History*, Working Paper No. 12 (Tucson: Southwest Institute for Research on Women, 1982), 10.

23. Patai, "U.S. Academics and Third World Women," 139.

24. Mourning Dove, *Cogewea, the Half-Blood: A Depiction of the Great Montana Cattle Range*, ed. Lucullus Virgil McWhorter, introduction by Dexter Fisher (Lincoln: University of Nebraska Press, 1981), viii.

25. Cited in Krupat, *Voice in the Margin*, 112.

26. Ramón Saldívar, *Chicano Narrative: The Dialectics of Difference* (Madison: University of Wisconsin Press, 1990), 156.

27. Krupat, *Voice in the Margin*, 225.

28. Kevin Dwyer, *Moroccan Dialogues: Anthropology in Question* (Baltimore: Johns Hopkins University Press, 1982), 260–261, 263.

29. The interviewers' extensive commentary would probably preclude Neil M. Cowan and Ruth Schwartz Cowan's *Our Parents' Lives: The Americanization of Eastern European Jews* (New York: Basic Books, 1989) from inclusion as a "first-person" study according to Blauner's definition. The Cowans' use of oral interview is extensive, however, and provides one particularly striking illustration of intra-racial mediation in which the "object" of study is situated ethnographically. See, in particular, "A Note on the Text": "In order to protect the anonymity of the people we interviewed, we have changed people's names and various identifying details in their stories. In doing this, we have tried to remain both historically and demo-graphically sensible, transforming an Isaac into an Aaron perhaps, but not into a Jason or a Lance; moving someone from Boston to Philadelphia perhaps, but not from Chicago to Paterson or New London. Further to protect anonymity, but also to assure readability, we have created composite characters: *defining types of peo-ple and then merging several individual voices into one character who represents the type*—a professional who was born in the United States, for example, or a factory worker who was born and lived abroad until her teens" (xxiv; emphasis added).

30. Genaro Padilla, "The Mexican Immigrant as °: The (de)Formation of Mexi-can Immigrant Life Story," in Robert Folkenflik, ed., *The Culture of Autobiogra-phy: The Constructions of Self-Representation* (Stanford: Stanford University Press, 1993), 128.

31. Of course, this formulation needs to grant that cultural reproduction oper-ates within a political system that assigns different traditions unequal values. See Johannes Fabian's critique of anthropology, *Time and the Other: How Anthropol-ogy Makes Its Object* (New York: Columbia University Press, 1983), for an ex-tended analysis of the ways in which time becomes, in anthropological discourse, "much like language or money . . . a carrier of significance, a form through which we define the content of relations between the Self and the Other" (ix). Fabian argues that anthropology denies its subject "coevalness," demonstrating instead "a persistent and systematic tendency to place the referent(s) of anthropology in a Time other than the present of the producer of anthropological discourse" (31).

32. James Clifford, *The Predicament of Culture: Twentieth-Century Ethnogra-phy, Literature, and Art* (Cambridge: Harvard University Press, 1988), 51.

33. See, for instance, Elizabeth Fox-Genovese, "My Statue, My Self: Autobio-graphical Writings of Afro-American Women," in Shari Benstock, ed., *The Private Self: Theory and Practice of Women's Autobiographical Writings* (Chapel Hill: University of North Carolina Press, 1988); or my own " 'I Made the Ink': (Literary) Production and Reproduction in *Dessa Rose* and *Beloved*," *Signs* 16, 2 (Summer 1990).

34. I would also note here that the writing of James Fenimore Cooper, the archetype for many later literary evocations of the "noble savage," represents Chin-gachgook as an "abstraction" (*The Last of the Mohicans* [1826; New York: Penguin,

1987], 341). More generally, "Indian fortitude" turns "each dark and motionless figure into stone" (341). Once again an "ethnic Other" serves as model.

35. Lejeune's assumption here about responsibility is undercut by his earlier point about collaboration. It seems to me that there are openings in Lejeune which his own prose tends to foreclose, and it is those openings I would like to address here.

36. Chan recalls in her editor's preface to Lee, *Quiet Odyssey*, that her own prompting did not always lead Lee to disclosure. "Anything else?" she recalls asking. "Certainly there are other things I remember, but I'd rather not tell about them" (xvii). The editor also recognizes this unwillingness to speak as a strategy of resistance to her own "not entirely-successful efforts to elicit more information from her. As I interviewed her, I came to realize that the story told here is what Mary Paik Lee wants to pass down to posterity: It is a self-conscious testament, complete unto itself" (137–38).

37. Salazar, "A Third World Woman's Text," 101, quoting p. 247 of Menchú's autobiography. See also Carole Boyce Davies's "Collaboration" for her gloss on speaker-editor relations in Marjorie Shostak's *Nisa: The Life and Words of a !Kung Woman* (Cambridge: Harvard University Press, 1981), in which she provides a way to read in Nisa's agency in the collaborative project (9).

38. What I am suggesting here is that we take into account how the context of feminist scholarship within which such narratives are produced tends to amplify any gesture of a particular speaker's that articulates a distinctively feminine authority. While I do not devalue the ways speakers position themselves as women, it seems to me that feminine authority is often very clearly expressed in the text because it is not only in the speaker's but in the editor's interest to do so.

39. Thanks to Genaro Padilla for first posing this question about Lejeune's assumption here.

40. Mamie Garvin Fields with Karen Fields, *Lemon Swamp and Other Places: A Carolina Memoir* (New York: Free Press, 1983). Further citations will appear in the text. Kevin Dwyer's analysis in *Moroccan Dialogues* of the relation between editorial introduction and narrative proper in ethnographic texts provides another demonstration of how such a division between "explanation" and "data" reasserts the (anthropological) editor as solitary subject/author: "In the anecdotal account, to the contrary, anthropologist and informant may both appear as subjects, but the fieldwork experience is still used to erect a barrier between Self and Other. First, the anecdotal account is explicitly opposed to the 'ethnography' and usually appears either as the introduction to the ethnography proper, or fills alone an entire volume. Here, the anthropologist's experience is sharply divided into its 'personal' aspects, exemplified in anecdotal 'tribulations' (as Malinowski revealingly called them) . . . and 'work,' which produces the 'data' in which personal experience supposedly plays no role. With this opposition, the author reiterates and reinforces the immunity of the Self: the activity of the Other remains the object of anthropologi-

cal 'explanation' and analysis while the Self's restricted to the anecdote, is sheltered from them" (266).

41. Patricia Zavella, "Recording Chicana Life Histories: Refining the Insider's Perspective," in Elizabeth Jameson, ed., *Insider/Outsider Relationships with Informants*, Working Paper No. 13 (Tucson: Southwest Institute for Research on Women, University of Arizona, 1982), 20–21.

42. Judith Stacey, "Can There Be a Feminist Ethnography?" in Gluck and Patai, eds., *Women's Words*, 116.

43. Elizabeth Jameson, "May and Me: Relationships with Informants and the Community", in Jameson, ed., *Insider/Outsider Relationships,* 11.

44. Borland, " 'That's Not What I Said,' " 72.

45. Personal communication, January 1993.

46. Sarah Rice, *He Included Me: The Autobiography of Sarah Rice,* transcribed and ed. Louise Westling (Athens: University of Georgia Press, 1989). Further citations will be included in the text.

47. Davies, "Collaboration," 12.

48. See especially chapter 5 of Judith Rollins, *Between Women: Domestics and Their Employers* (Philadelphia: Temple University Press, 1985).

49. This dialogue between transcriber and speaker over who will control the text also provides a metaphor for the dialogic nature of cultural authority. Just as the attempt to hide editorial intervention reveals the speaker's own exertion of agency, so efforts to write the American cultural script as a monolithic storyline of dominant versus dying cultures affirm, despite themselves, the fact that politically oppressed groups articulate authority through cultural practice. By pointing to the way in which an apparently fixed subjectivity is the outcome of a relation between editor and speaker, such life histories remind us that the plot of cultural demise is itself produced; it is merely one description of the complicated relation between political power and cultural practice.

50. The weight of editorial authority preempts the speaker's narrative in a similar fashion in *Quiet Odyssey.* Sucheng Chan's expansive introduction provides political and historical context for Mary Paik Lee's story. Nevertheless, her rigorously scholarly appendices, which "fact-check" Lee's recollections, tend, coming at the close of this text, to pull the rug from under Lee's feet. Again the issue is whether Lee's self-scripting is read as such or, as Chan directs readers to do, is glossed as an illustration of Korean American history.

51. Daniel, Introduction to Byerly's *Hard Times Cotton Mill Girls,* x.

52. Arnold Krupat, *For Those Who Come After: A Study of Native American Autobiography* (Berkeley: University of California Press, 1985), 68.

53. The death of the speaker coincides with narrative closure in *Motherwit* as well: "I was a good midwife. One of the best as they say. This book was the last thing I had planned to do until God said well done. I consider myself—in fact if I leave tomorrow—I've lived my life and I've lived it well" (177).

54. I am indebted to Barbara Christian's suggestive allusions to Pauline Hopkins's 1900 novel *Contending Forces* when I invoke its title here (personal communication, March 1990).

Chapter Four

1. Gregorita Rodríguez, *Singing for My Echo: Memories of Gregorita Rodríguez, a Native Healer of Santa Fe,* as told to Edith Powers (Santa Fe: Cota Editions, 1987). Further references will be included in the text.

Note also the presumptuousness of address in the decision to call an older woman by the diminutive, a form of the name more appropriate as a familial endearment than as a professional appellation. This forced intimacy is characteristic as well of *La Partera* and of address in Bobette Perrone, H. Henrietta Stockel, and Victoria Krueger, eds., *Medicine Women, Curanderas, and Women Doctors* (Norman: University of Oklahoma Press, 1989). Further references to this latter book will appear in the text.

2. And see the editorial introduction of Mrs. Rodríguez in this book, which emphasizes her work not as a midwife but as a politico. They first met her, the editors recall, "at a New Mexican political function in the early 1970s. She was surrounded by incumbents and candidates for local offices, all of whom sought her political support, not her medical advice. In Santa Fe, Gregorita Rodríguez is a political powerhouse . . . whose ties into the large ethnic community can control and guarantee a block of votes any contender would be happy to have" (107).

3. [Jesusita Aragón as edited by] Fran Leeper Buss, *La Partera: Story of a Midwife* (Ann Arbor: University of Michigan Press, 1980); Onnie Lee Logan, *Motherwit: An Alabama Midwife's Story,* as told to Katherine Clark (New York: E. P. Dutton, 1989); Jewel Babb, *Border Healing Woman: The Story of Jewel Babb as Told to Pat Ellis Taylor* (Austin: University of Texas Press, 1981). Further citations to these works will be given in the text.

4. Tey Diana Rebolledo, "Tradition and Mythology: Signatures of Landscape in Chicana Literature," in Vera Norwood and Janice Monk, eds., *The Desert Is No Lady: Southwestern Landscapes in Women's Writing and Art* (New Haven: Yale University Press, 1987), 102.

5. In an essay on the language of Victorian medical journals in England, Mary Poovey notes that many physicians aimed at a radical separation between obstetrics and midwifery: "It is interesting to note that W. Tyler Smith was intent upon eliminating the very word *midwife* from medical language and in sharply distinguishing between scientific, male-administered obstetrics and unscientific, female-dominated 'midwifery.' 'We may confidently hope,' he states in his first obstetric lecture, 'that hereafter the sign of the escape of midwifery from the midwife will be . . . obscure and insignificant, and that the very term *midwifery* will be relegated on account of its derivation': *Lancet,* 1847, vol. 2:371" (" 'Scenes of an Indelicate

Character': The Medical 'Treatment' of Victorian Women," *Representations* 14 (1986): 158.

This quotation from *Congratulations* (circa 1941), Beth-El Hospital's magazine for new mothers, provides a further illustration of the physician as agent of patriarchal control: "You are at home in your hospital, the home in which your baby first opened astonished eyes on this perplexing world. Very likely you have never thought of a hospital as a home, but that's precisely what it is—a place of refuge and solace for those in need of medical and surgical aid, where they may be assured of scientific care. What a comfort to think that your baby, and you too, have available such medical skill and modern nursing technique! . . . So here you are comfortably propped up in bed, in a home-like room, with a smiling nurse in attendance. . . . Then there's the doctor whose visits are presaged by everyone bustling about to have things in readiness. Could there ever be another man so kind and understanding! You can tell the goodlooking young intern is as devoted to him as you are. . . . Then one fine day, your nurse comes in and says, 'The doctor is letting you sit up for ten minutes today!' " (Cited in Neil M. Cowan and Ruth Schwartz Cowan, *Our Parents' Lives: The Americanization of Eastern European Jews* [New York: Basic Books, 1989], 188).

6. Discussions such as Aragón's acknowledge the role of hegemony in particular cultural practices such as midwifery. See Cowan and Cowan for descriptions of recommended child-care practices as a means to "educate" (read: "assimilate") recent Jewish immigrants: "Earlier in the century, in the shtetls of Lithuania, the ghettos of Warsaw, or even the tenements of Chicago, a pregnant Jewish woman might, if she had a question or a problem, consult her mother or her sister, or perhaps a midwife, a rabbi, or a neighbor. By the second decade of the century, such a woman, if she were living in the United States, would be more likely to consult a 'professional'—an outsider, someone who was neither Jewish nor a member of the community. The midwives, rabbis and relatives had been replaced by specialists—physicians, nurses. . . . [The reformers] hoped to alter the child-rearing practices of the nation's most recent immigrants [so as to produce] . . . the best type of citizen for a democratic republic. . . . The obvious course of action was to establish a national standard for the care of mothers and infants and persuade parents across the land to adhere to it" (177, 180–81). See chapter 3 for a more extended discussion of this issue.

7. For another illustration of the conflict between Aragón's own assessment of her work and editorial reinterpretation of it, see chapter 9 of *Medicine Women, Curanderas, and Women Doctors*. Despite its publication some seventy years after Dr. Underwood's dramatization of "voodoo obstetrics," the editors' introduction to Aragón provides us with a similarly fantastic picture, complete with monstrous incubi and blood, blood, blood: "Headless babies, infants with deformed and bleeding spines, tiny rotting fingers being expelled separately, one at a time in some cases—Jesusita had seen it all before she was fifteen. Blood, blood, and more blood

in the bed, on the floor, sometimes even soaking into the whitewashed adobe walls, was part of her young life" (115).

8. Josiah Macy Jr. Foundation, *The Midwife in the United States: Report of a Macy Conference* (New York: S-H Service Agency, 1968), 25.

9. Adrienne Rich, *Of Woman Born: Motherhood as Experience and Institution,* as quoted in Poovey, " 'Scenes of an Indelicate Character,' " 138.

10. Bernard R. Ortiz de Montellano discusses this change in the method of delivery in "Aztec Survivals in Modern Folk Medicine," *Grito del Sol* 2 (1979): 11–27, suggesting that medical reliance on a supine delivery ignores the specific contexts of rural and working-class maternity and carries largely negative consequences for the mother in labor: "Doctors in Mexico have been trying for years to get midwives to adopt the 'modern' prone position for their clients. Ironically, this modern position has been strongly criticized on the grounds that it does not allow the force of gravity to help, that it makes spontaneous childbirth more difficult, and thus requires chemical intervention, the use of forceps, and episiotomies. In this case, modern medicine is attempting to replace a perfectly valid practice by a technique which may be acceptable in a hospital setting but is clearly inferior in many cases, and particularly in rural situations where a midwife is in attendance, and where medical facilities are not available" (16).

11. See the discussion of the discourse of scientific progress in chapter 1.

12. Because readers see this defense of her integrity only once does not, of course, mean that Aragón herself did not call attention to areas of contention in other instances, but merely that the editor has chosen to include only this particular acknowledgment of potential conflict between herself and the speaker. Indeed, one might consider the editor's description of the interview process as providing a further (metatextual) instance both of this conflict and of Aragón's strategy for negotiating it in such a way as to maintain authority over the script: "While we worked on the tapes Jesusita would answer the phone or door as many as eight times an hour. The interruptions came from many sources; some were her friends, from both out of town and in Las Vegas, who had come to share news or to ask for help with their troubles or to bring herbs to use in her healings. She also had patients arrive at her door . . . or people coming for other reasons, asking her advice" (9). Such "interruptions" may allow Aragón to disrupt the flow of Buss's questioning in order to refashion the narrative according to her own design. Significantly, this same pattern of interruptions is described by Aragón herself in the text as the way she obtained the upper hand over the factory boss who was attempting to direct her work there.

13. For other examples of Logan's authorization of explicit censure through direct appeal to her editor, see pages 36, 43, and 86.

14. Such self-authorizing remarks are typical of the narrative as a whole. See, for instance, the discussions of resistance to an explicitly racist medical authority

on pages 107 and 166, and the assertion of medical skill, to the detriment of the physician, on page 142.

15. Such religious rhetoric surfaces again and again in *Motherwit* as a strategy both for defying white medical authority and for reinforcing her own. See, for instance, the assertions on 84, 91, 105, and 145.

16. Philippe Lejeune, "The Autobiography of Those Who Do Not Write," in his *On Autobiography* (Minneapolis: University of Minnesota Press, 1989).

Chapter Five

1. John R. Commons, *Races and Immigrants in America* (1907; New York: Macmillan, 1920), 127, 132–33. Further references will be cited in the text.

2. Jacob A. Riis, *The Battle with the Slum* (New York: Macmillan, 1902), 215. Further citations will appear in the text.

3. Manuel Gamio, *The Mexican Immigrant: His Life-Story* (Chicago: University of Chicago Press, 1931), 64. Further references will be cited in the text. This generalization is not without its qualifications, however. See, for instance, Señora Ruhe Lopez, who insists, "I have never had any trouble with the Americans; they have always treated me well" (231). But this assertion of racial harmony is radically undercut by the statements that follow it: "Once when I was introduced to an American family they asked me if I was Spanish and when I said I wasn't, that I was Mexican, they then said that the Mexicans weren't as clean nor as white as I; but I told them that in Mexico there are people as white and blonde, as intelligent and clean as in any other country of the world" (231). At a later point in her testimony, Señora Lopez, who is married to an Anglo, works to distinguish herself from Anglo women ("I think of myself as a very modern woman, following the American style but I am not extreme like the American women" (232).

4. Moses Rischin, *The Promised City: New York's Jews, 1870–1914* (Cambridge: Harvard University Press, 1962), 259–60.

5. Mary Antin, *The Promised Land* (Boston: Houghton Mifflin, 1912). Further references will be cited in the text.

6. Emma Goldman, *Living My Life* (New York: A. A. Knopf, 1970), 12. Additional citations will be included in the text.

7. Louis Levine, *The Women's Garment Workers: A History of the International Ladies' Garment Workers' Union* (New York: B. W. Huebsch, 1924), vii.

8. Alice Kessler-Harris, "Organizing the Unorganizable: Three Jewish Women and Their Union," in Milton Cantor and Bruce Laurie, eds., *Class, Sex, and the Woman Worker* (Westport: Greenwood Press, 1977), 147; Anzia Yezierska, *Breadgivers* (1925; New York: Persea Books, 1975).

9. Rose Pesotta, *Bread upon the Waters,* ed. John Nicholas Beffel (New York: Dodd, Mead, 1944) (further references will appear in the text), and cf. Rose Pes-

otta, *Days of Our Lives* (Boston: Excelsior Publishers, 1958). Rose Schneiderman with Lucy Goldthwaite, *All for One* (New York: Paul S. Erikson, 1967) (further references will appear in the text).

10. As I will suggest in my discussion of Mary Antin's *The Promised Land* and Elizabeth Stern's *My Mother and I* later in this chapter, the question of literary attention to anti-Semitism in Russia is far less problematic. Indictments of Russian brutality toward those living in the Pale, in fact, work as a trope of Jewish immigrant autobiography, and, in part, rehearse received notions of the United States as a promised land—haven for the oppressed of foreign shores.

11. Quoted in Kenneth L. Kann, *Comrades and Chicken Ranchers: The Story of a California Jewish Community* (Ithaca: Cornell University Press, 1993), 121.

12. It is worth noting that the language of class speaks for Jewish culture well beyond the turn of the century, as Depression-era texts like Herbert Gold's *Jews Without Money* (New York: International Publishers, 1930) (whose title clearly plays off of representations of the Jew as both wealthy and miserly) and more contemporary Jewish American literature attest.

13. Elizabeth Gertrude Stern [Levin], *My Mother and I* (New York: Macmillan, 1917). Further citations will appear in the text.

14. Susan A. Glenn, *Daughters of the Shtetl: Life and Labor in the Immigrant Generation* (Ithaca: Cornell University Press, 1990), 3–4. See Neil M. Cowan and Ruth Schwartz Cowan, *Our Parents' Lives: The Americanization of Eastern European Jews* (New York: Basic Books, 1989), for a more conventional (that is, less questioning) assessment of cultural change: "If our grandparents had ambivalent feelings about the tradition they had left behind, our parents had even more, for our parents—many of whom were born in America, all of whom spent their youth here—wanted to become Americans, wanted to assimilate" (252).

15. National Council of Jewish Women, Pittsburgh Section, *By Myself I'm a Book! An Oral History of the Immigrant Jewish Experience in Pittsburgh* (Waltham, Mass.: American Jewish Historical Society, 1972), 130.

16. Glenn, *Daughters of the Shtetl,* 3.

17. In this sense Russian-Jewish autobiography by women demonstrates how the experience of racial oppression acts to confirm ethnicity. See also Moses Rischin: "The Jews of Eastern Europe gloried in their separateness with no need to apologize and less to explain. Rendered conspicuous by their dress, language, and customs and confined in their occupations and habitats, they knew they were Jews, anchored in religious traditions by their needs, their convictions, their communal life, and the state of the surrounding peasantry" (*The Promised City,* 34). One could argue that such conditions, which make the representation of ethnicity relatively straightforward vis-à-vis the cultural outsider, ironically allow more room for writers to problematize other issues—in this case, gender.

18. Jacob A. Riis, *Children of the Tenements* (New York: The Macmillan Company, 1903) 56.

19. Pauline Leader, *And No Birds Sing* (London: Routledge, 1932). Further references will be cited in the text.

20. See, for instance, María Amparo Ruiz de Burton's *The Squatter and the Don*, ed. Rosaura Sánchez and Beatrice Pita (1885; Houston: Arte Público Press, 1992); Frances Harper's *Iola Leroy; Or, Shadows Uplifted* (1892; Boston: Beacon Press, 1987); and the work of Charles Chesnutt and Pauline Hopkins in books like *The Marrow of Tradition* (1901; Ann Arbor: University of Michigan Press, 1969) and *Contending Forces: A Romance Illustrative of Negro Life North and South* (1900; New York: Oxford University Press, 1988).

21. Richard Rodriguez, *Hunger of Memory: The Education of Richard Rodriguez* (New York: Bantam Books, 1982).

22. Richard Tuerk, "At Home in the Land of Columbus: Americanization in European-American Immigrant Autobiography," in James Robert Payne, ed., *Multicultural Autobiography: American Lives* (Knoxville: University of Tennessee Press, 1992), 114.

23. Alice Wexler provides a useful account of the "cantonist" system of drafting young Jewish boys into military service: "Imposed in 1827, [the cantonist system] made Jewish boys subject to military service under special conditions not applied to non-Jews. Theoretically draftable at age 18, in practice Jewish boys were literally kidnapped as children—ages 12, or even younger—and sent to special institutions where they received military training. As soldiers, they were required to serve in the army for 25 years. The real purpose of the cantonist system was not military but social: to separate Jewish children from their cultural milieu and force them to convert to Christianity. Similarly, the official government schools and the later Jewish 'Crown' schools (much like the government schools but without their heavily Christian emphasis) aimed, overtly or covertly, at assimilation" (Preface to *Emma Goldman: An Intimate Life* [New York: Pantheon, 1984], 5).

24. Tuerk, "At Home in the Land of Columbus"; Raymund A. Paredes, "Autobiography and Ethnic Politics: Richard Rodriguez's *Hunger of Memory*," in Payne, ed., *Multicultural Autobiography*, 282. See 281–84 for Paredes's discussion of Antin.

25. Theodore Roosevelt is frequently used as an index for cultural conversion in turn-of-the-century immigrant narrative. Riis's famous *Battle with the Slum*, for instance, is dedicated to Roosevelt, "whose whole life is a rousing bugle-call to arms for the right, for good citizenship, and an inspiration to us all" (dedication page).

26. I am borrowing this expression for a culturally contingent gender identity from Maxine Hong Kingston's *The Woman Warrior: Memoirs of a Girlhood Among Ghosts* (New York: Vintage, 1975).

27. I am indebted to Sandra Gunning for calling my attention to this point.

28. See Antin for a similarly equivocal view of education and language as the site simultaneously of cultural change and of tradition. If her mastery of English is

the means by which she takes possession of America (205) and is thus a way of denying the link with the Jewish life of Plotsk, the words Antin uses to describe the writing of her book reinstate this community. The act of remembrance will "put my grandfather's questions into words and set to music my father's dream," she claims (214). And, in a less gender-inflected formulation, "The tongue am I of those who lived before me, as those that are to come will be the voice of my unspoken thoughts" (214).

Ernesto Galarza in *Barrio Boy* (Notre Dame: University of Notre Dame Press, 1971) provides another account of the relation between writing and ethnic identity. In this bildungsroman, too, the act of writing simultaneously distinguishes the subject *from* and connects him *to* an ethnic immigrant community.

29. Barbara Mayer Wertheimer, *We Were There: The Story of Working Women in America* (New York: Pantheon, 1977), 297–98.

30. Levine, *The Women's Garment Workers*, 22–23.

31. Joseph Schlossberg, *The Rise of the Clothing Workers*, Educational Pamphlets, No. 1 (New York: Amalgamated Clothing Workers of America, 1921), 29–31.

32. Douglas Monroy, "La Costura en Los Angeles, 1933–1939: The ILGWU and the Politics of Domination," in Magdalena Mora and Adelaida R. Del Castillo, eds., *Mexican Women in the United States: Struggles Past and Present* (Los Angeles: Chicano Studies Research Center Publications, 1980), 173.

33. Glenn, *Daughters of the Shtetl*, 181. Jewish labor historians are virtually in perfect accord in identifying Jewish labor struggles as a form of ethnic practice. Besides Rischin's *The Promised City* and Henry J. Tobias's *The Jewish Bund in Russia: From Its Origins to 1905* (Stanford: Stanford University Press, 1972), see also Melvyn Dubofsky, who suggests that "what politics accomplished for the Irish, trade-unionism promised New York's Jews" (*When Workers Organize: New York City in the Progressive Era* [Amherst: University of Massachusetts Press, 1968], 17). In *The Women's Garment Workers*, Louis Levine describes workers who had begun to disestablish themselves from the synagogue as having "made the step from passive acquiescence in socialist and anarchist leadership to an active acceptance of their creeds. To them, socialism or anarchism became their religion and their philosophy, the source of their intellectual and imaginative life" (31). Susan Glenn argues: "More than simply a means of alleviating the economic insecurities of the Jewish working class, both in Russia and in America the twin causes of socialism and union organization became a critical vehicle for articulating the frustrations and longings of Jewish men and women" (*Daughters of the Shtetl*, 178).

34. Tobias, *The Jewish Bund in Russia*, 245.

35. Rischin, *The Promised City*, 166, 159.

36. Ann Schofield, "The Uprising of the 20,000: The Making of a Labor Legend," in Joan M. Jensen and Sue Davidson, eds., *A Needle, a Bobbin, a Strike:*

Women Needleworkers in America (Philadelphia: Temple University Press, 1984), 174.

37. Glenn, *Daughters of the Shtetl,* 192.

38. Rischin, *The Promised City,* 43, 157.

39. As quoted in Rischin, *The Promised City,* 167.

40. The writings of labor organizers and labor historians alike testify to this connection. See, for instance, Schlossberg's bulletin ("The foundation and background of [American labor movement spokespeople] was the struggle against Czarist autocracy in Russia") (*The Rise of the Clothing Workers,* 10), as well as Louis Levine, Moses Rischin, Susan Glenn, and Henry Tobias. Commons's *Races and Immigrants in America* (my compendium for stereotypes) also implicitly documents the relation between Jewish resistance to Russian anti-Semitic legislation and socialist practice: "The government and the army join with the peasants, for, true to the character of this versatile race, the Jews are leaders of the revolutionary and socialistic patriots who seek to overthrow the government and restore the land to the people" (92).

41. Henry Roth's novel *Call It Sleep* (New York: Avon Books, 1934) provides an interesting working out of this gendered metaphor of immigrant labor. Like Pauline Leader, Roth depicts the life of the Jewish wife as that of a slave (40, 157), but where much of earlier immigrant autobiography celebrates this labor as the embodiment of Jewish practice by mourning its loss as a loss of faith, Roth represents the mother as laboring without the solace of spiritual recompense. "I don't know why they made Friday so difficult a day for women,"David's mother says (70); despite her toil to prepare her home for the Sabbath, she is a skeptic denied the comfort of faith.

42. See, for instance: "Father decided my name should be changed from Rachel to Rose. He said it sounded nicer. In the same way my brothers got their names of Charles and Harry, which also were not really translations of their original Hebrew names of Ezekiel and Aaron, and Mother became Dora" (27).

43. Alice Kessler-Harris, "Where Are the Organized Women Workers?" in Nancy Cott, ed., *A Heritage of Her Own: Toward a New Social History of American Women* (New York: Simon and Schuster, 1979), 347.

44. Françoise Basch's Introduction to Theresa Malkiel, *The Diary of a Shirtwaist Striker* (1910; New York: ILR Press/Cornell University Press, 1990), 52. The Anglo-American labor press, by contrast, notes the activity of women in such a way as to slight, by inference, the immigrant worker. Consider one journalist's description of American-born ILGWU organizer Josephine Casey: a "charming young Southern woman of most attractive personality," she is described as "cultured, broadminded, and refined . . . a type distinctly different from the anarchist strike-leading individual so often pictured as a trades union leader" (Eric Foner's citation from a Kalamazoo newspaper, 1 March 1912, as quoted by Karen Mason in "Feel-

ing the Pinch: The Kalamazoo Corsetmakers' Strike of 1912," in Carol Groneman and Mary Beth Norton, eds., *"To Toil the Livelong Day": America's Women at Work, 1780–1980* (Ithaca: Cornell University Press, 1987), 143.

45. Wexler, Preface to *Emma Goldman*, 8. Whatever their other disagreements, feminist labor historians are virtually of one mind on the subject of Jewish women's active participation in efforts to organize the garment industry. Schofield, Glenn, Kessler-Harris, and Wertheimer, among others, all cite various combinations of cultural tradition and financial necessity as encouraging the militancy of Jewish American working women. Glenn's *Daughters of the Shtetl* provides a particularly thorough working out of this argument: "Women occupied a paradoxical place in Eastern European Jewish society in the late nineteenth and early twentieth centuries. On the one hand, they were excluded from the main lines of public authority in matters civic and religious; on the other, they played a central role in economic life and were charged with the important task of maintaining the fundamental religious rituals of private life. . . . [This] freed them to participate as quasi-independent brokers in the public world of the marketplace and vested them with the rights and responsibilities of breadwinners. But it limited their activities to work and domestic cares, privileging higher pursuits, such as education, for man" (8). Glenn distinguishes Jewish women from white American women in this respect: "Whereas American middle-class women had traditionally sought to politicize their role as moral guardians and, at the same time, to differentiate their civic contribution from men's, Jewish daughters aimed to politicize their role as breadwinners, striving to join with men in the common struggles of the working-class immigrant community" (215). Even those critics who most closely rely on the separate-spheres model of labor nevertheless conclude by recognizing the public contributions of Jewish women to union work. Thus Kessler-Harris: "To choose a militant and active future among a people who valued marriage and the family as much as did most Eastern European Jews must have been extraordinarily difficult. Women who decided to be continuously active in the labor movement knew consciously or unconsciously that they were rejecting traditional marriage. . . . These women were not entirely beyond the pale, since American-Jewish culture urged women into marriage while its injunction to self-sufficiency encouraged a militant sense of independence" (146–47).

46. Schofield, "The Uprising of the 20,000," 179.

47. King-kok Cheung, *Articulate Silences: Hisaye Yamamoto, Maxine Hong Kingston, Joy Kogawa* (Ithaca: Cornell University Press, 1993).

48. Critical reports of the history of American labor prior to the feminist revisions of the early 1980s do not act as much of a corrective. The patronizing intonation of Louis Levine's evaluation of the repercussions of the Uprising of the 20,000 is unmistakable: the strike, he announces, has "revealed woman to herself as few incidents in history have done and in ways never to be forgotten" (166). Melvyn Dubofsky's account is even more dismissive of feminine organizing capabilities:

" 'the uprising of 20,000' illustrates that the most unlikely candidates for unionization could be united for organized economic action. . . . Even Samuel Gompers praised the girls for laying the foundations for future progress in the garment trades. . . . The girls themselves learned that working-class solidarity presented the most favorable avenue to equitable treatment" (57–58).

49. Basch, Introduction, 21.

50. Elizabeth Hasanovitz, *One of Them: Chapters from a Passionate Autobiography* (Boston: Houghton Mifflin, 1918).

51. Ann Schofield, Introduction to Pesotta, *Bread upon the Waters*, xvii.

52. Wexler, Preface to *Emma Goldman*, 88.

53. Joan M. Jensen, "Inside and Outside the Unions: 1920–80," in Jensen and Davidson, eds., *A Needle, a Bobbin, a Strike*, 187. In fact, Monroy suggests that Pesotta's attention to cultural difference led to a (limited) success in organizing in Los Angeles: "Pesotta and the ILGWU leadership in Los Angeles exhibited a more enlightened attitude towards Mexicanos and their culture than the rest of the AFL and the ILGWU. . . . Pesotta did much to reach the Mexicano community. During the 1933 strike the ILGWU did short broadcasts at 7:00 pm on a Mexican cultural society's radio program until it was shut down. . . . The leadership also produced a four-page, semi-weekly newspaper, *The Organizer*, in Spanish and English. . . . Photos of Labor Day parades show those on the ILGWU's Spanish Branch float regaled in Mexican costumes. However . . . among those officers elected to the board of Local No. 90, Mexicanos only numbered 6 out of 19, and held none of the important positions" ("La Costura en Los Angeles," 175–76).

54. Kessler-Harris, "Organizing the Unorganizable," 151.

Chapter Six

1. Rose Cohen, *Out of the Shadow* (New York: George H. Doran, 1918), 197. Further references will be included in the text.

2. For a particularly encyclopedic display of anti-Semitic preoccupations concerning Russian-Jewish immigration to the United States, see John R. Commons, *Races and Immigrants in America* (1907; New York: Macmillan, 1920). Commons' book is sweepingly indiscriminate in its racism, but for the purposes of this argument I will restrict my citations to a small sampling from the chapter he devotes to Jewish immigrants. Of Jewish people in Eastern Europe he makes the following pronouncement: "Astute politicians and dashing military leaders, they [Magyars] are as careless in business as the Slavs, and the supremacy which they maintained in politics has slipped into the hands of the Jews in economics. In no other modern country has the Jew been so liberally treated, and in no other country have public and private finance come more completely under his control. . . . In the Austrian dominions of former Poland the Jew likewise has become the financier, and both the Ruthenian and the Pole, unable to rise under their burden of debt, contribute

their more enterprising peasants to America" (81–82). And later: "That which most of all has made the Jew a cause of alarm to the peasants of Eastern Europe is the highest mark of his virtue, namely, his rapid increase in numbers. A high birth-rate, a low death-rate, a long life, place the Jew as far above the average as the negro is below the average" (94–95); "Thus it is that this marvellous and paradoxical race, the parent of philosophers, artists, reformers, martyrs, and also of the shrewdest exploiters of the poor and ignorant, has, in two decades, come to America in far greater numbers than in the two centuries preceding" (93).

3. Moses Rischin cites the first phrase as Burton J. Hendricks's but goes on to document this anti-Semitic paranoia as endemic rather than exceptional to American letters: *The Promised City: New York's Jews, 1870–1914* (Cambridge: Harvard University Press, 1962), esp. 254–60. The second phrase is taken from Rose Pesotta, *Days of Our Lives* (Boston: Excelsior Publishers, 1958), 237.

4. Regenia Gagnier, "The Literary Standard, Working-Class Autobiography, and Gender," in Susan Groag Bell and Marilyn Yalom, eds., *Revealing Lives: Autobiography, Biography, and Gender* (New York: State University of New York Press, 1990), 94.

5. Cf. Moses Rischin, *The Promised City: New York's Jews, 1870–1914* (Cambridge: Harvard University Press, 1962); Melvyn Dubofsky, *When Workers Organize: New York City in the Progressive Era* (Amherst: University of Massachusetts Press, 1968); Philip S. Foner, *Women and the American Labor Movement*, 2 vols. (New York: Free Press, 1979 and 1980); Susan Estabrook Kennedy, *If All We Did Was to Weep at Home: A History of White Working Class Women in America* (Bloomington: University of Indiana Press, 1979); Susan A. Glenn, *Daughters of the Shtetl: Life and Labor in the Immigrant Generation* (Ithaca: Cornell University Press, 1990).

6. In *Give Us Bread But Give Us Roses: Working Women's Consciousness in the United States, 1890 to the First World War* (London: Routledge, 1983), Sarah Eisenstein provides a case in point by detailing the focus of her study: "We need to see whether women, through dealing with their conflicts and problems, developed new forms or elements of consciousness. For instance, in their trade union activity, perhaps they developed ideas that might be said to represent a particular working women's consciousness" (14–15). To develop a notion of the "representative" in a study of consciousness appears self-defeating. Defining a single type of working-class subjectivity, after all, runs the risk of reproducing the objectifying conditions assembly-line workers are subjected to, in that it may develop a series of manufactured self-portraits more striking for their uniformity than their distinctiveness. While she concedes that the primary texts she consults (autobiographies of unionized women like Rose Schneiderman's cowritten *All for One* (Rose Schneiderman with Lucy Goldthwaite, *All for One* [New York: Paul S. Erikson, 1967]) (further citations appear in the text) are hardly blueprints for the struggles and

considerations of working women generally, Eisenstein nevertheless insists on using them as such.

7. Publishing history and citation as documented by Françoise Basch in her Introduction to Theresa Malkiel, *The Diary of a Shirtwaist Striker* (1910; New York: ILR Press/Cornell University Press, 1990), 62–63. Further references will appear in the text.

8. The following critical misapprehension illustrates some of the difficulties involved in using narrative as documentary without sufficient regard for its literary contexts. Theresa Malkiel's novel, *The Diary of a Shirtwaist Striker*, retells the story of the Copper Union strike of 1909 (popularly known as the Uprising of the 20,000) and details the history of its largely Jewish organizing efforts from the vantage point of a non-Jewish first-person narrator. This rhetorical strategy enables Malkiel to acknowledge the anti-Semitism directed at Jewish labor organizers as well as to affirm a sense of Jewish culture and ethnic pride, via the apprehension of a grudgingly respectful cultural other. The relation between culture and class is marked, then, from the outset of the novel. Initial hostility is converted into respect: "It's a good thing, this strike is; it makes you feel like a real grown-up person. But I wish I'd feel about it like them Jew girls do. Why, their eyes flash fire as soon as they commence to talk about the strike—and the lot of talk they can put up—at times they make a body feel like two cents" (81). Presumably mistaking this fictional "diary entry" for autobiographical observation, Moses Rischin cites it as support for an analysis of ethnocentrism in the labor movement. Attributing the observation to a "young black worker," he quotes the passage as evidence of the " 'mixed feelings towards the more activist Jewish workers' " in the Cooper Union strike (quoted by Ann Schofield, "The Uprising of the 20,000: The Making of a Labor Legend," in Joan M. Jensen and Sue Davidson, eds., *A Needle, a Bobbin, a Strike: Women Needleworkers in America* [Philadelphia: Temple University Press, 1984], 176). Ironically, a Jewish novelist's affirmation of culture has been transformed into an illustration of the ethnic conflict the writer has attempted to defuse by voicing it. In its new guise as oral history, the comment was picked up by Ann Schofield, who, citing Rischin as her source, reproduced it to illustrate her own discussion of the Cooper Union strike.

9. Bella Brodzki and Celeste Schenck, eds., *Life/Lines: Theorizing Women's Autobiography* (Ithaca: Cornell University Press, 1988), 5, 9, 11; Susan Friedman, "Women's Autobiographical Selves: Theory and Practice," in Shari Benstock, ed., *The Private Self: Theory and Practice of Women's Autobiographical Writings* (Chapel Hill: University of North Carolina Press, 1988), 45; Sherna Berger Gluck and Daphne Patai, eds., Introduction to *Women's Words: The Feminist Practice of Oral History* (New York: Routledge, 1991), 5. See also Mary Jo Maynes's essay "Gender and Narrative Form in French and German Working-Class Autobiographies," in Personal Narratives Group, eds., *Interpreting Women's Lives: Feminist*

Theory and Personal Narratives (Bloomington: Indiana University Press, 1989), for a particularly concise example of this tendency to overgeneralize: "If the middle-class autobiography appeared as the genre par excellence of the individual, the working-class autobiographer was usually enmeshed in collectivity" (111). See in addition Carol Holly's "Nineteenth-Century Autobiographies of Affiliation: The Case of Catherine Sedgewick and Lucy Larcom," in Paul John Eakin, ed., *American Autobiography: Retrospect and Prospect* (Madison: University of Wisconsin Press, 1991), where Holly reads the feminine self more generally as a relational one.

The records of labor I have read by Russian Jewish immigrant women express the relationship between work and subjectivity in far more complicated terms than Maynes's essay or even Doris Sommer's " 'Not Just a Personal Story': Women's *Testimonios* and the Plural Self," in Brodzki and Schenck, eds., *Life/Lines,* a more nuanced appraisal of the testimonial writing of largely working-class Latin American women that nevertheless insists on "the construction of a collective self" as the defining paradigm of all such textual acts of "interpersonal rhetoric" (118).

Although she does not develop a sustained critique of the relational self, Julia Watson briefly points to some of the difficulties with this model in "Toward an Anti-Metaphysics of Autobiography," in Robert Folkenflik, ed., *The Culture of Autobiography: Constructions of Self-Representation* (Stanford: Stanford University Press, 1993). Critiquing Susan Friedman's "model of selfhood," Watson suggests, "Although interpersonal relationships and a sense of community are assuredly important in many women's self-definition, their modification by social circumstances, and sometimes their complete absence, are also marked in the above autobiographers" (70).

10. Minh-ha, "Commitment from the Mirror-Writing Box," in Gloria Anzaldúa, ed., *Making Face, Making Soul/Haciendo Caras: Creative and Critical Perspectives by Women of Color* (San Francisco: Aunt Lute Foundation Books, 1990), 252.

11. Thus I would distinguish my own position from "the handful of critics who study working-class literature" who, according to Janet Zandy, editor of *Calling Home: Working-Class Women's Writings—An Anthology* (New Brunswick: Rutgers University Press, 1990), affirm that "a collectivist rather than individualistic sensibility is a key difference between bourgeois art and working-class art" (12).

12. Investigation into turn-of-the century working conditions in New York City, as quoted by Louis Levine, *The Women's Garment Workers: A History of the International Ladies' Garment Workers' Union* (New York: B. W. Huebsch, 1924), 22.

13. Gagnier, "The Literary Standard, Working-Class Autobiography, and Gender," 103. Gagnier's assessment is made about twentieth-century British working-class autobiography, but the sense of dislocation between a reading public assessed as middle-class and the working-class writer seems to me to characterize much labor autobiography.

14. Nor does the collaborative nature of this project make Schneiderman any easier to locate. In fact, the absence of editorial acknowledgment of the textual process discourages unreflected assignment of authorial agency. While the title page frames the text as the product of a joint venture (the book is "by Rose Schneiderman with Lucy Goldthwaite"), the nature of Goldthwaite's assistance is never spelled out. Nor does any editorial introduction supplement the brief "author's" preface, which is signed by Schneiderman alone. Left with no insight into the relationship that produced the text (did the collaboration begin as an oral history, with Goldthwaite transmuting the spoken word into print? or did editorial intervention take the form of research assistance or stylistic appraisal?), we cannot with any degree of certainty assume that either particular rhetorical inflections or overall literary design is idiosyncratic to Schneiderman.

15. On the WTUL see Elizabeth Weiner and Hardy Green, "A Stitch in Our Time: New York's Hispanic Garment Workers in the 1980s" in Jensen and Davidson, eds.,, *A Bobbin, a Needle, a Strike:* "Established in 1905, the WTUL, an organization founded by female unionists and upper-middle-class reformers, offered needed financial and moral support for militant activity. Its paternalistic and benevolent style was not unfamiliar to women and those who came from immigrant families seemed particularly impressed with its Americanizing aspects. Young immigrant girls spoke with awe of the 'fine ladies' of the WTUL and did not object to the folk-dancing classes that were part of the Chicago League's program" (356). At the same time that Schneiderman rhetorically indebts herself to the WTUL ("My own story is inextricably interwoven with the history of the New York Women's Trade Union League, an organization composed of women from the trade-union movement and their allies, dedicated to helping working women through trade unionism," 5) she critiques their classism. Consider how the collective subject in the following anecdote helps Schneiderman maintain a strong working-class consciousness in the face of the slights directed at her by some of the wealthy women affiliated with the ILGWU: "We were going to hold a street meeting that evening and went to see Elizabeth Babcock, the leading suffragist, to discuss details. She was shocked at the idea of a street meeting and said that she could not possibly be seen there. It was a very hot day and I remember that she received us out on the porch. If she had given us a glass of iced tea or had asked us to sit down we would have been very grateful. But she did neither and we went away terribly disappointed in her lack of vision and hospitality" (125). See also Schneiderman's allegation that the WTUL was "being supported by the National Association of Manufacturers, " an accusation "they never denied" (126).

16. So as not to reiterate Schneiderman's own self-deprecatory rhetoric I cite a sample of these acknowledgments below: "Three days before the strike, Schlesinger sent in Meyer Perlstein to manage it. I was furious because Schlesinger evidently did not believe in my ability to see things through" (117); "When the MacNamaras confessed, his chances were ruined. It was a great blow to me *per-*

sonally, from which I took a long time to recover, for my youth and confidence in the labor movement would not let me believe that trade unionists would do such a thing" (4; emphasis added); "In January, 1903, we were chartered as Local 23, and I was elected secretary. It was such an exciting time. A new life opened up for me. All of a sudden I was not lonely anymore. I had shop and executive-board meetings to attend as well as the meetings of our unit" (50); "I helped all I could but I was always under the manager's thumb, and I was glad when the International assigned me to New England. I was not always unhappy in Philadelphia for I had dear friends there" (113); "The next stop was Worcester, another anti-union town, and I had the devil's own time there. I spent Christmas in a hotel room reading Dostoyevsky's *Crime and Punishment* and feeling very blue" (115).

Perhaps the clearest example of this anecdotal form of autobiographical assertion is provided by the following: "He [George Meany] asked me to come up to the platform and it was then that Eleanor Roosevelt said to the audience that I had taught her all she knew about trade unionism. I think it was an exaggerated statement but it was one of the very proud moments of my life. But to get back to the so-called 48-hour-week law. After it was passed, the minimum-wage bill finally became law in Governor Lehman's second administration, only to be declared unconstitutional in 1936 by the U.S. Supreme Court" (257).

17. Patricia Meyer Spacks, "Selves in Hiding," in Estelle C. Jelinek, *Women's Autobiography: Essays in Criticism* (Bloomington: Indiana University Press, 1980), 114.

18. Schneiderman's telescopic description of early childhood provides a structural analogy for her oblique method of authorizing her adult self. Here, an ostensibly self-deprecatory description of her small size only emphasizes the heroic quality of her efforts: "I was a tiny baby and, alas, like my mother and my grandfather, I have been tiny ever since—four-and-a-half feet tall. But I began to walk and talk when I was all of nine months old and I remembered many things from those early years" (13).

19. Documented by Ann Schofield, Introduction to Rose Pesotta, *Bread upon the Waters* (1944; New York: ILR Press, 1987), ix.

20. Spacks, "Selves in Hiding," 118–19, 125; Blanche Gelfant, "Speaking Her Own Piece: Emma Goldman and the Discursive Skeins of Autobiography," in Eakin, ed., *American Autobiography*, 241. Emma Goldman, *Living My Life*, 2 vols. (1931; New York: Dover Press, 1970). Further citations will appear in the text.

21. Alice Wexler describes the self-constructed Goldman legend in more detail in the preface to her biography, *Emma Goldman: An Intimate Life* (New York: Pantheon, 1984): "The demonic legend that surrounded her during her years in America: an image created partly by a hostile government and sensationalizing press, but one that she herself exploited to popularize her ideas. . . . There is her own myth of herself as earth mother and as tragic heroine, which she dramatized in her massive autobiography. . . . Goldman's heroic legend was a great part of her

power as an inspiration to others; indeed, her public persona was perhaps her most original creation. Goldman wished to live her life as a heroine: to invent herself as mother earth, martyr, messiah, 'a voice in the wilderness,' as she often described herself" (xvii–xviii).

22. Spacks, "Selves in Hiding," 118.

23. Like her essays, articles, and personal correspondence, Goldman's autobiographical writings merit close and sustained critical attention. My own interest in her work for the purposes of this study, however, is to develop a reading *model* rather than providing an exhaustive reading of her oeuvre.

24. Anxiety about her status as litterateur would undoubtedly only have been aggravated by Alexander Berkman's heavy-handed bragging about the extent of his own editorial interpolations in what Wexler, following his lead, frames as a collaborative effort: "We know from Berkman's diaries the extent to which he changed, cut, and polished the manuscript. 'The Mss., after I correct it, looks worse than an ordinary battlefield,' he boasted one day. 'Some pages: half of it crossed out by me, the other half every word, literally, changed by me' " (xvii–xviii).

25. Glenn, *Daughters of the Shtetl*, 128, 129.

26. Gelfant,"Speaking Her Own Piece," 236–37.

27. Gelfant,"Speaking Her Own Piece," 236.

28. Gelfant,"Speaking Her Own Piece," 238.

Coda

1. Rose Pesotta, *Days of Our Lives* (Boston: Excelsior Publishers, 1958), 254. Succeeding references will appear in the text.

2. Roman Vishniac, *A Vanished World* (New York: Farrar, Straus, and Giroux, 1983).

3. Fabiola Cabeza de Baca, *The Good Life: New Mexico Traditions and Food* (1949; Santa Fe: Museum of New Mexico Press, 1982); Gregorita Rodríguez, *Singing for My Echo: Memories of Gregorita Rodríguez, a Native Healer of Santa Fe,* as told to Edith Powers (Santa Fe: Cota Editions, 1987).

Works Cited

Abreu, Margaret. "In the New Mexico Kitchen." *New Mexico* (March 1940): 36.

Alarcón, Norma. "The Theoretical Subject(s) of *This Bridge Called My Back* and Anglo-American Feminism." In Hector Calderón and José David Saldívar, eds., *Criticism in the Borderlands: Studies in Chicano Literature, Culture, and Ideology.* Durham: Duke University Press, 1991.

Aleshire, Joan. "Exhibition of Women Artists (1790–1900)." In Elaine Hedges and Ingrid Wendt, eds., *In Her Own Image: Women Working in the Arts.* Old Westbury, New York: Feminist Press, 1980.

Andrews, William L. *Sisters of the Spirit: Three Black Women's Autobiographies of the Nineteenth Century.* Bloomington: Indiana University Press, 1986.

———. *To Tell a Free Story: The First Century of Afro-American Autobiography, 1760–1865.* Urbana: University of Illinois Press, 1986.

Angelou, Maya. *All God's Children Wear Traveling Shoes.* New York: Random House, 1986.

———. *I Know Why the Caged Bird Sings.* New York: Random House, 1969.

Antin, Mary. *The Promised Land.* Boston: Houghton Mifflin, 1912.

Anzaldúa, Gloria. *Borderlands/La Frontera: The New Mestiza.* San Francisco: Spinsters/Aunt Lute Book Company, 1987.

Anzaldúa, Gloria, ed. *Making Face, Making Soul/Haciendo Caras: Creative and Critical Perspectives by Women of Color.* San Francisco: Aunt Lute Foundation Books, 1990.

[Aragón, Jesusita, as told to] Fran Leeper Buss. *La Partera: Story of a Midwife.* Ann Arbor: University of Michigan Press, 1980.

Babb, Jewel. *Border Healing Woman: The Story of Jewel Babb as Told to Pat Ellis Taylor.* Austin: University of Texas Press, 1981.

Baker, Houston A., Jr. *Black Literature in America.* 1969. New York: McGraw-Hill, 1971.

———. *Blues, Ideology, and Afro-American Literature: A Vernacular Theory.* Chicago: University of Chicago Press, 1984.

Baldwin, James. *The Fire Next Time.* 1962. New York: Vintage, 1993.

———. *Shadow and Act.* New York: Random House, 1955.

Baraka, Amiri [LeRoi Jones]. *Black Magic: Collected Poetry, 1961–1967.* Indianapolis: Bobbs-Merrill, 1969.

———. *Blues People: Negro Music in White America.* New York: William Morrow, 1963.

———. *The LeRoi Jones/Amiri Baraka Reader.* Ed. William J. Harris. New York: Thunder's Mouth Press, 1991.

———. "The Myth of a 'Negro' Literature." In Gladys J. Curry, ed., *Viewpoints from Black America.* 1962. Englewood Cliffs, New Jersey: Prentice-Hall, 1970.

Benstock, Shari, ed. *The Private Self: Theory and Practice of Women's Autobiographical Writings.* Chapel Hill: University of North Carolina Press, 1988.

Blackburn, Regina. "In Search of the Black Female Self: African-American Women's Autobiographies and Ethnicity." In Estelle C. Jelinek, *Women's Autobiography: Essays in Criticism.* Bloomington: Indiana University Press, 1980.

Blauner, Bob. "Problems of Editing 'First-Person' Sociology." *Qualitative Sociology* (Spring 1987): 46–64.

Boelhower, William. "The Making of Ethnic Autobiography in the United States." In Paul John Eakin, ed., *American Autobiography: Retrospect and Prospect.* Madison: University of Wisconsin Press, 1991.

Borland, Katherine. " 'That's Not What I Said': Interpretive Conflict in Oral Narrative Research." In Sherna Berger Gluck and Daphne Patai, eds., *Women's Words: The Feminist Practice of Oral History.* New York: Routledge, 1991.

Braxton, Joanne M. *Black Women Writing Autobiography: A Tradition Within a Tradition.* Philadelphia: Temple University Press, 1989.

Brenkman, John. *Culture and Domination.* Ithaca: Cornell University Press, 1988.

Brodzki, Bella, and Celeste Schenck, eds. *Life/Lines: Theorizing Women's Autobiography.* Ithaca: Cornell University Press, 1988.

Buss, Fran Leeper. See Aragón, Jesusita.

Buss, Fran Leeper, ed. *Dignity: Lower Income Women Tell of Their Lives and Struggles—Oral Histories Compiled by Fran Leeper Buss.* Ann Arbor: University of Michigan Press, 1985.

Byerly, Victoria. *Hard Times Cotton Mill Girls: Personal Histories of Womanhood and Poverty in the South.* Ithaca: ILR Press, 1986.

Cabeza de Baca, Fabiola. "Los Alimentos y Su Preparación." Extension Circular 129. New Mexico: New Mexico College of Agriculture and Mechanic Arts, Agricultural Extension Service, 1934.

———. "Boletín de Conservar." Extension Circular 106. New Mexico: New Mexico College of Agriculture and Mechanic Arts, Agricultural Extension Service, 1931.

———. *The Good Life: New Mexico Traditions and Food.* 1949. Santa Fe: Museum of New Mexico Press, 1982.

———. *Historic Cookery.* 1949. Las Vegas, New Mexico: La Galería de los Artesanos, 1970.

———. "New Mexican Diets." *Journal of Home Economics* (34 November 1942): 668–669.

———. *We Fed Them Cactus.* 1954. Albuquerque: University of New Mexico Press, 1989.

Calderón, Hector, and José David Saldívar, eds. *Criticism in the Borderlands: Studies in Chicano Literature, Culture, and Ideology.* Durham: Duke University Press, 1991.

Calta, Marialisa. "Take a Novel, Add a Recipe, and Season to Taste." *New York Times,* 17 February 1993, B1, B3–B4.

Carmichael, Stokely. "Power and Racism." In Gladys J. Curry, ed., *Viewpoints from Black America.* 1962. Englewood Cliffs, New Jersey: Prentice-Hall, 1970.

———. "Toward Black Liberation." In Larry Neal and LeRoi Jones, eds., *Black Fire.* New York: William Morrow, 1968.

Cervantes, Lorna Dee. *Emplumada.* Pittsburgh: University of Pittsburgh Press, 1981.

Cheung, King-kok. *Articulate Silences: Hisaye Yamamoto, Maxine Hong Kingston, Joy Kogawa.* Ithaca: Cornell University Press, 1993.

Chin, Frank. "Come All Ye Asian American Writers of the Real and the Fake." In Jeffery Paul Chan, Frank Chin, Lawson Fusao Inada, and Shawn Wong, eds., *The Big Aiiieeeee! An Anthology of Chinese American and Japanese American Literature.* New York: Meridian, 1991.

Cliff, Michelle. "Object into Subject: Some Thoughts on the Work of Black Women Artists." In Gloria Anzaldúa, ed., *Making Face, Making Soul/Haciendo Caras: Creative and Critical Perspectives by Women of Color.* San Francisco: Aunt Lute Foundation Books, 1990.

Clifford, James. *The Predicament of Culture: Twentieth-Century Ethnography, Literature, and Art.* Cambridge: Harvard University Press, 1988.

Clifford, James, and George E. Marcus, eds. *Writing Culture: The Poetics and Politics of Ethnography.* Berkeley: University of California Press, 1986.

Cohen, Rose. *Out of the Shadow.* New York: George H. Doran, 1918.

Commons, John R. *Races and Immigrants in America.* 1907. New York: Macmillan, 1920.

Cooper, James Fenimore. *The Last of the Mohicans.* 1826. New York: Penguin, 1987.

Cowan, Neil M., and Ruth Schwartz Cowan. *Our Parents' Lives: The Americanization of Eastern European Jews.* New York: Basic Books, 1989.

Culley, Margo. "What a Piece of Work Is 'Woman'!" In Margo Culley, ed., *American Women's Autobiography: Fea(s)ts of Memory.* Madison: University of Wisconsin Press, 1992.

Curry, Gladys J., ed. *Viewpoints from Black America.* 1962. Englewood Cliffs, New Jersey: Prentice-Hall, 1970.

Darden, Norma Jean, and Carole Darden. *Spoonbread and Strawberry Wine: Recipes and Reminiscences of a Family.* New York: Fawcett Cress, 1978.

Davies, Carole Boyce. "Collaboration and the Ordering Imperative in Life Story Production." In Sidonie Smith and Julia Watson, eds., *De/Colonizing the Subject: The Politics of Gender in Women's Autobiography.* Minneapolis: University of Minnesota Press, 1992.

de Cordova, Lorenzo. *Echoes of the Flute.* Santa Fe: Ancient City Press, 1972.

Del Castillo, Adelaida R., ed. *Between Borders: Essays on Mexicana/Chicana History.* Encino, California: Floricanto Press, 1990.

Dewhurst, C. Kurt, Betty MacDowell, and Marsha MacDowell, eds. *Artists in Aprons: Folk Art by American Women.* New York: E. P. Dutton in association with the Museum of American Folk Art, 1979.

Dubofsky, Melvyn. *When Workers Organize: New York City in the Progressive Era.* Amherst: University of Massachusetts Press, 1968.

Dwyer, Kevin. *Moroccan Dialogues: Anthropology in Question.* Baltimore: Johns Hopkins University Press, 1982.

Edgar, J. Clifton. "The Education, Licensing and Supervision of the Midwife." *American Journal of Obstetrics and the Diseases of Women and Children* 73 (March 1916): 385–398. In Judy Barrett Litoff, ed. *The American Midwife Debate: A Sourcebook on Its Modern Origins.* Westport: Greenwood Press, 1986.

Eisenstein, Sarah. *Give Us Bread But Give Us Roses: Working Women's Consciousness in the United States, 1890 to the First World War.* London: Routledge, 1983.

Ellison, Ralph. *Invisible Man.* 1947. New York: Vintage, 1972.

Elsasser, Nan, Kyle MacKenzie and Yvonne Tixier y Vigil. *Las Mujeres: Conversations from a Hispanic Community.* Old Westbury, New York: Feminist Press, 1980.

Esquivel, Laura. *Like Water for Chocolate: A Novel in Monthly Installments with Recipes, Romances and Home Remedies.* Trans. Carol Christensen with Thomas Christensen. New York: Doubleday, 1992.

Fabian, Johannes. *Time and the Other: How Anthropology Makes Its Object.* New York: Columbia University Press, 1983.

Fergusson, Erna. *Mexican Cookbook.* Albuquerque: University of New Mexico Press, 1934.

Fields, Mamie Garvin, with Karen Fields. *Lemon Swamp and Other Places: A Carolina Memoir.* New York: Free Press, 1983.

Fischer, Michael M. J. "Ethnicity and the Post-Modern Arts of Memory." In James Clifford and George E. Marcus, eds., *Writing Culture: The Poetics and Politics of Ethnography.* Berkeley: University of California Press, 1988.

Fisher, M. F. K. *The Gastronomical Me.* 1943. San Francisco: North Point Press, 1989.

Foner, Philip S. *Women and the American Labor Movement.* 3 vols. New York: Free Press, 1979 and 1980.

Forten, Charlotte L. [Grimké]. *The Journal of Charlotte L. Forten: A Free Negro in the Slave Era.* Ed. Ray Allen Billington. 1953. New York: W. W. Norton, 1981.

Foster, Frances Smith. "Autobiography After Emancipation: The Example of Elizabeth Keckley." In James Robert Payne, ed., *Multicultural Autobiography: American Lives.* Knoxville: University of Tennessee Press, 1992.

Fox-Genovese, Elizabeth. "My Statue, My Self: Autobiographical Writings of Afro-American Women." In Shari Benstock, ed., *The Private Self: Theory and Practice of Women's Autobiographical Writings.* Chapel Hill: University of North Carolina Press, 1988.

Franklin, Benjamin. *The Autobiography of Benjamin Franklin.* 1915. New York: Penguin, 1986.

Friedman, Susan. "Women's Autobiographical Selves: Theory and Practice." In Shari Benstock, ed., *The Private Self: Theory and Practice of Women's Autobiographical Writings.* Chapel Hill: University of North Carolina Press, 1988.

Gagnier, Regenia. "The Literary Standard, Working-Class Autobiography, and Gender." In Susan Groag Bell and Marilyn Yalom, eds., *Revealing Lives: Autobiography, Biography and Gender.* New York: State University of New York Press, 1990.

Galarza, Ernesto. *Barrio Boy.* Notre Dame: University of Notre Dame Press, 1971.

Gamio, Manuel. *The Mexican Immigrant: His Life-Story.* Chicago: University of Chicago Press, 1931.

Gayle, Addison. "Cultural Strangulation: Black Literature and the White Aesthetic." In Houston A. Baker Jr., ed., *Black Literature in America.* 1969. New York: McGraw-Hill, 1971.

Gelfant, Blanche. "Speaking Her Own Piece: Emma Goldman and the Discursive Skeins of Autobiography." In Paul John Eakin, ed., *American Autobiography: Retrospect and Prospect.* Madison: University of Wisconsin Press, 1991.

Glenn, Evelyn Nakano. *Issei, Nisei, War Bride: Three Generations of Japanese American Women in Domestic Service.* Philadelphia: Temple University Press, 1988.

Glenn, Susan A. *Daughters of the Shtetl: Life and Labor in the Immigrant Generation.* Ithaca: Cornell University Press, 1990.

Golden, Marita. *Migrations of the Heart: An Autobiography.* New York: Ballantine, 1983.

Goldman, Anne. " 'I Made the Ink': (Literary) Production and Reproduction in *Dessa Rose* and *Beloved*." *Signs* 16, 2 (Summer 1990): 313–330.

Goldman, Emma. *Living My Life.* 2 vols. 1931. New York: Dover, 1970.

Groneman, Carol, and Mary Beth Norton, eds. *"To Toil the Livelong Day": America's Women at Work, 1780–1980.* Ithaca: Cornell University Press, 1987.

Grubb, Alan. "House and Home in the Victorian South: The Cookbook as Guide." In Carol Bleser, ed., *In Joy and in Sorrow: Women, Family, and Marriage in the Victorian South, 1830–1900.* New York: Oxford University Press, 1991.

Hardin, E. R. "The Midwife Problem." *Southern Medical Journal* 18 (May 1925): 347–350. In Judy Barrett Litoff, ed., *The American Midwife Debate: A Sourcebook on Its Modern Origins.* Westport: Greenwood Press, 1986.

Harper, Frances. *Iola Leroy; Or, Shadows Uplifted.* 1892. Boston: Beacon Press, 1987.

Harris, Jessica B. *Iron Pots and Wooden Spoons: Africa's Gifts to New World Cooking.* New York: Atheneum, 1989.

Hasanovitz, Elizabeth. *One of Them: Chapters from a Passionate Autobiography.* Boston: Houghton Mifflin, 1918.

Hedges, Elaine, and Ingrid Wendt, eds. *In Her Own Image: Women Working in the Arts.* Old Westbury, New York: Feminist Press, 1980.

Higginbotham, Evelyn Brooks. "African-American Women's History and the Metalanguage of Race." *Signs* 17 (Winter 1992): 251–274.

Holly, Carol. "Nineteenth-Century Autobiographies of Affiliation: The Case of Catherine Sedgewick and Lucy Larcom." In Paul John Eakin, ed., *American Autobiography: Retrospect and Prospect.* Madison: University of Wisconsin Press, 1991.

Holt, Hamilton, ed. *The Life Stories of (Undistinguished) Americans as Told by Themselves.* 1906. New York: Routledge, 1990.

hooks, bell. *Talking Back: thinking feminist, thinking black.* Boston: South End Press, 1989.

Hopkins, Pauline E. *Contending Forces: A Romance Illustrative of Negro Life North and South.* 1900. New York: Oxford University Press, 1988.

Hurston, Zora Neale. *Dust Tracks on a Road: An Autobiography.* Ed. Robert Hemenway. 1942. Urbana: University of Illinois Press, 1984.

Jameson, Elizabeth. "May and Me: Relationships with Informants and the Community." In Elizabeth Jameson, ed., *Insider/Outsider Relationships with Informants.* Working Paper No. 13. Tucson: Southwest Institute for Research on Women, University of Arizona, 1982.

Jameson, Fredric. *Postmodernism; Or, The Cultural Logic of Late Capitalism.* Durham: Duke University Press, 1990.

Jaramillo, Cleofas M. *Cuentos del Hogar.* El Campo, Texas: Citizen Press, 1939.

———. *The Genuine New Mexico Tasty Recipes.* 1939. Santa Fe: Seton Village Press, 1942.

———. *Romance of a Little Village Girl.* San Antonio: Naylor, 1955.

——. *Sombras del Pasado/Shadows of the Past*. Santa Fe: Ancient City Press, 1941.

Jefferson, Thomas. *Notes on the State of Virginia*. 1787. New York: W. W. Norton, 1982.

Jelinek, Estelle C. *The Tradition of Women's Autobiography: From Antiquity to the Present*. Boston: G. K. Hall, 1986.

——. "Women's Autobiography and the Male Tradition." In Estelle C. Jelinek, ed., *Women's Autobiography: Essays in Criticism*. Bloomington: Indiana University Press, 1980.

Jelinek, Estelle C., ed. *Women's Autobiography: Essays in Criticism*. Bloomington: Indiana University Press, 1980.

Jensen, Joan M. "Canning Comes to New Mexico: Women and the Agricultural Extension Service 1914–1919." In Joan M. Jensen, ed., *New Mexico Women: Intercultural Perspectives*. Albuquerque: University of New Mexico Press, 1986.

——. "Inside and Outside the Unions: 1920–80." In Joan M. Jensen and Sue Davidson, eds., *A Needle, a Bobbin, a Strike: Women Needleworkers in America*. Philadelphia: Temple University Press, 1984.

——. "Oral History of Working Class Women in the Southwest." In Nancy E. Loe, ed., *A Sense of Community: A Framework for Women's Oral History*. Working Paper No. 12. Tucson: Southwest Institute for Research on Women, 1982.

——. *With These Hands: Women Working on the Land*. Old Westbury, New York: Feminist Press, 1981.

Jensen, Joan M., and Sue Davidson, eds. *A Needle, a Bobbin, a Strike: Women Needleworkers in America*. Philadelphia: Temple University Press, 1984.

Jensen, Joan M., and Darlis A. Miller, eds. *New Mexico Women: Intercultural Perspectives*. Albuquerque: University of New Mexico Press, 1986.

Jones, LeRoi. *See* Baraka, Amiri.

Kann, Kenneth L. *Comrades and Chicken Ranchers: The Story of a California Jewish Community*. Ithaca: Cornell University Press, 1993.

Kennedy, Diana. *The Art of Mexican Cooking: Traditional Mexican Cooking for Aficionados*. New York: Bantam, 1989.

——. *The Cuisines of Mexico*. 1972. New York: Harper and Row, 1986.

Kennedy, Susan Estabrook. *If All We Did Was to Weep at Home: A History of White Working Class Women in America*. Bloomington: University of Indiana Press, 1979.

Kessler-Harris, Alice. "Organizing the Unorganizable: Three Jewish Women and Their Union." In Milton Cantor and Bruce Laurie, eds., *Class, Sex, and the Woman Worker*. Westport: Greenwood Press, 1977.

——. "Where Are the Organized Women Workers?" In Nancy Cott, ed., *A Heritage of Her Own: Toward a New Social History of American Women*. New York: Simon and Schuster, 1979.

Kingston, Maxine Hong. *The Woman Warrior: Memoirs of a Girlhood Among Ghosts*. New York: Vintage, 1975.

Krupat, Arnold. *Ethnocriticism: Ethnography, History, Literature*. Berkeley: University of California Press, 1992.

———. *For Those Who Come After: A Study of Native American Autobiography*. Berkeley: University of California Press, 1985.

———. *The Voice in the Margin: Native American Literature and the Canon*. Berkeley: University of California Press, 1989.

Leader, Pauline. *And No Birds Sing*. London: Routledge, 1932.

Lee, Don E. *Black Pride*. New York: Broadside Press, 1968.

———. *Think Black*. New York: Broadside Press, 1969.

Lee, Mary Paik. *Quiet Odyssey: A Pioneer Korean Woman in America*. Ed. Sucheng Chan. Seattle: University of Washington Press, 1990.

Lejeune, Philippe. *On Autobiography*. Minneapolis: University of Minnesota Press, 1989.

Leonardi, Susan. "Recipes for Reading: Summer Pasta, Lobster à la Riseholme, and Key Lime Pie." *PMLA* 3 (May 1989): 340–347.

Levine, Louis. *The Women's Garment Workers: A History of the International Ladies' Garment Workers' Union*. New York: B. W. Huebsch, 1924.

Leyson, Rosemary Cho. "The Visit Home." In Gloria Anzaldúa, ed., *Making Face, Making Soul/Haciendo Caras: Creative and Critical Perspectives by Women of Color*. San Francisco: Aunt Lute Foundation Books, 1990.

Lionnet, Françoise. *Autobiographical Voices: Race, Gender, Self-Portraiture*. Ithaca: Cornell University Press, 1989.

Litoff, Judy Barrett. *American Midwives: 1860 to the Present*. Westport: Greenwood Press, 1978.

Logan, Onnie Lee. *Motherwit: An Alabama Midwife's Story*. As told to Katherine Clark. New York: E. P. Dutton, 1989.

Macy, Josiah Jr., Foundation. *The Midwife in the United States: Report of a Macy Conference*. New York: S-H Service Agency, 1968.

Malkiel, Theresa. *The Diary of a Shirtwaist Striker*. 1910. New York: ILR Press/Cornell University Press, 1990.

Marcus, Jane. "Invisible Mediocrity: The Private Selves of Public Women." In Shari Benstock, ed., *The Private Self: Theory and Practice of Women's Autobiographical Writings*. Chapel Hill: University of North Carolina Press, 1988.

Martin, Patricia Preciado. *Images and Conversations: Mexican Americans Recall a Southwestern Past*. Tucson: University of Arizona Press, 1983.

Mason, Karen. "Feeling the Pinch: The Kalamazoo Corsetmakers' Strike of 1912." In Carol Groneman and Mary Beth Norton, eds., *"To Toil the Livelong Day": America's Women at Work, 1780–1980*. Ithaca: Cornell University Press, 1987.

Mason, Mary G. "The Other Voice: Autobiographies of Women Writers." In James

Olney, ed., *Autobiography: Essays Theoretical and Critical.* Princeton: Princeton University Press, 1980.

Maynes, Mary Jo. "Gender and Narrative Form in French and German Working-Class Autobiography." In Personal Narratives Group, eds., *Interpreting Women's Lives: Feminist Theory and Personal Narratives.* Bloomington: Indiana University Press, 1989.

Menchú, Rigoberta. *I . . . Rigoberta Menchú: An Indian Woman in Guatemala.* Ed. Elisabeth Burgos-Debray. New York: Verso, 1984.

Minh-ha, Trinh H. "Commitment from the Mirror-Writing Box." In Gloria Anzaldúa, ed., *Making Face, Making Soul/Haciendo Caras: Creative and Critical Perspectives by Women of Color.* San Francisco: Aunt Lute Foundation Books, 1990.

Misch, Georg. *A History of Autobiography in Antiquity.* Trans. E. W. Dickes. Cambridge: Harvard University Press, 1951.

Mitford, Jessica. "Teach Midwifery, Go to Jail." *This World (San Francisco Chronicle),* 21 October 1990, 8.

Mohanty, Chandra Talpade. "Introduction. Cartographies of Struggle: Third World Women and the Politics of Feminism." In Chandra Talpade Mohanty, Ann Russo, and Lourdes Torres, eds., *Third World Women and the Politics of Feminism.* Bloomington: Indiana University Press, 1991.

Monroy, Douglas. "La Costura en Los Angeles, 1933–1939: The ILGWU and the Politics of Domination." In Magdalena Mora and Adelaida R. Del Castillo, eds., *Mexican Women in the United States: Struggles Past and Present.* Los Angeles: Chicano Studies Research Center Publications, 1980.

Moraga, Cherríe. *The Last Generation.* Boston: South End Press, 1993.

———. *Living in the War Years: Lo Que Nunca Pasó por Sus Labios.* Boston: South End Press, 1983.

Mourning Dove. *Cogewea, the Half-Blood: A Depiction of the Great Montana Cattle Range.* Ed. Lucullus Virgil McWhorter. Introduction by Dexter Fisher. Lincoln: University of Nebraska Press, 1981.

National Council of Jewish Women, Pittsburgh Section. *By Myself I'm a Book! An Oral History of the Immigrant Jewish Experience in Pittsburgh.* Waltham, Massachusetts: American Jewish Historical Society, 1972.

Neal, Larry. *Black Boogaloo: Notes on Black Liberation.* San Francisco: Journal of Black Poetry Press, 1969.

Olney, James. "Autobiography and the Cultural Moment: A Thematic, Historical, and Bibliographical Introduction." In James Olney, ed., *Autobiography: Essays Theoretical and Critical.* Princeton: Princeton University Press, 1980.

Olney, James. *Metaphors of Self: The Meaning of Autobiography.* Princeton: Princeton University Press, 1972.

Olney, James, ed. *Autobiography: Essays Theoretical and Critical.* Princeton: Princeton University Press, 1980.

Omi, Michael. *Racial Formation in the United States from the 1960s to the 1980s.* New York: Routledge, 1986.

Ortiz de Montellano, Bernard R. "Aztec Survivals in Modern Folk Medicine." *Grito del Sol* 2 (1979): 11–27.

Padilla, Genaro M. "Imprisoned Narrative? Or, Lies, Secrets, and Silence in New Mexico Women's Autobiography." In Hector Calderón and José David Saldívar, eds., *Criticism in the Borderlands: Studies in Chicano Literature, Culture, and Ideology.* Durham: Duke University Press, 1991.

———. "The Mexican Immigrant as °: The (de)Formation of Mexican Immigrant Life Story." In Robert Folkenflik, ed., *The Culture of Autobiography: The Constructions of Self-Representation.* Stanford: Stanford University Press, 1993.

———. *My History, Not Yours: The Formation of Mexican American Autobiography.* Madison: University of Wisconsin Press, 1993.

Paredes, Raymund A. "Autobiography and Ethnic Politics: Richard Rodriguez's *Hunger of Memory.*" In James Robert Payne, ed., *Multicultural Autobiography: American Lives.* Knoxville: University of Tennessee Press, 1992.

———. "The Evolution of Chicano Literature." In Houston A. Baker Jr., ed., *Three American Literatures.* New York: Modern Languages Association, 1982.

Patai, Daphne. "U.S. Academics and Third World Women: Is Ethical Research Possible?" In Sherna Berger Gluck and Daphne Patai, eds., *Women's Words: The Feminist Practice of Oral History.* New York: Routledge, 1991.

Perrone, Bobette, H. Henrietta Stockel, and Victoria Krueger, eds. *Medicine Women, Curanderas, and Women Doctors.* Norman: University of Oklahoma Press, 1989.

Personal Narratives Group, eds. *Interpreting Women's Lives: Feminist Theory and Personal Narratives.* Bloomington: Indiana University Press, 1989.

Pesotta, Rose. *Bread upon the Waters.* Ed. John Nicholas Beffel. New York: Dodd, Mead, 1944.

———. *Days of Our Lives.* Boston: Excelsior Publishers, 1958.

Poovey, Mary. " 'Scenes of an Indelicate Character': The Medical 'Treatment' of Victorian Women." *Representations* 14 (1986): 137–168.

Porter, Carolyn. "Are We Being Historical Yet?" *South Atlantic Quarterly* 87 (Fall 1988): 743–786.

Raynaud, Claudine. "Rubbing a Paragraph with a Soft Cloth? Muted Voices and Editorial Constraints in *Dust Tracks on a Road.*" In Sidonie Smith and Julia Watson, eds., *De/Colonizing the Subject: The Politics of Gender in Women's Autobiography.* Minneapolis: University of Minnesota Press, 1992.

Reagon, Bernice Johnson. "My Black Mothers and Sisters: Or, On Beginning a Cultural Autobiography." *Feminist Studies* 8 (Spring 1982): 81–95.

Rebolledo, Tey Diana. "Narrative Strategies of Resistance in Hispana Writing." *Journal of Narrative Technique* 20, no. 2 (Spring 1990): 134–146.

———. "Tradition and Mythology: Signatures of Landscape in Chicana Literature." In Vera Norwood and Janice Monk, eds., *The Desert Is No Lady: South-western Landscapes in Women's Writing and Art.* New Haven: Yale University Press, 1987.

Rice, Sarah. *He Included Me: The Autobiography of Sarah Rice.* Transcribed and ed. Louise Westling. Athens: University of Georgia Press, 1989.

Riis, Jacob A. *The Battle with the Slum.* New York: Macmillan, 1902.

――――. *Children of the Tenements.* New York: Macmillan, 1903.

Rischin, Moses. *The Promised City: New York's Jews, 1870–1914.* Cambridge: Harvard University Press, 1962.

Rodríguez, Gregorita. *Singing for My Echo: Memories of Gregorita Rodríguez, a Native Healer of Santa Fe.* As told to Edith Powers. Santa Fe: Cota Editions, 1987.

Rodriguez, Richard. *Hunger of Memory: The Education of Richard Rodriguez.* New York: Bantam Books, 1982.

Rollins, Judith. *Between Women: Domestics and Their Employers.* Philadelphia: Temple University Press, 1985.

Rosenblatt, Roger. "Black Autobiography: Life as the Death Weapon." In James Olney, ed., *Autobiography: Essays Theoretical and Critical.* Princeton: Princeton University Press, 1980.

Roth, Henry. *Call It Sleep.* New York: Avon Books, 1934.

Ruiz de Burton, María Amparo. *The Squatter and the Don.* Ed. Rosaura Sánchez and Beatrice Pita. 1885. Houston: Arte Público Press, 1992.

Ruoff, A. LaVonne Brown. "John Joseph Mathews's Talking to the Moon: Literary and Osage Contexts." In James Robert Payne, ed., *Multicultural Autobiography: American Lives.* Knoxville: University of Tennessee Press, 1992.

Salazar, Claudia. "A Third World Woman's Text: Between the Politics of Criticism and Cultural Politics." In Sherna Berger Gluck and Daphne Patai, eds., *Women's Words: The Feminist Practice of Oral History.* New York: Routledge, 1991.

Saldívar, Ramón. *Chicano Narrative: The Dialectics of Difference.* Madison: University of Wisconsin Press, 1990.

Saldívar-Hull, Sonia. "Feminism on the Border: From Gender Politics to Geopolitics." In Hector Calderón and José David Saldívar, eds., *Criticism in the Borderlands: Studies in Chicano Literature, Culture, and Ideology.* Durham: Duke University Press, 1991.

Sarris, Greg. *Keeping Slug Woman Alive: A Holistic Approach to American Indian Texts.* Berkeley: University of California Press, 1993.

Sayre, Robert. "Autobiography and the Making of America." In James Olney, ed., *Autobiography: Essays Theoretical and Critical.* Princeton: Princeton University Press, 1980.

Schlossberg, Joseph. *The Rise of the Clothing Workers.* Educational Pamphlets, No. 1. New York: Amalgamated Clothing Workers of America, 1921.

Schneiderman, Rose, with Lucy Goldthwaite. *All for One.* New York: Paul S. Erikson, 1967.

Schofield, Ann. "The Uprising of the 20,000: The Making of a Labor Legend." In Joan M. Jensen and Sue Davidson, eds., *A Needle, a Bobbin, a Strike: Women Needleworkers in America.* Philadelphia: Temple University Press, 1984.

Shange, Ntozake. *Sassafras, Cypress and Indigo.* New York: St. Martin's Press, 1982.

Smart-Grosvenor, VertaMae. *Vibration Cooking; Or, The Travel Notes of a Geechee Girl.* 1970. New York: Ballantine, 1986.

Smith, Sidonie. *A Poetics of Women's Autobiography: Marginality and the Fictions of Self-Representation.* Bloomington: Indiana University Press, 1987.

———. *Subjectivity, Identity, and the Body: Women's Autobiographical Practices in the Twentieth Century.* Bloomington: Indiana University Press, 1993.

Smith, Sidonie, and Julia Watson, eds. *De/Colonizing the Subject: The Politics of Gender in Women's Autobiography.* Minneapolis: University of Minnesota Press, 1992.

Sommer, Doris. " 'Not Just a Personal Story': Women's *Testimonios* and the Plural Self." In Bella Brodzki and Celeste Schenck, eds., *Life/Lines: Theorizing Women's Autobiography.* Ithaca: Cornell University Press, 1988.

Sone, Monica. *Nisei Daughter.* 1953. Seattle: University of Washington Press, 1987.

Stacey, Judith. "Can There Be a Feminist Ethnography?" In Sherna Berger Gluck and Daphne Patai, eds., *Women's Words: The Feminist Practice of Oral History.* New York: Routledge, 1991.

Stein, Gertrude. *The Autobiography of Alice B. Toklas.* 1933. New York: Random House, 1955.

Stern, Elizabeth Gertrude [Levin]. *My Mother and I.* New York: Macmillan, 1917.

Stewart, James T. "The Development of the Black Revolutionary Artist." In Larry Neal and LeRoi Jones, eds., *Black Fire.* New York: William Morrow, 1968.

Takaki, Ronald. *Strangers from a Different Shore: A History of Asian Americans.* New York: Penguin, 1989.

Taylor, Pat Ellis. *Border Healing Woman: The Story of Jewel Babb.* Austin: University of Texas Press, 1981.

Texas State Board of Health. Bureau of Child Hygiene. "Report on the Midwife Survey in Texas, January 2, 1925." 1924. In Judy Barrett Litoff, ed., *The American Midwife Debate: A Sourcebook on Its Modern Origins.* Westport: Greenwood Press, 1986.

Tobias, Henry J. *The Jewish Bund in Russia: From Its Origins to 1905.* Stanford: Stanford University Press, 1972.

Tucker, Susan. *Telling Memories Among Southern Women: Domestic Workers and*

Their Employers in the Segregated South. Baton Rouge: Louisiana State University Press, 1988.

Tuerk, Richard. "At Home in the Land of Columbus: Americanization in European-American Immigrant Autobiography." In James Robert Payne, ed., *Multicultural Autobiography: American Lives.* Knoxville: University of Tennessee Press, 1992.

United States Department of Labor. *Proceedings of Conference on Better Care for Mothers and Babies: Held in Washington, D.C., January 17–18, 1938.* Bureau Pub. No. 246. Washington, D.C.: U.S. Government Printing Office, 1938.

Véa, Alfredo Jr. *La Maravilla.* New York: Dutton, 1993.

Villareal, José Antonio. *Pocho.* New York: Doubleday, 1959.

Vincent, David. *Bread, Knowledge, and Freedom: A Study of Nineteenth-Century Working Class Autobiography.* London: Europa, 1981.

Watson, Julia. "Toward an Anti-Metaphysics of Autobiography." In Robert Folkenflik, ed., *The Culture of Autobiography: Constructions of Self-Representation.* Stanford: Stanford University Press, 1993.

Watson, Julia, and Sidonie Smith. "Introduction: De/Colonization and the Politics of Discourse in Women's Autobiographical Practices." In Sidonie Smith and Julia Watson, eds., *De/Colonizing the Subject: The Politics of Gender in Women's Autobiography.* Minneapolis: University of Minnesota Press, 1992.

Weiner, Elizabeth, and Hardy Green. "A Stitch in Our Time: New York's Hispanic Garment Workers in the 1980s." In Joan M. Jensen and Sue Davidson, eds., *A Needle, a Bobbin, a Strike: Women Needleworkers in America.* Philadelphia: Temple University Press, 1984.

Wertheimer, Barbara Mayer. *We Were There: The Story of Working Women in America.* New York: Pantheon, 1977.

Wexler, Alice. *Emma Goldman: An Intimate Life.* New York: Pantheon, 1984.

Williams, J. Whitridge. "Medical Education and the Midwife Problem in the United States." *Journal of the American Medical Association* 58 (January 1912): 1–7. In Judy Barrett Litoff, ed., *The American Midwife Debate: A Sourcebook on Its Modern Origins.* Westport: Greenwood Press, 1986.

Wong, Hertha D. "Pictographs as Autobiography: Plains Indian Sketchbooks of the Late Nineteenth and Early Twentieth Centuries." *American Literary History* (Summer 1989): 295–316.

———. *Sending My Heart Back Across the Years: Tradition and Innovation in Native American Autobiography.* New York: Oxford University Press, 1992.

Wong, Jade Snow. *Fifth Chinese Daughter.* New York: Harper and Brothers, 1945.

Wong, Sau-ling Cynthia. "Autobiography as Guided Chinatown Tour? Maxine Hong Kingston's *The Woman Warrior* and the Chinese American Autobiographical Controversy." In James Robert Payne, ed., *Multicultural Autobiography: American Lives.* Knoxville: University of Tennessee Press, 1992.

———. "Immigrant Autobiography: Some Questions of Definition and Approach." In Paul John Eakin, ed., *American Autobiography: Retrospect and Prospect.* Madison: University of Wisconsin Press, 1991.

———. *Reading Asian American Literature: From Necessity to Extravagance.* Princeton: Princeton University Press, 1993.

Wood, Jim. "In the Mexican Kitchen." *Image (San Francisco Examiner)*, 10 March 1991, 30.

Yezierska, Anzia. *Breadgivers.* 1925. New York: Persea Books, 1975.

———. "Wild Winter Love." In Anzia Yezierska, *Hungry Hearts and Other Stories.* 1920. New York: Persea Books, 1985.

Zandy, Janet, ed. *Calling Home: Working-Class Women's Writings—An Anthology.* New Brunswick: Rutgers University Press, 1990.

Zavella, Patricia. "Recording Chicana Life Histories: Refining the Insider's Perspective." In Elizabeth Jameson, ed., *Insider/Outsider Relationships with Informants.* Working Paper No. 13. Tucson: Southwest Institute for Research on Women, University of Arizona Press, 1982.

Zinn, Maxine Baca, Lynn Weber Cannon, Elizabeth Higginbotham, and Bonnie Thornton Dill. "The Costs of Exclusionary Practices in Women's Studies." In Gloria Anzaldúa, ed., *Making Face, Making Soul/Haciendo Caras: Creative and Critical Perspectives by Women of Color.* San Francisco: Aunt Lute Foundation Books, 1990.

Zook, Kristal Brent. "Light-Skinned-ded Naps." In Gloria Anzaldúa, ed., *Making Face, Making Soul/Haciendo Caras: Creative and Critical Perspectives by Women of Color.* San Francisco: Aunt Lute Foundation Books, 1990.

Index

234 *Index*

Compositor:	Maple-Vail Book Manufacturing Group
Text:	10/13.5 Caledonia
Display:	Caledonia
Printer:	Maple-Vail Book Manufacturing Group
Binder:	Maple-Vail Book Manufacturing Group

ISBN 0-520-20096-9